"THEY CANNOT KILL US ALL"

"THEY CANNOT KILL US ALL"

AN EYEWITNESS ACCOUNT OF SOUTH AFRICA TODAY

Richard Manning

A PETER DAVISON BOOK

Houghton Mifflin Company
Boston 1987

Library of Congress Cataloging-in-Publication Data

Manning, Richard, 1950–
They cannot kill us all.

"A Peter Davison book."
1. South Africa — Race relations. 2. South Africa —
Politics and government — 1978–   . I. Title.
DT763.M356   1987   968.06'3   87-10036
ISBN 0-395-43781-4

Printed in the United States of America

S 10 9 8 7 6 5 4 3 2 1

The author is grateful for permission from the International Defence & Aid Fund for Southern Africa to quote from Nelson Mandela's *The Struggle Is My Life*.

Map by George Ward

For Diane, who shared the adventure

Oh, it was a very simple story that Gerrit van Biljon told me. And as he spoke I could see it was a story that would go on forever. . . . No there was nothing at all in that story. It was the sort of thing that happens every day. It was just something foolish about the human heart.

Herman Charles Bosman
The Wind in the Trees

Contents

Introduction

It was an education of a lifetime, living in South Africa. Nowhere have I loved living as much — and regretted leaving more — than there.

I was in South Africa with my family, as Johannesburg bureau chief for *Newsweek* magazine, for 270 revolving degrees on the compass, nine months to the day, before the government ordered my expulsion. It was without doubt the most intense nine months of my life, and that is probably why I loved it so. Into those months were crammed the lifetimes of scores — hundreds — of South Africans I met, black and white, and their stories, burdens, and hopes.

To my sadness, black and white hopes intersected so violently, and with such force, that to describe their collision accurately was also to describe the nature of that collision. Civil war. The South African government looked with disapprobation on being described as a party to, and a cause behind, that civil war, so it ordered my deportation. Yet my expulsion, the later expulsion of other reporters, and a blanket crackdown on news reporting in general could not disguise realities: the civil war continues, and the hopes and dreams of South Africans, black and white, still remain as they were before, unfulfilled. This book is about that civil war, those varied, splintered hopes, and the force and energy behind them.

Inherent in all civil wars is a sense of drift, of uncertainty. I came to see how South Africa was, in the words of Matthew

Arnold, "Wandering between two worlds, one dead, / The other powerless to be born." The South African government itself admitted in 1985 that apartheid was "dead." Yet there was no clear heir to apartheid, not even a sense of what the heir would look like or when it would be born. Its birth still continues in the fetid townships, the barren homelands, and the marbled halls of power in Cape Town and Pretoria. So, in another sense, this book is also about the birthing pains of a new nation. And the death throes of the old.

There is pain in both birth and death, and one cannot live among the people of South Africa, black and white, without wanting to diminish their future pain. That may not be possible, since their futures lie primarily in their own hands. But one can hope that wisdom will come to guide them, that whites will come to see blacks as something other than chattel, and that blacks will come to gain a measure of humanity in a country that has denied them the right to be human.

There is a great temptation, in viewing South Africa, to think of all whites as villains and all blacks as heroes. I came to see that one of the hideous complexities of South African life is the falseness of that assumption. I could not leave South Africa condemning all whites because I count some of the whites I met there as the most moral people I have ever met. And I met black children whose hatred was so vibrant, so alive, that it scared me, literally, almost to death.

Yet I came to learn that it was apartheid itself that had made the children that way. So in a final sense this book is also about the success of apartheid, which by 1985 had accomplished what it set out to achieve nearly forty years before — separate worlds for black and white, those worlds never meeting, never crossing.

But in South Africa the destinies of black and white will be forever intertwined. Blacks and whites need each other to sort out the future of their violent and tortured land. The task before them, especially before the white, will be to discover what can be done, before all die, to ensure that all will not have to die.

* * *

Many helped with this book and made its writing possible. They are to be thanked. The editors of *Newsweek* made this book possible by sending me to Johannesburg in the first place and then granting me a leave of absence to write it on my return. Yet without their encouragement, and especially the kind and thoughtful editing of Kenneth Auchincloss and Tom Mathews, I might have burned out under the pressure of the seven-day and five-thousand-word weeks that often seemed never to end. Also deserving of thanks is my longtime colleague Lynn James, of *Newsweek*'s foreign staff in New York, for her help with African languages and her willingness to put up with a tired grump at 3:00 A.M. on Sundays, Johannesburg time.

Peter Younghusband was a *Newsweek* fixture in South Africa for more than fifteen years as special correspondent in Cape Town before he left in early 1986 for greener pastures. As my combination colleague, tutor, and friend after I arrived in Johannesburg, he provided not only invaluable political guidance but also warm companionship and a friendship that I will always value as permanent. I owe him an enormous debt of thanks.

We were a small and mostly merry band in Jo'burg, outmanned by the competition by a factor of three to one but far from outclassed. Mark Peters, our photographer, was a tireless worker as well as a welcome partner on many trips around South Africa. His great good humor kept our lives sane, even if his driving sometimes put our lives at risk. Beverley Raath, our office manager, tutored me patiently in the intricacies of Afrikaans and translated paragraphs and whole articles for me when I needed them. Nhlanhla Mbatha brought me access to whole areas of South Africa I would never have had without him. Louise Gubb, Greg English, David Turnley, and Patrick Durand helped us mollify hungry photo editors in New York with their excellent pictures. We were all more than colleagues — we were friends as well. I will always be grateful for their help, but above all for their friendship.

Few foreign correspondents would be able to operate above water in South Africa without the help, patience, and broken sleep of Edmund "Fingers" van der Merwe, whose Media Services International was our lifeline to the outside world. I cannot count the number of Saturday nights I kept Fingers up beyond midnight, transmitting revisions, changes, and checkpoints to New York through his computers in Cape Town and Paarl. Fingers made my life easier, and I thank him.

This book has benefited from my association with one of the most hard-working and professional groups of people I have ever known, Johannesburg's foreign press corps. There are too many to mention all of them, but two deserve special thanks. Christopher Wilson of AP–Dow Jones guided me through the complexities of South Africa's foreign debt freeze, introduced me to the beauty of Herman Charles Bosman's short stories, and spent endless hours with me over calamari and chips, talking subjects as diverse as the Afrikaner's will to rule and the young comrades' will to kill. Chris also became my best friend in Johannesburg. Alan Cowell of the *New York Times*, deported six months after my expulsion, was easily the most experienced — and expert — reporter in South Africa during my time there. His expertise did not, however, stop him from sharing ideas, views, and perspectives with a far less experienced Africa hand. I think back fondly on afternoons and evenings we spent with him and his family, my young son and his young daughter smearing each other with finger paint as we talked of Africa, the Afrikaners, gold, diamonds, and the world.

This book also benefited from the hard work and diligence of Rollene Saal, who did what literary agents say is impossible — finding a publisher in the month of August. My editor, Peter Davison, brought many things to this book, not the least of which was his poet's eye for language. His encouragement, prodding, and suggested changes in the structure and tone of this book were offered with a warmth and tact that made writing it easier and more of a labor of love than it was when I began it. And few authors with nothing more in hand than a deportation order and twelve suitcases can claim an editor who finds them a house to live in so the book can get written. Peter Davison is very good in the above-and-beyond department.

Yet in the end this book was helped most by the love and warmth of my family. My wife, Diane, and son, Matthew, gave up comfortable lives and schools in the United States to accompany me to Africa. Then they turned around again a year later to return to a third house and a third school in less than thirteen months, with uncounted numbers of suitcases, planes, and hotel rooms along the way. They have supported me in ways that most husbands and fathers have no reason to expect and that any husband or father would count himself lucky to have been given. In turn, I count myself lucky to have had my father, Robert Manning, encourage me to write this book and encourage me in its writing, kindly and from close by, right through to its end.

Perhaps he did so because he came to visit us in Africa — my father slipped in a month before we had to leave — and saw for himself the beauty and squalor of the land that I showed him and that he had seen briefly twenty-six years before. South Africa is a place that stays with you, like a low-level virus you catch and carry for the rest of your life, unable to shake off. It's the people who do it — who make you want to go back — all the fractious and splintered people who make you go beyond everything you've grown up with, to accept the notion that a white racist could be sincere or that a black murderer could be, too.

The people, their voices, and what the voices cry. For all South Africans, black and white, embrace the same desperate hope, if for different reasons: "They cannot kill us all."

One

WAIT-A-BIT

My DATEBOOK for that day, Monday, June 23, 1986, contains only three entries. I wrote the last one very late that night while I was on the phone with my editors in New York, scratching it in, perhaps, to give a finality to the day, the week. 10:00 — file from home office; 15:30 — Press Briefing, Pretoria; 18:00 — Expulsion Order.

I was not too surprised when the expulsion order came. Six weeks earlier the minister in charge of government propaganda had attacked *Newsweek*, and me personally, before Parliament. The government had banned the previous week's issue of *Newsweek*, which carried a cover story I had reported called "South Africa's Civil War — the Making of a Bloodbath." The issue that hit the newsstands in South Africa that day, June 23, contained four inked-out paragraphs.

The country was eleven days into what looked to be a permanent state of emergency, and the government had made no secret of its animosity toward the press. I had begun to notice a frostiness at the Pretoria press briefings, the official in charge answering my questions in cold monosyllables, as if to say, "We're not going to have to live with this guy much longer." For the past week, every time I popped into the Associated Press office, people looked up with surprise and said, "You're still here?"

It was like living in a twilight zone. Eight days had passed since

I'd handed my wife a list of vital phone numbers — the lawyer, the U.S. ambassador — in case I was picked up and arrested. I had also given her power of attorney to terminate bank accounts and leases. Driving the twenty miles home from Pretoria earlier that afternoon of June 23, I felt a curious sense of relaxed resignation as I passed through the bright winter sunlight on the limitless and brown South African veld.

It was a drive I always enjoyed, speeding across the high plains, climbing gradually to a ridge just north of Johannesburg. One could see the whole city from that ridge. In the spring the northern suburbs glowed lavender with jacaranda blossoms. On summer afternoons the giant post office and TV towers were tall needle silhouettes against the dark thunderheads that gathered over the Witwatersrand. I always used to race into town, then, to avoid the fantastic thunderstorms that hit the city like clockwork at 4:30. It was a beautiful place.

That winter afternoon the city looked bright and clear from the ridge, a city of Oz under a blinding sun and crystal sky. I was resigned to the sad notion of leaving the country three years sooner than I had hoped. But since there was nothing I could do about doom, I figured I might as well relax. So I played a tape of early Beatles songs, sang along, and turned up the volume so high that the rear speakers blew. Why not enjoy the music before I had to face it.

I was in the kitchen cooking dinner when the phone rang in my office across the *stoep*, or back porch. It was Johann Spies, the evening telex operator at the downtown offices we foreign journalists shared. "Hullo, Rick," he said. "I've got a telex here, and it's very bad news."

I asked him what it was. "Oh, Rick, it's very bad. Very bad." Several thoughts flashed through my mind at once. Was it the expulsion order? Or was it my father? Had something happened to him? Or my brothers? "Johann, I think you'd better just read me the telex."

"It's very bad news," he said for the third time.

"Look, Johann," I repeated with a laugh. "I think you'd better just read me the damn telex. Just tell me who it's from and then read it."

"It's from Stoffel Botha," Johann said, and I relaxed. The minister of home affairs would not be telexing me about my family. I was just going to get thrown out of the country. That was all. I sat back in my stiff chair and listened to the other shoe drop.

Johann read the three-paragraph telex, which explained that the government considered it in the public interest that I leave the country, that I could appeal the expulsion order in writing, and that if the appeal failed I would have to be out of the country by midnight on Thursday. No specific reason was given for the expulsion, nor would any be forthcoming. "Thanks, Johann," I croaked. "Just put the telex in my box and I'll pick it up in the morning. See you tomorrow."

"Rick," he said, "I'm so sorry. I wish I didn't have to be the one to tell you this, but the telex said I had to find you. I'm so sorry."

"That's all right. I hear the Red Sox are in first place now anyway."

"What?"

"Never mind. I'll explain tomorrow."

I put down the phone and went back across the *stoep* and into the kitchen, where dinner was busily burning. I could hear my wife and five-year-old son upstairs, noisily painting a cabinet. What a mess, I mumbled, pouring myself a stiff Scotch. What in the name of God are we going to do — with ourselves, our furniture, our lives, our house.

Jesus, the house, I thought, and chuckled. What a house. When we moved to Johannesburg we looked at about thirty houses to rent, but I disqualified most of them because they could have doubled for any house in the San Fernando Valley. I wanted a *pozzie* — South African slang for house, short for "position" — that was South African, and this house was South African.

It was a giant cube of red and tan sandstone, sitting in the

middle of two acres of indigenous garden, which in turn sat in
the middle of eight acres of raw *bundu,* or bush. Our landlord,
who had the improbable name Victor Hugo, had raised strelit-
sias — birds of paradise — and aloes, the beautiful South African cactuses that bloom in winter, and the garden was filled with
them, along with bougainvillea, stinkwood trees, banana palms,
and giant green ferns called *monstro delicioso,* delicious monsters.
We awoke on any morning to a panorama of South African
fauna, and it was beautiful.

The house, like most houses in white neighborhoods, had a
pool, an odd circular thing with a fountain running into it off a
rock, and the fountain attracted finches and hornbills and all
other sorts of South African birds. I would often sit out on the
patio, by the *monstro delicioso,* or in my office across the *stoep* and
just watch them.

And of course at our *pozzie* we wore our *cozzies* in the pool —
South African slang for swimsuits, short for "bathing costumes."
And from time to time we'd have peaches and weebits around
the pool — attractive young ladies, not food — and they were
usually pursued by baby veal, young eligible men in their twenties, or so they were described by a woman friend of mine in her
thirties.

When you met somebody you'd say "Howzit?" and when you
left you'd say "See you just now" instead of "See you later." If
you liked something, you'd pronounce it *"lekker* good." And if
you didn't like something, you'd *whinge* — complain — and then
more often than not be told to *voertsak* — fuck off — and then
you'd "gap it" — leave. How, I thought, sitting in that lekker big
kitchen, whinging and about to gap it, was I ever going to stop
talking South African?

I got up and walked across the long open hallway to the
lounge — the living room — and sat before the coal fire I'd lit
an hour before. The room was the size of a college classroom
and was glassed on two sides. Even though it had fired brick
walls and stone floors, like many South African homes, it was

warm and airy. And for the first time in five years we actually
had a dining room, also brick and stone but warm and pleasant,
because Victor Hugo had left us his family's stinkwood dining
room table and chairs. We would sit in the dining room on summer evenings, with the glass doors open wide, just listening to
the birds and the rustling of the trees in the soft summer wind.

We could also do that in the bedrooms, big and airy and glass-
walled as well. The whole place was big; the shower stalls in the
bathrooms were big enough, I often thought, to park a Volkswa-
gen. We knew we'd never live in a house like it again, and because of the dollar/rand exchange rate and because Victor Hugo
had given us a break on the rent, we were paying less than one
thousand dollars a month for it. And now we were going to have
to leave it.

And my God, I thought, wandering back to the oversized
kitchen with the ancient Fuchsware electric stove that occasionally blew every fuse in the house, what were we going to do with
Victor Hugo? We had signed a three-year lease. What were we
going to do about that?

And school. This meant that my son Matthew was going to get
yanked out of school in the middle of the winter term. It meant
leaving a school and a teacher he loved, and I stood in the cold
kitchen thinking of how to tell him we were going to have to
leave Pippa and Tim and Adam, Adil and Gare. We had just
bought Matthew a dog for his birthday. What in God's name
were we going to do with an eleven-week-old puppy?

I thought of my wife, Diane, and what it would mean for her
to be uprooted for the second time in less than a year, having to
pack and move again, without my help this time because I'd be
gone. And she would have to leave her friends, good friends she
had made in only nine months.

And I thought of Ann Molefe, our housekeeper, and her husband, Saul. They had been living in a wing of our house when
we rented it, a black couple in their twenties. As I glanced out
the kitchen window, I noticed their two young daughters and a

nephew cheerily swinging on the tire swing. Where would they
all go if Victor couldn't rent the house?

And Joel. He was the Hugos' gardener, so I figured he'd probably be okay. But I was bothered anyway because the thirty-year-
old Joel would probably suffer a drop in pay and, besides, I liked
him. He had been completely mystified by Americans and our
ways of doing things and could never really get used to my cleaning the pool and backwashing the ancient filter and cutting
brush. "This is what the president of the United States does
on weekends," I told Joel one Sunday, as I hung from a tree
branch.

"Sir?" he said, uncomprehending.

"This is what Americans do to relax."

He walked away, shaking his head and smiling. Americans, I
could almost hear him thinking, are crazy.

I opened a window and put the smoking dinner next to it.
New York and the lawyers would have to wait. I walked slowly
to the foot of the stairs. "Diane?" I called. Suddenly I realized I
didn't know what to say. Jesus Christ, I had never rehearsed this.
"Diane?"

"Up here in the bathroom. We're washing these brushes. Matthew, you're getting paint all over everything."

"I'll come up."

"What is it? What's with your voice?"

The sound of running water and splashing brushes grew
louder as I trudged up the stairs to our bathroom. I could hear
Matthew squealing. I slowly rounded the corner and stood still
at the far end of the long blue-tiled room, leaning on the garage-
sized shower stall.

"What is it? Your voice sounded so funny."

"It happened."

"What?" My wife's voice rose, louder at the end, higher.

"It happened. I've been ordered to leave the country. Three
days. I can appeal it but I don't think it means anything.
Deported."

"*Sssssshhhhiit,*" she barked. "Those *bastards!*" And she threw the paint brush into the shower stall. Matthew started to cry and began asking what was going on. For a while our bathroom was a maelstrom of me trying to explain to him and Diane trying to explain to him and me trying to explain to her and the puppy running around biting my shoes. I slumped against the cold blue tile, drew a breath, and sighed.

"I'm sorry," I moaned. "It's all my fault." Diane came over to me then, and Matthew.

"Don't be sorry. It's been wonderful." And we hugged, then, the three of us, alone in a blue-tiled bathroom as the last rays of the sunset lit up the pale azure African sky, and the sky twinkled through our tears.

The next three days were a blur of meetings, phone calls, and farewell lunches. We filed the written appeal, but I knew it would fail because the expulsion order left no room for a personal appeal. I knew that the written appeal was simply a way for the government to avoid a Supreme Court case, and I told my editors in New York not to hold out any great hope.

I also told David Hoffe, our Johannesburg lawyer, that the only thing that really mattered to me was the manner of my expulsion. I did not want a couple of burly Afrikaner cops to pick me up and throw me into the back of a van while my five-year-old son watched. It had happened to others in the past. If the appeal failed, I asked him, could he please arrange for the heavies to be kept away for as long as possible so I could say a normal goodbye to my family.

I got word that the appeal had failed at 4:00 P.M. on that last day, Thursday. David Hoffe came into my downtown office, where I was waiting with Diane and Matthew and several friends. We had all just returned from a three-hour lunch of calamari and chips — for some reason the press corps' staple — and we were all feeling very mellow.

The restaurant manager had brought us several bottles of free wine, and Alan Cowell of the *New York Times* brought two bottles of champagne. We all knew the appeal would fail, and the atmosphere at our last lunch reminded me of Edna St. Vincent Millay's *Recuerdo:* "We were very tired, we were very merry." At one point my wife picked up her third glass of champagne, toasted the crowd, and repeated Dooley Wilson's invasion-of-Paris line from *Casablanca:* "Sure takes the sting out of being occupied, don't it, Mr. Rick," at which we all fell apart, ordered another bottle of gratis wine, and started doing Bogart imitations.

So when Hoffe arrived, we were ready. He had struck a deal, he said. If I could get to the airport by six o'clock, then Stoffel Botha would keep his heavies away.

I quickly ran through the corridors, saying goodbye to my colleagues and friends in the foreign press. At last I came to Johann and Marie Spies, standing behind the wall of glass that separated the telexes and IBMs from the hallway.

Marie (pronounced in South Africa with the accent on the first syllable: *Mar*-ie) worked the telexes on the day shift, and she and Johann were just switching over. They looked like two sad Afrikaner salt and pepper shakers: both in their fifties, Johann bald and portly, Marie white-haired and plump. They both came out of the glass cubicle to say goodbye. I had worked with them every day for nine months, and Marie had done her best to improve my Afrikaans, occasionally even complimenting my accent.

I shook hands with Johann, who again said he was sorry, but it was as if he was apologizing for all of Afrikanerdom because this time he looked bashful and ashamed. *"Tot siens,"* I said to Marie. Goodbye, but closer to *au revoir.* Her eyes filled with tears and she gave me a big hug. "I don't know what they're doing to this country," she whispered. "I don't know what they think they're doing."

I got to the airport by six and the heavies did stay away, as agreed. The goodbye, for all my efforts, was far from normal because Matthew was tired and cranky, and he screamed horribly when I had to pass the barricades and check in.

I said a final goodbye to Matthew and Diane and our friends through a sheet of Plexiglas. Mark Peters, *Newsweek*'s photographer, waited until I was up a set of stairs and could hear him over the Plexiglas before he boomed the bureau motto at the top of his lungs, a line we had used many times about editors, police, and government officials: "Fuck 'em if they can't take a joke!"

We were all beyond caring when everyone stopped and stared at us: a gap-toothed Rhodesian photographer grinning maniacally while holding a crying five-year-old on his shoulders; a blond American woman holding her sides and laughing; a twenty-three-year-old black South African with fist raised in a black power salute; and me, at the top of a flight of stairs, grinning sadly at them all and waving goodbye. *We were very tired, we were very merry, / We had gone back and forth all night on the ferry.*

I didn't notice Stoffel Botha's plainclothes toughs until after I'd passed through emigration and was about to leave the terminal for my waiting plane. They stuck out in the crowd, two big beefy guys wearing sharkskin suits and loud ties, which is the way many Afrikaner cops and officials dress. They were standing by the door to the tarmac, and I walked straight over to them.

"Mr. Manning," said one of them, and he introduced himself as Colonel Van der something and his colleague as Major Du something. "We're here to take you to your plane." They spoke in the broad guttural spits that is the way of many Afrikaners, especially rural Afrikaners, when speaking English.

"You know, I'd just like to thank you for staying away and letting me be with my family. It made it easier. It meant a lot to me. Thanks."

"Not at all, Mr. Manning," said the colonel, taking my elbow softly and turning me toward the waiting 747. "Our orders are simply to see that you get on the plane. This way, please."

We began walking across the winter asphalt. "You know," I

said to the colonel as we walked. "I love your country and I'm very sorry to leave it. I'm sorry to see things the way they are."

The two cops maintained a tight, but far from hostile, silence. We reached the foot of the stairway. "Hier is ons," I said — here we are — and the two policemen smiled.

"Goodbye, Mr. Manning," said the colonel, raising his voice above the din of the engines and sticking out his hand. I shook it, and the hand of the major as well. "Have a good flight." I took one step up onto the ramp.

"You know," I said to them. "None of this was personal. I just hate to see you guys fucking up your country." All three of us shrugged. I walked up the ramp and they walked back to the terminal. They were still there, watching, when the 747's doors slammed shut and we began to taxi away. *Tot siens.* Goodbye, Afrikaners.

Alan Paton, perhaps the best-known South African writer in the West, once called the Afrikaners "a people of rock and stone in a land of rock and stone." Athol Fugard, the playwright, likened the Afrikaner to the aloe — tough, indigenous, and thorny. Above all, the Afrikaner is — and was and shall be — the farmer.

The word *Boer,* by which the Afrikaners were known for many years, means "farmer" in Afrikaans. South Africa's ruling political party, the National Party (NP), was founded largely on Afrikaner farm support in 1914. In winning election after election since coming to power in 1948, the National Party has looked to and depended on the farm vote as its "solid South."

The men and women who led the Great Trek into the interior of the continent in the last century were farmers. Those farmers — and farmers in general — have been glorified in national lore much as the frontiersmen have been in the United States. And it was fifty thousand farmers, Boers, who took on the British Empire in the bloody war of independence of 1899–1902, only to lose.

I spent some time with those mainstream Afrikaners. It was early in 1986, a time of great political upheaval. I wanted to see if the Boers still supported the party of the Boer, the NP, so Mark Peters and I drove off over the brown Transvaal veld, north through fields of grazing cattle and high corn, past Potgietersrus and Pietersburg, Blinkwater and Vivo, to a little town called Alldays near the Limpopo River. We stopped at a small shop that specialized in everything from taxidermy to VCR rentals and bought a couple of oversized straw baskets. The people there told us that if we wanted a good local farmer, we had to go see Hannes Luus.

Meeting Johannes Jacobus Luus, cotton farmer on the Limpopo, was like meeting a ghost of the Afrikaner past. Take away the tan shorts and shirt and replace them with tweeds and moleskins, and fifty-five-year-old Hannes Luus could have passed for a Burger off to fight the British at Ladysmith. His beard was cut in the classic Boer fashion of the 1890s, with full whiskers on the cheeks and chin only. The skin of Luus's face and hands bore the nut brown shade common to Afrikaner farmers. In South Africa the word *rooienek* — redneck — is a derisive term reserved for coddled city folk, usually of British origin. *Rooieneks* can't take the sun; hence they don't belong. Luus belongs. His crinkled eyes peered warily from under the brim of a soft army field hat as he watched us coming up the drive.

"Goeie more," I said. "Hoe gaan dit vandag?" He relaxed a little at the Afrikaans greeting. "Baie goed, dankie," he replied. Then he scowled, and his big hands clutched a briar pipe as I explained I was an American journalist and wanted to talk to him.

"My English isn't all that good," he said in his thick rural accent that rolls all *r*'s and hits the letters *p, t, d, c,* and *k* like a hammer. His vowels came out elongated and slightly nasal, as though they were coming from the other end of a cardboard tube, the way it is with many Afrikaners speaking English. "I don't want you to be making me out as some illiterate."

Three Dobermans played at his bare feet. "And I'll talk to you about anything except politics," he continued. "I won't talk politics. And unless you tell it like I tell it, then I'll come down to Jo'burg and get you." I looked at the Dobermans and agreed to his terms. I figured it was pointless to argue the obvious at that stage — that in South Africa it's impossible *not* to talk politics. He'd get around to it sooner or later. And it didn't take long.

We sat in his *voorkammer,* or living room, which was decorated with accouterments of the Afrikaner past — ox wagon paintings, game heads, and samplers. Luus sat on a deep fabric couch, but the rest of the furniture was made of thick and heavy wood, very rural, very Afrikaner. The shades were drawn against the harsh summer sun, and the wood-paneled room was cool, dark, and breezy.

A summer wind soughed through the tipianas and blue gums outside, and we started talking about cotton and center pivot irrigation and drought. Life must be pretty good up here, I said, with cotton selling well, and he harrumphed. "Not near as good as it once was," he growled, fingering the fabric of his tan cotton shorts. "Things have changed too much in the last few years. I see it happening and I don't like it. Reform. I can't support the NP any longer." Hannes Luus then talked politics for two hours.

In 1980 Pieter Willem (P. W.) Botha told white South Africans that they would have to "adapt or die." Botha, then prime minister and later state president, saw African realities. White-ruled Rhodesia was in the process of becoming black-ruled Zimbabwe. The neighboring Portuguese colonies of Mozambique and Angola had become independent and black-ruled. In modern Africa three million whites could no longer hope to subjugate a majority of twenty-five million blacks forever. Changes would have to be made.

Botha set out on a program to reform apartheid. South Africa's nine hundred thousand Indians and 2.8 million Coloreds, persons of mixed race, were given their own houses in Parliament.* The Prohibition of Mixed Marriages Act, which outlawed marriage between the races, was repealed. So were the pass laws, the regulations that made it mandatory for all blacks to carry passes and that limited a black's ability to move about the country. Nonwhites were allowed by law to form trade unions, and many central business districts were opened to black-owned businesses. Blacks who had been denied South African citizenship when they became citizens of their "independent" homelands were promised their citizenship back again.

Things began to change slowly, in a halting jog trot designed to further black status, but not so fast as to scare the wits out of traditional Afrikaners.

Hannes Luus sat in his *voorkammer* trying to explain why he was against reform. He was having trouble finding the right words in English, and that bothered him because he was an intelligent and articulate man. He took off his hat and scratched the back of his neck with his pipe stem. His tan shorts and shirt rumpled as he thought. "I can tell it to you better in Afrikaans," he said. "The best thing for the black man in South Africa is for the white man to have *voogskap* . . . *voogskap, voogskap* . . . to be a guardian. Yes, the best thing for the black man is for the white man to have guardianship over him."

"Separate development" — a euphemism for apartheid — must stay. Luus leaned forward on his couch, his hat off and his balding brow wrinkled in deep thought. His bare head made his

---

*Nonwhite South Africans resent being called Indian, Colored, and African as much as they resent the separate worlds created for them by apartheid. Nonwhites — a term they also dislike because it draws attention to the racial distinctions they wish to destroy — prefer to be called simply "black." This book respects their wishes, and as often as possible those people the Afrikaners categorize as Africans, Indians, and Coloreds are identified simply as "black," except in cases where the maze of South African politics calls for discussion of Colored or Indian townships, politicians, and houses in Parliament.

1890s-style beard all the more prominent. He really did look like a Boer, I thought.

"My view," he said earnestly, "is that we should continue with separate development and not power sharing. I can't see why the homelands system* can't work. The blacks can have their own politics in their own areas." His words were coming out in a strange version of English Afrikaans: "bleks ken hef deirrre une politikes in deirrre une arreass." "And I say that not because I hate the black man. I don't. But because I think it best that he develop on his own. The blacks in South Africa live the best lives of all blacks in all of Africa, and they should be told what is best for them in South Africa." He paused and scratched his beard.

"It's a matter of civilization." Luus sat up straight and gestured with his pipe. I could tell these were words he deeply believed. This was Afrikaner credo, and as he spoke he had the look and tone of someone explaining to a child why there are tides or lakes or rivers. One of the most frightening aspects of apartheid, I was discovering, was the simplistic logic behind it.

Luus stretched his long, bare arms before him, and I could see the lily white skin under his tan cotton shirt, accentuating the same kind of "farmer's tan" I'd seen in Nebraska and Iowa. "White civilization is far higher than black civilization, and how the hell can you mix two different civilizations and two different levels? You can't." The back of one hand slapped across the palm of the other, making a sharp crack in the still room. "It doesn't work. The mixing of the races in the United States doesn't

---

*A major component of apartheid and separate development was the establishment of the ten "self-governing" tribal homelands. There the nation's twenty-five million blacks "of African ancestry" were to carry on their "own" political affairs, though at the pleasure of the government in Pretoria. The homelands, patchwork and sometimes disjointed, are Bophuthatswana, Ciskei, Gazankulu, KaNgwane, KwaNdebele, KwaZulu, Lebowa, QwaQwa, Transkei, and Venda. Four of them — Bophuthatswana, Ciskei, Transkei, and Venda — are "independent," though no government other than South Africa's recognizes them.

work." He looked at me sympathetically, as if he knew I must understand.

Luus began to talk faster, nimbly. "Here in South Africa, if you give blacks full political rights then they'll want to take over the government. If you give them full political rights then they'll take over civilization. Everywhere else that's been done in Africa the level of civilization has come down. If separate development is abolished, then I don't think South Africa will have a future. The civilization — the infrastructure and everything else — will come down." He pushed his hands, palm down, to the floor.

Luus sat up straight again. "That is why it is fitting and proper for the white man to have guardianship: to ensure that South Africa will have a future." Luus slapped his bare knee and nodded his head several times. Yes, he seemed to be thinking, yes, he had explained a national ethos to perfection.

I came across many men and women like Hannes Luus, people who believe with absolute self-assurance that they are right and that their beliefs are morally correct. And, I found, arguing politics with an Afrikaner was like talking geography with the Flat Earth Society.

"I do believe in one man, one vote," Luus said. He stretched his long legs and wiggled the toes of his bare feet. Then he jumped forward on his couch and shook his pipe under my nose. "Most Afrikaners believe in one man, one vote. But the black man's vote must come in his own country — in Venda or Ciskei, Transkei, Bophuthatswana, and the rest. Every person in South Africa has a vote. The Vendas on my farm have a vote." He paused, like a lawyer about to deliver the climax of his argument. "In Venda." And he popped his pipe in his mouth, satisfied.

Luus began to talk faster. All the rust was gone from his English, and his eyes began to crinkle in the way that eyes crinkle when the speaker is trying to make a difficult point. "I believe you can have power sharing on a higher level, like in a President's Council, as P.W. has hinted at, like sort of a mini-commonwealth." Luus raised his left hand toward the ceiling; he lowered his right to the floor, as if he were holding an invisible stack of cups. "But not on a lower level. No. The blacks sell their labor in South Africa, but they should be required to vote in their own country." And he brought his hands together again, in a loud clap that shook the stillness of the country room.

"Now you," he said to me, leaning forward even farther on his couch, so that I thought he might fall off. He spoke in something of a sing-song, stabbing his hand in the air with each point. "You sell your labor here in South Africa, but you don't vote here. You vote in the United States. It should be the same way with blacks. They can work here, like you do, and vote at home, like you do." Again Luus nodded several times, pleased with the logic of his argument.

Hannes Luus is a kind man in the context of his society. He gets up every day at first light and works alongside his workers in the fields. His workers are well fed and well cared for. Once a month he loads up his biggest farm truck and drives his laborers seventy-five miles southeast to their Venda homeland for an extended visit. To his mind, and in his society, that is the very model of Christian charity. It sounded to me as if he shared many of the same beliefs as his leaders, and I told him so.

"Nah," he growled, pushing his hands at me derisively. "There are certain blacks who have become permanent city dwellers under this government." He scowled, and the tone of his voice turned down, sad. "Botha is going to let them stay that way, and he wants to give them power sharing. Now that's not right in my view, and that's why I don't vote for the NP anymore."

Luus's voice began to lilt in a foxtrot, one-two, one-two rhythm. "Blacks can move to Soweto and work there if they want to. But politically the black must have his vote in Venda or KwaZulu. The black man's political rights must be in his homeland." Luus put his hat back on, stuck his pipe back in his mouth, and glowered.

An hour later Luus stood in the shade of his largest flamboyant tree, bidding us goodbye. I could tell that his is a full life and, though troubled, a happy life. One daughter attends university and three others are at boarding school nearby. His wife has time for leisure, and the day we visited she was off in the city shopping. The living looked easy and the cotton was high. Seven hundred hectares of it stretched before him, most of it drenched in a fine mist of irrigated spray.

The tipianas and bougainvillea were in full bloom, and they gave the afternoon a pinkish glow while a group of fifteen or twenty black women and children sat in the dusty shade of the flamboyant. In their midst was Hannes Luus, a paternal *voog*, it seemed, among his children.

His hands were on his hips and his pipe was stuck firmly in his mouth. The Dobermans skittered nearby. "Write it like I tell it," he repeated, no threat to his voice. "That's the way we feel up here. Send me a copy of your article, and if it's not right, I'll come down to Jo'burg and punch you in the nose."

I sent him a copy. The article I wrote highlighted his belief in *voogskap* and separate development, and it must have pleased him because I never heard back.

I drove away from Hannes Luus's farm that afternoon shaking my head in disbelief. At that point the country was eighteen months into a period of prolonged unrest that had seen more than one thousand blacks killed amid protest and demands for an end to apartheid. I had spent the last four months filing dispatches on black anger and impatience, telling readers that black South Africans would settle for nothing short of the complete dismantling of the system.

I had spoken with many blacks, and I could see their determination to be liberated. I had seen the dark glow in the eyes of black youths as they burned cars and threw rocks at army troop carriers, known as Casspirs, or Zola Budds, because they are short and quick.

And here I had just left a man who never wanted to see an end to apartheid. What is more, the man I had just left was no wild-eyed fringe radical; rather, he represented the mainstream of his people. Where on earth would it all end? Why are these Afrikaners so Goddamned obstinate? Can't they see reality? Yet, I was discovering, there were reasons for the Afrikaner's intransigence — finite and tangible reasons. History, I was in the process of finding, was still very close to the Afrikaner.

An indigenous, thorny shrub grows in the northern Transvaal along the banks of the Limpopo. I got snarled up in several on Hannes Luus's farm because Mark Peters insisted on taking a picture of Luus in the middle of the dried-up river. To get down to the riverbed, we had to crawl through thickets of those thorn bushes, and every time we came close to one, the thorns grabbed our cotton shirts and pants and held on tight. "Jesus, Peters," I moaned, trying to untangle myself from the thorns. "Lekker great idea to come down here. What the hell are these things?"

"Wait-a-bits." He laughed, trying to get the thorns out of his canvas camera bag. "You know, as in 'Wait a bit, not so fast.' " We both chuckled, and on many later occasions as we drove around the country together, Peters would park his car next to wait-a-bit bushes so I would have to climb through them, cursing and laughing, to get to wherever we were going.

And as we went around the country talking to many Afrikaners, hearing them explain why they are what they are, listening to their logic, it seemed to me that the Afrikaner's own history acts on him like the wait-a-bit. It holds him back and keeps him from walking forward into a peaceful future beyond apartheid. As long as Hannes Luus and others resist change, I was learning, their leaders will be slow to change. And the wait-a-bit thorns are deeply embedded in Afrikaners like Johannes Jacobus Luus.

If the thorns are deep, that is because the Afrikaner's history has been long and cruel. Afrikaners talk about history a lot, and I learned a lot of history from the Afrikaners I met.

The Dutch East India Company founded an outpost at the Cape of Good Hope in 1652. The governors of the company

intended the small colony to be nothing more than a provision-
ing station for ships bound from the Netherlands to the rich
colonies in the East Indies. Immigration was not encouraged because it would not increase profits. In all of the eighteenth century, for example, the Dutch East India Company allowed only
sixteen hundred Hollanders to immigrate to the Cape — the
number of legal and illegal immigrants entering the United
States in one day in the mid-1980s. Today there are approximately three million descendants of the Dutch settlers — Afrikaners — in South Africa; by comparison, the population of the
United States passed the three million mark during the Revo-
lutionary War.

The colony's tiny size and isolation quickly produced two developments, and both were to have lasting significance. One was
the emergence of slave labor. The company wanted the ships
provisioned quickly and cheaply — so the Afrikaners turned to
slaves. The use of slave labor in the small colony soon grew into
a near total dependence on cheap black labor in general as the
colony expanded. Before long, a basic attitude had become ingrained into the white South African psyche: the black man is a
unit of labor and the white man is his *baas*, or master.

The second development was prompted by distance. The colonists quickly came to feel themselves cut off from the rest of
the world, and it was an unsympathetic world at that — from
the penurious governors in Amsterdam to the hostile Hottentots
and Bushmen on the Cape Flats. The colonists began to feel
themselves more African than European. What did Europe
know, or care, about their situation? They would make it on
their own, the White Tribe of Africa, without anyone meddling
in their affairs. This attitude was the basis of an Afrikaner world
view that would last to the present day.

One early wave of immigrants had an important impact on
the colony and on its burgeoning self-image — French Protes-
tants, or Huguenots, forced to flee Catholic France. The Huguenots brought a strict brand of Calvinism and a strong belief
that they had been chosen by God to civilize the end of the earth.

That belief eventually grew into the popular Afrikaner myth that the Afrikaners had a covenant with God to spread civilization and, by extension, to preserve it.

Calvinism also gave the Afrikaner a sense of slavish obedience to tribal authority. Calvinist communities of the seventeenth and early eighteenth centuries required order and obedience, whether in Massachusetts, Switzerland, or Africa, and the reasons were clear and omnipresent: do what the presbyter says, or fall victim to Catholics or hostile natives. Obey — and conform — or leave. The first leaders of the National Party played on that sense of tribal obedience in the 1930s and 1940s as they organized Afrikaners for the overthrow of the English-dominated United Party. Conform for the good of Afrikanerdom, the Afrikaners were told; only by obeying the leadership of the Tribe and voting NP will the Tribe be able to survive. The Afrikaners conformed, and the National Party has won every general election since 1948.

Natural environment and demographics played as great a role in developing the Afrikaner world view as did cultural factors. Hostile Bushmen and Hottentots populated the Cape Flats. Hostile Xhosas lay up the coast in the eastern Cape, and beyond them were the Zulus, in what is now the province of Natal. Migration to the interior was as actively discouraged by the Dutch East India Company as immigration to the colony itself, and the tiny young colony remained clustered close to Cape Town for nearly all of its first 150 years.

Yet movement to the interior could not be stopped, and it accelerated in the early nineteenth century. On one hand the steady migration was set in force by the lure of an immense continent. On another hand it came in response to a new social structure and a new and alien government in Cape Town.

The British took over the Cape Colony from the Dutch in the middle of the Napoleonic Wars, and they brought their laws and customs with them. The British and the Afrikaners shared the colony amicably for a generation, but then the issue of slavery turned the slow migration to the interior into a flood.

The Afrikaners were outraged when the British Empire outlawed slavery in 1834, because their grazing and farming economy had come to depend completely on slaves. Then they were further outraged by the Crown's compensation program: compensation — thirty pounds for each slave, less one pound ten shillings sixpence for the papers — would come only after a formal representation was made in person to the Crown in London. Since few Afrikaners could afford boat passage to Britain — and since even fewer had the inclination to grovel before a "foreign" Parliament — as many as twelve thousand of them decided the time had come to leave the Cape for good and start a new country of their own in the interior. So began the Great Trek, east and then north into the vast interior.

When they reached what is now the province of Natal, the Afrikaners found a newly unified Zulu nation. In the summer of 1838 the leaders of the Great Trek went to sign a peace treaty with the Zulu king, Dingane. No sooner were the leaders inside Dingane's camp than Dingane had them all killed.

Then Dingane sent his *impis* — battalions — out after the Afrikaner wagons. That night the wagons were not outspanned and circled into *laager,* the traditional joining of the wagons into a defensive camp, perhaps because most of the men had gone to Dingane's camp. The wagons were spread casually at a place called Bloukrans when Dingane's *impis* fell on them. Forty men, 50 women, and 180 children were killed that night at Bloukrans. The Afrikaners later built a town near there, and they called it Weenen, which means simply "weeping" in Afrikaans.

The Afrikaners who were farther back in the trek quickly began looking for revenge. They got it on December 16, 1838, the most celebrated day on the Afrikaner calendar — the Day of the Covenant. The Afrikaners positioned their *laager* next to a river so that one full flank was protected from easy attack, and there they waited for the Zulus to fall on them. Five thousand Zulus died that day at the Battle of Blood River. The way ahead was clear, and the Afrikaners headed north over the Drakensberg Mountains, where they eventually succeeded in founding two independent Boer republics, the Orange Free State and the Transvaal Republic.

They had no way of knowing it when they crossed the mountains, but the Afrikaners were stumbling into the richest mineral deposit in the world. In 1868, one of the biggest diamond stores on earth was found in the far western Orange Free State. Then, in 1886, the largest gold seam in the world was discovered in the Witwatersrand area of the Transvaal. However, the British Empire and Cecil John Rhodes, entrepreneur and later prime minister of the Cape Colony, were not about to let those mineral riches remain in the hands of what they considered a bunch of illiterate farmers. So the British simply annexed the diamond area into the Cape Colony. Later, beginning in 1899, they drew the Transvaal into what has become known as the Boer War and conquered the entire region.

For many Afrikaners, the Boer War ended yesterday. At a formal dinner one evening I was sitting with John Maree and his wife. Maree is one of the most successful Afrikaner businessmen in South Africa, past chairman of Barlow Rand and ARMSCOR, the state-owned munitions company, and then chairman of ESCOM, the state-owned utility. He is an intelligent, handsome man with the rugged good looks of an aged Sean Connery. What, I asked him, had he been taught about the Boer War?

He put down his knife and fork. A cloud came over his face, and the man seemed to transform right before my eyes from an amiable and personable businessman into an angry, glowering Boer. "My wife is Anglo, and she calls it the Boer War," he growled. A roughness came into his speech, and gone was all refinement. His vowels broadened and his tongue smacked the consonants like a plumber's wrench on a pipe. "To us it was the Second War of Independence, and it was when the English stole our country from us."

I once asked another Afrikaner friend what sort of treatment the Boer War got in his household. He leaned back in his chair and mentioned one of the bloodiest battles of the war, where the

Boers outflanked a British force one night in January 1900 and killed every last man. "Spion Kop," my friend said, a dark gleam in his eye, like a farmer gloating over a slaughtered pig. "My grandfather told me of how we strung the Poms up like biltong [beef jerky] on the wire at Spion Kop."

For three years, fifty thousand Afrikaners, old men and boys included, held off a quarter of a million English, Canadians, Australians, and New Zealanders. The war began in the southern spring of 1899 when two Afrikaner forces invaded Natal and defeated the main British army. Then they surrounded the British forces at Ladysmith and Mafeking. But the following year saw the breaking of those sieges and the British capture of Bloemfontein, the capital of the Orange Free State, and Pretoria, the capital of the Transvaal. The British commander in chief, Lord Roberts, thought the war was over and went home. He left his chief of staff, Lord Kitchener, to mop up.

But the Afrikaners fought on for another two years. They organized into *commandos* — an Afrikaans word that came into English out of the Boer War — and fought the British from one end of the country to the other on horseback. The British were being beaten until Kitchener formed a new strategy and brought the war to the Afrikaners where they least expected it. Home.

Kitchener's forces roamed the Transvaal and the Orange Free State burning the farmhouses and crops of known Afrikaner combatants. Cattle and other livestock numbering in the millions were slaughtered indiscriminately. The women and children left on the farms were taken and herded into concentration camps.

In these camps the British withheld meat from the wives and children of men on commando. Reports and editorials appeared in the *Times* of London saying that the Afrikaners were used to living in close quarters anyway, so the camp conditions were nothing new. Other reports said that Boers did not like fresh air and had never given milk to their children, so the children were missing nothing. Official policy coming out of Whitehall said that the camps were a response to Kitchener's scorched-earth campaign: there was no food on the land, so the camps were needed to provide food and shelter for the women and children. In the last eighteen months of the war, six thousand women and twenty thousand children under sixteen died in the camps, most of them from typhoid, measles, and dysentery.

The treatment of the Boers in English concentration camps created a furor at the time, and the British were vilified world-wide. Boer relief was briefly an international *cause célèbre*. Yet what is known of the Afrikaners today comes chiefly from Anglo South African writers and English historians chronicling English wars. A standard English history text shows how little is remembered. "The Boers betook themselves to guerrilla warfare and did all the damage that mobility and marksmanship could inflict," wrote Sir George Clark in his 1971 *English History: A Survey*. "Roberts having gone home in triumph, it was Kitchener who had to spend more than a year, with heavy losses of life, in building blockhouses and stretching barbed wire, and also, to the accompaniment of fierce if misdirected criticism, in rounding up and providing for the women and children."

The deaths of twenty-six thousand people represented more than the simple loss of ten percent of the Afrikaner population. It was the equivalent of putting Afrikanerdom through a national abortion a generation deep. Dead were not only the children but the future bearers of children. The existence of children, sometimes eight in a family, had given the Afrikaner nation insurance that the land would continue under Afrikaner ownership. When the British killed the children, they put the Afrikaners' future on their inhospitable continent in immediate jeopardy. And the Afrikaners responded with eighty years of hatred of all things British and all peoples outside the Tribe.

It is easy to wonder what South Africa would be like today if those twenty-six thousand had not died. It is conceivable that the Afrikaner might have felt himself more secure in his world. He might not have felt the need to resort to artificially imposed white supremacy. A larger Afrikaner population might not have felt the need to protect itself against the black majority with the extreme severity of formal apartheid. A less bitter people might not have chosen to look on all outside the Volk — the White Tribe — with hatred and might not have viewed the forty-five years after the Boer War with a single-minded rapacity aimed at winning back control of the country. It is a great irony of history that eighty-five years ago the Afrikaners were the world's darlings and today are the world's villains. It is an even greater irony that the one set of circumstances may have helped bring about the other.

The war left the Afrikaners beaten and broken. Their homes were burned and their fields were barren. Their livestock were decimated. Furthermore, they were made to live under the control of the British, speak English in schools, the courts, and Parliament, and fight the Britons' wars for them. In all things the Afrikaner was very much a second-class citizen — at best second class — in this new and British land. But mostly the Afrikaner was poor.

The condition of the rural Afrikaner — eighty percent of the Afrikaner population — between 1903 and the Second World War was Okie in its poverty, restlessness, and despondence. It is almost impossible now to imagine that eighty years ago some Afrikaners were working on farms owned by black farmers, but many Afrikaners were poorer than their black neighbors and hired themselves out during plowing season.

Between 1929 and 1932 the Carnegie Corporation commissioned a Special Inquiry into Poverty and Development in South Africa, and its findings told a tale of squalor. Commissioners found Afrikaner families living in one-room reed huts and mud huts. One commissioner asked schoolchildren to write down what they ate for breakfast, for lunch, and for dinner. Most of them wrote down simply "pap," short for mealiepap, a gruel made from cornmeal. A commissioner visiting a woman in her one-room hut was given a cup of coffee and a spoon but no sugar. The spoon, he was told, was for fishing flies out of the coffee. One third of the homes inspected were found "unsuitable for civilized life." The commissioners discovered that because of years of isolated rural life, inbreeding had become common and had produced, by their estimate, twenty-seven thousand retarded children. Over half the school age population had not finished primary school. The commission estimated that approximately three hundred thousand Afrikaners, or half the Afrikaans-speaking population, were "very poor."

Many Afrikaners left the squalor of the countryside for the cities, just as, two generations later, blacks moved from their impoverished homelands to the large urban areas. What attracted whites to Johannesburg fifty years ago was what attracts blacks to the Witwatersrand today — the gold mines run by the English mining companies. Some Afrikaners moved in with relatives, but many lived in what can only be described as slum housing.

In the early 1930s the city of Johannesburg fired black janitors so it could give the jobs to poor Afrikaners. Port Elizabeth, South Africa's automotive capital, had a white homeless problem so great that its mayor collected General Motors' huge wooden packing crates and distributed them to poor whites for shelter.

The Carnegie Corporation commissioned a second Inquiry into Poverty and Development in South Africa in the 1980s. Fifty years after the first inquiry, the second found that many of the same conditions, and much of the same squalor and poverty, still exist. It found terrible rural poverty and disease, overcrowding, and widespread malnutrition. But not among Afrikaners. Into the place once held by the Afrikaner, the Afrikaner had put the black.

In short, what happened was that two Afrikaner organizations founded in the 1910s, the National Party and the Afrikaner Broederbond, eventually succeeded in their two long-term goals: taking the government from the ruling English and advancing the Afrikaner into domination of society.

Like many in the West, I approached South Africa thinking — wrongly, as I learned — that apartheid was simply the separation of the races by law. It did not take me long to find that it is more than that: actually, a policy of divide and rule designed to put the Afrikaner at the top of society and keep him there, by law, forever. And apartheid began with the National Party, founded in 1914 to give the Afrikaner his own political party in the English-dominated Parliament. Its earliest members were farmers and miners, who needed a voice most.

The Afrikaner Broederbond, or Band of Brothers, was formed in 1918 as a secret "cultural" society dedicated to the political and economic advancement of the Afrikaner over the heads of the Coloreds of Cape Town, the Indians of Durban, the English of Natal, and the black Africans of the hinterland. Throughout the 1920s and 1930s, Broederbond and NP meetings combined aspects of revival meeting, political rally, and university lecture. Organize. Get out the vote. Be proud to be an Afrikaner. Vote Afrikaner and vote NP. Speak Afrikaans and no English. Afrikaners were told to conform and unite for the good of the Tribe. They did conform, and the National Party came to power in the 1948 election. Afrikaners continued to conform, and the NP continued to win elections. Only in the 1980s did that conformity begin to come unglued — over the issue of ceding a degree of domination to "aliens," blacks.

The issue in 1948 was apartheid, an ordinary Afrikaans word meaning "separateness," but first used in a political context only five years before. Apartheid was an NP policy to advance what was then a segregated society into a society where white supremacy would be the law of the land.

The NP accused the ruling United Party, an Anglo-Afrikaner coalition formed in the 1930s, of being "soft" on white supremacy. The NP by contrast presented a platform that was anything but soft. Land previously reserved for blacks would become formal homelands, promised the NP. Mixed marriages would be outlawed. There would be no mixed residence and no mixed schooling. The vote would be taken away from persons of mixed

race, or Coloreds, who had been given the vote because they
shared the Afrikaner's blood and used the Afrikaner's language
as their first tongue. Few gave the NP a chance of winning.
When the South African Parliament dissolved before the election in 1948, the United Party had eighty-nine seats and the NP
had forty-nine. To win a majority the NP would have to win
twenty-eight new seats, and a swing of that magnitude had never
taken place in South African history.

The National Party won thirty new seats. When Parliament
reconvened, the NP had seventy-nine seats to the United Party's
sixty-five. (One of the new M.P.'s was a thirty-two-year-old Nationalist from George in the Cape Province named P. W. Botha.)
The Afrikaners had won. They had their country back. All that
remained was to consolidate power so as never to lose it again.
One jubilant elevator attendant quipped to an opposition politician that election night, "From now on, a *kaffir* is a *kaffir* again."*
Enter apartheid.

One of the most pernicious aspects of apartheid, I learned, was
that its surface trappings — its outward appearance — disguised
the real energy and logic behind the system. I found that what
apartheid looks like to the average white South African bears no
relation to what apartheid in action looked like to me.

I was in black townships and at riots. I was at rallies and in
churches. White South Africans do not see black townships or
homelands. They are remote. Afrikaners see few blacks, often
only those who work for them. They do not see how the majority
of blacks live, and I learned how many Afrikaners remain bliss-
fully ignorant of black protest. It didn't hit me like a thunder-
bolt. It was just a slow dawning — after talking to many of them

---

Kaffir, the Arabic word for "unbeliever," was used by Arab slave traders of
the seventeenth century to describe the black slaves they sold to the Dutch in
the Cape Colony. The Afrikaners took the word into their own language,
where it came to have the same colloquial meaning as "nigger."

and learning their history — that to Afrikaners apartheid is not about discrimination or racism. To Afrikaners apartheid is about what they see around them every day — often the only thing. Privilege.

Following the 1948 elections it became the law that whites — Afrikaners — have privilege, because Afrikaners had no privilege in the past. Now only whites could have well-paying jobs. Only whites could go to the best schools and universities. The whites — and that meant principally Afrikaners — would have their due at last.

From legally sanctioned privileges for whites, it was an easy next step to assign legally underprivileged status to nonwhites. It became the law that blacks could not own land in white areas because land ownership would be a privilege reserved for whites. Blacks could not own businesses in the white cities; that would be a privilege reserved for whites. By law blacks could not hold certain "reserved" jobs. They could not legally form unions. They could not use the same stairways, elevators, and washrooms used by whites.

By law blacks would have their own schools. Black schools, previously under the control of English missionaries, would come under government control. Later it became law that those schools would teach blacks nothing of usefulness in the modern world. Learning would be a privilege reserved for whites.

At the center of apartheid lay a system of social and economic safety nets for the Afrikaner. The National Party guaranteed the Afrikaner job security by passing laws mandating that all public servants be not only white but bilingual. Since few English speakers were fluent in Afrikaans, the jobs went to Afrikaners. The recession-proof public sector thereby became virtually an Afrikaner franchise.

Today, for example, sixty percent of the Afrikaans-speaking population works for the government in some capacity. While the pay is not high, the benefits are very good. Any public employee can buy a house or flat with no money down and the backing of a government bond in its place. Since a civil servant can go to school part time at full pay, South Africa abounds with Afrikaners holding Ph.D.'s, and many insist on being addressed as "Doctor." If a public employee wants to buy a car, the government again supports the purchase. One of the strangest sights I saw in South Africa took place outside the Union Buildings in Pretoria during a hailstorm. Scores of civil servants came rushing into the parking lot and began madly moving their cars into the shelter of trees in the park below. A close look at the cars told why the civil servants were so eager to get them out of the hail. They were all Mercedes and BMW sedans.

The NP had come through on its original promises, and its adherence to the original 1948 program accounted for its continued success at the polls. Afrikaners always knew where the NP stood, and it was easy for them to support their party because the NP's "message" was clear: white supremacy would live forever.

It was only when NP leaders began to tamper with the original apartheid formula that their constituency began to fragment. While many blacks in the 1980s found P. W. Botha's reforms inadequate — and took to the streets to show their anger over them — many white farmers, public employees, mineworkers, and shopkeepers saw *any* reform of apartheid as the NP "going soft" on the vital issue of preservation of white supremacy and privilege. The Afrikaners began to see their lives and livelihoods threatened as much by the ruling NP as by mobs of angry blacks.

By the end of 1985 all of us covering the South African scene could see many disturbing signs on the horizon: the NP vote dropped precipitously in six by-elections in October of that year, and the far right parties, the Conservative Party (CP) and the Herstigte Nasionale Party (HNP), which favor a retention of apartheid, made significant gains. Many whites were becoming outspoken in their criticism of the government, urging the NP to scrap the reform program altogether and crush black protest. In the meantime, black unrest continued to mount, as more and more blacks took to the streets and demanded the immediate dismantling of apartheid.

We awaited the opening of Parliament in Cape Town in February 1986 with a mixture of dread and optimism. We could see that P. W. Botha was at a crossroads. He was going to have to decide — soon — which road to take: continue reforms at the risk of alienating his white constituency or end reform and squash black protest to keep the fragmenting White Tribe united.

It was around that time that I sought out a cross section of white South Africans to test their politics. I wanted to see how support for the NP was running: Was it deep? Was it mere rote allegiance to a purveyor of largesse? Or was there no support? If it was deep, I reasoned, then there was a good chance that P. W. Botha would continue with his program of reform. The leadership, I had been told many times, does not move forward without the Tribe behind it.

For some of the reporting I went to Port Elizabeth in the eastern Cape. P.E., as the city is called, is South Africa's industrial heartland: Detroit, Akron, and Pittsburgh rolled together and dropped into the humidity of Jacksonville, Florida. P.E. lacks the charm and grace of Cape Town, the bustle of Johannesburg, and the jacaranda trees of Pretoria. Its beachfront falls second to Durban's. I wanted to find some very ordinary people — post office clerks, public employees — and the very ordinary city of P.E., with its high industrial unemployment and high level of racial strife, seemed a good place to look.

Mark Peters and I ended up in Algoa Park, a tough blue-collar suburb even seedier than P.E. itself. Low-slung government housing dominated the landscape — great gray slabs of concrete set on concrete stilts for carports. The only color to the place was the laundry hanging from the balcony rails. The buildings could have passed for council flats in London or public housing in the Monongahela Valley outside Pittsburgh; the only thing that distinguished Algoa Park was the warm and salty Indian

Ocean breeze under the cloudless African sky. Peters and I drove slowly through the town, getting hostile stares from every face we saw. The Tennessee twang of Patsy Cline on a distant radio seemed out of place with poor white kids on the asphalt, playing cricket.

Outside one of those concrete slabs we found Nic De Vos, post office clerk for thirty-one of his forty-seven years and as ordinary as his city. A small, mousy man dressed in brown shirt and brown pants, De Vos was just getting home from work when we approached him and asked if we could spend some time talking to him. He agreed, staring through Coke bottle glasses and chain-smoking, his brown hair falling lazily over his forehead.

Talking with De Vos reminded me of times I had spent with down-on-their-luck autoworkers outside Detroit. They were Kentuckians from the hollers of Appalachia, and generations of mountain inbreeding had made their eyes dull and the eyes of their children even duller. As we talked, I could see that De Vos cared about absolutely nothing. After we left his small apartment in something of a stupor, Peters asked me how someone could be that far out of it, that cut off and dense. Easy, I said. That's what happens when the National Party takes care of everything. You don't have to care. You don't have to be interested. You don't have to feel anything. The party does it all. And produces shadow men like Nic De Vos.

De Vos showed us up to his second floor apartment, where his wife, Marie, was waiting in a drab brown housedress and a pair of fluffy brown mules. Marie De Vos had the look of an embalmed Pekinese dog. Her lifeless eyes never seemed to move, and she did not say a single word the entire time we were in her flat, even though she remained in the living room with us.

I'd seen their living room countless times in steel and tractor towns in the United States: sturdy blue upholstered couches and chairs, garish lamps, religious paintings and artifacts hanging from the beige walls — upscale Salvation Army secondhand. Periodically the four De Vos teenagers wandered through the room, and they had the dull-eyed, smudged-mouth look I'd seen in many North American white ethnic backwaters like South Boston, Chicago's Tenth Ward, and Asbestos, Quebec. They came and went like dusty sylphs as we talked with Nic De Vos about the quality of his life and his politics.

"I'm guaranteed a job for as long as I want it," De Vos mused, and his tone of voice was as lifeless as if he were reciting wall-paper colors. His voice level was as mousy as his stature. "I've got housing security and a pension fund for when the time comes to retire. The pay isn't all that great, but at the moment it's better than working in the private sector. The situation down here is that right now there are a lot of people out of work, and it's good just to have a job." I waited for De Vos to go on. He merely sat on the edge of his couch, nodding his head. It moved the way a spring-loaded head on a child's gewgaw nods. And with the same expression. Empty.

But surely, I suggested, he must be concerned about some of the violence in the townships. De Vos's living room was barely a mile from the black township of New Brighton, where some of the country's worst violence had taken place.

"We're a country with a lot of blacks." He shrugged, as if the thought had just occurred to him for the first time. He lit a cig-arette and frowned. "I guess it's difficult to handle all of them. I know there are riots in some places, and if they don't stop the riots I don't know what will happen. But I think the press over-states what's happening. Most blacks want to live in peace. I see them on the buses and in the streets and where I work, and they seem satisfied with life. I think most blacks are pretty happy." He stared at the floor as he did the gewgaw nod, blowing smoke into the air. "Yeah, the ones I see seem pretty happy with things."

I was finding it difficult to believe what I was hearing. In New Brighton, a mile from this man's living room couch, had been invented the brutal method of killing known as the Necklace, by which a police informer is bound neck and foot with gasoline-soaked automobile tires and then set alight. New Brighton had also been the site of the country's worst *tsotsi* violence — simple thuggery, hooliganism. And he thought blacks were happy with life? His wife took up the gewgaw nod, sitting primly on the couch with her feet together and her hands folded in her lap.

What about the government, I asked him. What did he think of the way they were handling things. "I think they're doing a good job," he said, a note of firmness coming into his voice for the first time. "You've got good blacks and bad blacks and it's difficult to handle them all. It's a tough job, and I support the National Party. Always, even if I don't always agree with it." He paused then, and his hand came up and scratched his head of mousy brown hair.

"There are some views, some personal things, that I don't agree with," he muttered lackadaisically, "but I've been a National Party supporter since I joined the post office in 1954, and I intend to stay with it. I'm not always pleased with the increases we get, like the last one for ten percent. That's only half of what inflation's running at. But I'm an NP man."

I asked De Vos if some of his differences with the NP over "views and personal things" were enough to make him leave the party. He lit another cigarette and started up the nod again. "The CP and the HNP do have their appeal," he replied dully, staring at his cigarette. "They're more like the old days. But I'm sticking with the NP." I waited for him to say more, to go on. But he merely continued the nod, smiling emptily at the green carpet on the floor. I looked over at Peters, who had a pained expression on his face, a silent plea to leave. We thanked the De Voses and left.

"That was a waste of fucking time," growled Peters as we loped back to our car. "That wanker didn't know a thing."

"Precisely," I said, smiling, "and that's why it wasn't a waste of time."

"What do you mean? He thinks all blacks are happy. Jesus. Lekker stupid." And Peters started imitating De Vos talking about happy blacks on buses.

"Don't you see?" That guy is a perfect example of what the NP does to people, a perfect example of government-imposed ignorance and stupidity," I said, opening the car door. "All he cares about is that he gets a ten percent raise from time to time, and that's it. But still, you heard what he said about the CP and the HNP. I think he's starting to see more than happy blacks on buses. Some of what's happening around here is starting to sink in. I'll give you odds he votes Conservative the next chance he gets."

"You're probably right. But, Jesus, was he ever dense."

"Brought to you by the producers of the Group Areas Act and the Separate Amenities Act. New and Improved."

"Batteries Not Included. Each Part Sold Separately." We laughed grimly and went off in search of more Afrikaners.

As we drove, Peters was so frustrated that he wanted to do handbrake slides — 360-degree turns caused by simultaneously accelerating, yanking up the handbrake, and spinning the steering wheel. Peters, a former scout in the Rhodesian army, could get wild at times, and after I'd left him in Alldays after seeing Hannes Luus he'd done handbrake slides all over the northern Transvaal, at one point ending up in a farmer's ditch. South Africa gets to you that way sometimes. I persuaded him to keep driving straight ahead.

We ended up talking about the *broedertwis*. Literally translated, the word means "brother fight," but the term has come to mean something closer to "blood feud." During that trip to P.E. and in our travels to other places, Peters and I saw how the *broedertwis* was beginning to tear Afrikanerdom in two. One side of the feud wanted to go on with reforms. The other wanted to end reforms and to crack down on black protest. If Nic De Vos was still teetering on the fence, he was merely occupying a position many others had abandoned years before on their journey toward intransigence.

We found Jan Leroux the next afternoon at the Port Elizabeth train station, where he worked as a baggage porter. The late afternoon rush hour was beginning, with a scene familiar in all South African cities. Black women passed by, *bubbas* — infants — on their backs in blankets, papoose-style. Many women carried bags of groceries on their heads. They all swarmed to the station to board the trains that would carry them away from the bulky, Georgian sandstone buildings of downtown Port Elizabeth.

Leroux and three other porters sat in the sun outside the station, leaning on their trolleys and passing the time of day. A black family struggled by with an overloaded trolley. Sacks and bags balanced precariously on the bars. Suddenly the trolley tipped over, and sacks, bags, and packages flew onto the sidewalk.

Leroux and his mates just sat in the sun, leaning on their handcarts. "P.W. says we don't have to marry them, just mix with them," Leroux muttered. "There's no place for just the European anymore. P.W. says we have to live with them. How can you?"

Leroux, sixty-three, had worked for the South African railway system all his life. Like many Afrikaners, he was a big, beefy man who looked as if he was brought up on a steady diet of potatoes, Castle beer, and *boerevors,* the fatty, bland South African equivalent of bratwurst. "I say the government gave up too much land to the blacks to begin with," Leroux intoned, still leaning on his handcart, his brown porter's cap pushed back cockily on his forehead, leaving only wisps of gray hair and long sideburns curling in the humidity. A neatly trimmed gray mustache hung below his knobby nose, and a mole on his left cheek bobbed up and down as he talked.

Leroux's voice sounded grainy and nasal, like flat notes being pushed through a trombone. "But once they put them in the homelands they should have kept them there," Leroux said, cocking his porter's hat. "They've let the blacks come out again and live in the cities and that's wrong. P.W. never looked at European people and gave *us* houses the way he's giving the blacks houses. He's never helped Europeans the way he's helping blacks."

I grunted inside at the incongruity. It is a bad joke the Afrikaners constantly and unconsciously play on themselves without thinking twice, and I'd heard it not just from Jan Leroux but from newspaper editors and businessmen: When is an African not an African? When he's an Afrikaner and insists he's a European.

Something else was familiar about Leroux. Perhaps because Afrikaners have been arguing politics for 350 years, many of them talk politics sounding and looking like professional politicians. Listening to Leroux was like getting a lecture from a South Side Chicago precinct captain. He continually jabbed his right forefinger at my nose, until I almost went cross-eyed, and he stood close to me in an aggressive posture.

The rush hour continued under the vivid Indian Ocean sky, and Leroux's three pals continued to loll lazily in the sun. "We pay taxes and the government gives the land to the blacks," Leroux asserted, the hard consonants steel on pavement. "That's fine up to a certain point. It would be fine if the blacks simply stayed in the Ciskei and Transkei. But no. The government allows the blacks to come here to the cities and take our jobs." He jutted his chin out combatively and waved a hand vaguely off to the east, as if pushing blacks into the two poor Xhosa homelands that lie 150 miles away in that direction.

Leroux's hands began to flail and he talked faster. "The government issues them money; why don't they just stay there! That's why I left the National Party and joined the Conservatives. The government wastes money it should be spending on the whites in the first place. The Conservatives do things the old way."

Leroux looked around him, pointing vaguely at blacks walking in the late afternoon sunlight. "Look what the blacks do," he said belligerently, shoving his finger under my nose again. "They come to the cities, and the government spends a fortune building schools for them. And the blacks just burn them down. How can you live with people like that?" End of subject. Leroux leaned back on a trolley, his arms folded cockily.

Peters and I left. "What was he whinging on about?" Peters asked. "Real motor mouth that one." He had been taking his pictures from a distance, trying to frame Leroux under the giant blue Port Elizabeth station sign. "He looked pretty upset."

"The next time you see your friend P. W. Botha, Mark, you might mention that he's not a very popular guy around here." I sighed. "I think we can kiss any notion of further reform good-bye." I looked out at the long crowds of blacks moving slowly toward the Port Elizabeth station, trudging glumly along the sidewalks. Many of them had the look of tired horses at the end of a long day in the fields, but they were a threat to men like Jan Leroux, who wanted them back in their homelands. It didn't seem possible and it made no sense. He had everything they did not have.

The anti-NP sentiment that Peters and I found in P.E. was nothing compared with what we found in the mining country to the north. Nowhere is the white backlash against reform as vicious as in the mines, where apartheid carries the name "job reservation."

Depending on whether a man is white or black, he is either a mineworker or a miner. The difference is more than semantic. A white mineworker is a "scheduled person," meaning that he is allowed by law to own a blasting certificate and can do the job reserved for holders of blasting tickets — pushing the plunger on a dynamite charge. Black miners are not allowed to be scheduled persons, and their job is hacking a hole for the dynamite and carting the coal or metal away. The differences between the two jobs are great in terms of pay, drudgery, and prestige. And if people like Dave Kuim of the all-white Mine Workers Union (MWU) could have their way, apartheid would stay on in the mines, and everywhere else, forever.

Kuim (pronounced like the Latin *cum*) is chief organizer for the fast-growing MWU in one of its fastest-growing areas, the Vaal Triangle. The triangle is a heavily industrialized region of the southern Transvaal and the northern Orange Free State that encompasses mini-Pittsburghs like Vereeneging, Vanderbijl

Park, and Sasolburg. These are hardscrabble towns, and the men we saw who work the mines and factories there are tough, lunch-bucket-and-a-beer types. The men coming out of the giant ISCOR steel mill in Vanderbijl at shift change could have passed for steelworkers shouldering their way out of a USX mill in Gary, Indiana: overalls and hardhats, grizzled hands, and whiskered faces.

The triangle is also one of the most conservative parts of the country: the men who work those mines and factories have benefited from job reservation for the last seventy years, and they don't want to give it up. As the fast-talking Kuim put it when I was barely through his door, "People here are not interested in reforms." Kuim likes it in the triangle. He is a man so antiblack that he left his native Durban in 1970 for the rigid segregation of the Orange Free State. Natal, he said, was too liberal. And he didn't like Natal because most of South Africa's Indian population of nine hundred thousand lives around Durban, descendants of the Indian cane cutters brought to work the Natal cane fields in the nineteenth century. By contrast, Indians were not even allowed into the Orange Free State until 1985.

"When it comes to wage increases, who suffers the most in this industry? The whites, that's who," Kuim barked, sitting in his small, bare office in Vanderbijl Park. It reminded me of Teamsters Union offices I'd visited around the American Midwest, where a picture of Jimmy Hoffa was often the only decoration on the walls. In Kuim's office the only picture on the walls was a black and white portrait of Arrie Paulus, the Teamster-style general secretary of the MWU. Kuim glanced over at it from time to time, with reverence.

"The whites suffer because the blacks are striking every five minutes," Kuim barked again, wagging his finger at me. "And when it comes time for a pay increase for whites, the companies say there are not enough profits for a raise. Because of the black strikes. Honestly. The world does not understand how much more the whites must suffer than the blacks."

Kuim, baby faced at forty-one, stood about six feet and

weighed more than three hundred pounds. He had the look of a former professional athlete gone grotesquely to seed, a rumpled and brown-haired heart attack just waiting to happen.

His collar flapped open because his neck was about four sizes too big for his shirt. His double chin looked like a goiter. So huge was his stomach that his blue necktie stopped abruptly only halfway to his belt, and the ten inches of white space between belt and tie seemed all the larger for its bareness.

"Whites go and make demands of management, and management says there's nothing available, so the whites go away emptyhanded," Kuim explained, thumping his desk, his words a fast rattle, his voice high and reedy. "If the blacks want something and they don't get it, they go on strike, and the white must tighten his belt. Every day the blacks will go to management and say, 'We don't like this white foreman. We won't work for him. Fire him.' And the company will fire him, just like that, for the sake of race relations."

Kuim's pace was quickening. His fingers snapped and his chin flapped. "And now they want to give blacks access to dynamite?" His voice rose toward a screech on the word *dynamite,* and he continued to raise it for emphasis, leaning back in his chair and holding his hands about a foot apart, as if ready to catch a ball.

"Do you know how dangerous and explosive the situation is going to be if blacks get their hands on dynamite? We've been lenient. We've been charitable." His tone softened, dropped; his voice drew out the vowels — *leeeenient, chaaaritaaable* — and then rose: "But there is this hate situation there on the job, and I hate to say where it's going to end. But it's not going to be pretty." Kuim paused, shaking his head, like a preacher pausing to let the idea of hellfire and brimstone sink in to his congregation.

"It's building up every day," he said, dropping his arms and leaning forward on his desk. "A place is being made for the black at the expense of the white, and many whites are simply not going to tolerate it. This is a very serious situation, and no one must underestimate the feeling of the mineworker on this issue."

There was violence in his voice, but it was soft, implied more by his wagging finger and wet lips than by his shouts. He spoke softly, and I was frightened by his baby face and his new quiet tone. "These reforms are a joke, and we're against them," and Kuim pounded his desk sharply, once, with a fat fist. "All of them. We want the black man in his place and the white man in his. We don't want to mix with them like the government is forcing us to do."

Kuim began to shake his head, and I sensed a feigned sorrow. "I don't know how much more we are going to bear this. We've been very patient on this, but the powder keg is beginning to burn. The kickback, the backlash, is coming. Sasolburg was only one example of that."

For a time Sasolburg was the only city in South Africa sending a member of the Herstigte Nasionale Party to Parliament. In the October 1985 by-elections, Louis Stofberg won election to the House of Assembly by 367 votes over the NP candidate, even though Stofberg and his party are from an earlier era. Stofberg raised a storm when he insisted that the word *kaffir* was not offensive and could be used as a term of endearment. One of the principal issues in the campaign was the presence of an interracial married couple in town. Stofberg and his HNP supporters decried the couple's presence as an abomination, and the HNP won its first election victory in fifteen years. One of Stofberg's most vocal and active organizers in that landmark election was Dave Kuim of the MWU.

"This government had no mandate to alter the situation and we were being forced to accept these changes without being consulted." Kuim's voice grew louder and he began to wave a pudgy finger. "Say you go into a bar, and you're a whiskey man. If the guy you go with makes you drink beer without even asking you, then you're going to resent it, aren't you? We did, and we showed 'em." Kuim pounded his desk again, with the flat of his hand, and the loud smack echoed in his small, bare office.

"The government says reforms will bring about harmony. But

just the opposite happens." He was no longer shouting. "Blacks
are being advanced over the heads of whites, and it's wrong. You
hear about the blacks and all their problems. Well, let me tell
you something. The hatred is beginning to boil up in the
whites." Kuim leaned over his desk, a sullen sneer on his lip. A
drop of spittle flecked his lower lip. "You wait."

He straightened up, his stomach pressed against the edge of
his desk. "In the next election held here in the triangle the NP
will fall," he said with the dark tone of a country preacher threat-
ening hell and damnation. "I said it in Sasolburg and I was right
then. I'm right on this one, too. If a national general election
were held right now the Conservatives would win enough seats
to become the official opposition in Parliament."

I found myself taking it all in. What he said made sense —
very eerie sense. There was something very sound about his tone
and argument, like a Boston Irishman explaining how the
mayor of Boston will never be a Republican.

"Wait a few more years, with more sanctions and more unrest,
and the Conservative Party will win the general election. You
wait." The soft threat of violence was back in his voice. "Whites
have had protection for three hundred years," he said, smiling.
"If whites are endangered they will turn to the party that will
preserve their protection and the status quo. It's going to be 1948
all over again. You wait." And he nodded with self-assurance, a
man certain he was in the right and would prevail.

I left Kuim's office and headed back to Johannesburg, trying
to make sense of it all. I'd seen Afrikanerdom and I was numb.
The wait-a-bit thorns seemed still so deeply embedded in so
many Afrikaners that I didn't see how they could change and
walk ahead into any kind of future without bloodshed. And I
was terribly bothered by the calm logic of it all. I felt as if I had
just spent a month listening to a series of bizarre math lectures
on how two plus two equals five. But there must be some hope
for continued reform. Surely there had to be Afrikaners who
had changed. I knew there had to be at least one, and I went to
see him one hot afternoon in February.

"It makes me laugh, and it makes me cry," said the old man, sitting in his book-lined study outside Pretoria. He was speaking English, but a heavy Afrikaans accent roughened his speech. The word *supremacist* came out with a hard *c* — *supremakist*. From time to time he simply lapsed into Afrikaans. "For whites in this country, three things dominate all thinking," he spat out. "Fear, fear, and fear. They fear they will be swamped and subjugated by blacks as they have subjugated the blacks for these so many years." There was anger in his voice, dark anger. "They know there is an account to be rendered, so they are afraid. But they think it is possible politically, biologically, and socially to remain in control — so evil, stupid, shortsighted, and blind are they."

It was late afternoon and Willem Kleynhans, in linen shorts and bare feet, was wound into a big leather chair in his study. I had spoken to him several times over the telephone, but I wanted to spend an afternoon with him to talk about the Tribe. He invited me out to his Pretoria house, and we sat in his study drinking tea and talking.

At one point Kleynhans put down his tea and began to gesture with a rusk, the hard biscuit South Africans enjoy with tea. His voice became more guttural, with rolling *r*'s like a Scotsman's and hard consonants ground as if with a bandsaw. "It's naive to think that PeeVee Botha and all the other Afrikaner leaders can easily switch and shed the policies of the past and expect the masses of Afrikanerdom to follow," the old man said, stuttering in aggravation. "If PeeVee Botha did away with the Group Areas Act he would be killed. At the very least he would be vilified by his own people and rejected as a traitor to the Volk and called not a true Afrikaner. Those are effective measures. I know."

I had wanted to talk to someone who had broken the yoke of conformity, to see what the consequences of rebellion are and to find out, essentially, how hard it is for an Afrikaner to change. I came to see through Willem Kleynhans how hard it is. Kleynhans is perhaps the best that Afrikanerdom has to offer. If things had gone differently he might today be in the Cabinet instead of in the political science department at the University of South Africa (UNISA), the Pretoria-based correspondence college that is the only source of higher education for many blacks.

He was very much of the Tribe. His father was a *penkopper,* a courier, during the Boer War. Willem went to Pretoria to study in 1940, and he rose to chairman of the Junior National Party in the Transvaal. Later, when he joined the faculty at the University of Pretoria, he was accepted into the Broederbond. Election day 1948 was one of the happiest days of his life, as his party came to power.

By the early 1950s Kleynhans was one of the NP's rising young stars — chief lecturer in his department at the age of thirty-five and a member of the Transvaal National Party Executive. The prime minister, J. G. Strydom, called him by his first name. After Kleynhans was expelled from the Volk, a friend wrote of "the great expectations that were cherished in Party circles for Willie Kleynhans."

Kleynhans is a thoughtful man of fundamental decency. When I came to visit him that baking hot February afternoon, he suggested that I move my car from his driveway onto his lawn, where it could rest in the shade of a tree. That sense of decency erupted in May 1955. "I began in my heart of hearts to question some of the values of the party," he remembered with a frown. "My conscience was starting to bother me." Prime Minister Strydom introduced a bill to pack the Senate with sympathetic NP votes so that a bill taking the vote away from Coloreds would pass. Kleynhans rebelled: it was wrong to disenfranchise anyone, much less Coloreds, who shared the Afrikaners' blood, language, history, and heritage, if not their skin color. He circulated a petition denouncing the Senate packing. In the end he found twelve other professors of a like mind, and he released the petition to the press.

"It was a very painful time," Willem Kleynhans recalled thirty-one years later. His voice was little more than a sigh. His tall, very thin frame was capped with a shock of steel gray hair plastered back over his skull. His hair and his bony nose combined to give him the look of an aging Dick Tracy. Although only sixty-six, he looked at least a decade older. The bones in his bare legs stuck out like knobs, and he looked very frail.

He threw his bare, thin arms in the air. "What we were subjected to because we refused to conform! What we were called! Communists, traitors, enemies of the Volk. Everything." Kleynhans was thrown out of his family, the Broederbond, and the National Party.

The pro-government daily *Die Transvaaler* assailed the petition as "unnationalist, uninformed, naive, disloyal, unbecoming and traitorous." One reader suggested that the names of the petitioners be engraved in red "so that our descendants can see who is fighting against the sincere efforts for the preservation of White South Africa." Poison-pen letters threatened everything from tarring and feathering to whipping. Kleynhans's experience left him with a jaded and cynical view of his countrymen. Apartheid touches all South Africans of all colors in a very personal, intimate way. The way it touched Willem Kleynhans was to leave him a pessimist. He referred to himself as a prophet of doom.

"You must understand conformity," he said, almost pleading. He leaned forward in his leather chair, his thin bones popping. "Why was it that the Afrikaner, through the National Party, became so all-powerful? It was because the masses were prepared to conform for the sake of hanging on to power. Two generations have been brainwashed with this sort of conformity. How do you eradicate it from their minds and undo what was done?" He brought his arms down in a sudden swoop, and they smacked the leather chair with a sharp crack.

"Take myself. I understand myself, so let's talk about me." Kleynhans began to talk so rapidly that his tongue had trouble keeping up, and he stuttered and gasped from time to time. "After thirty years of breaking away and refusing to swallow apartheid philosophies, still today at times I find that I am riddled with these white supremacist beliefs. And that's after thirty years." His voice rose at the end, a thin wail.

Kleynhans stood up and began to stalk about the room. It was a big room, and election posters from the United States and Britain hung amid the bookshelves. A Nixon-Agnew boater from the 1972 Miami convention lay incongruously on a table. "Can you imagine what it's like for someone like P. W. Botha, who stood firm on those beliefs until yesterday? *Hemmel* [heaven]. You can't tell me that it's going to be easy for people like him, or the mass of Afrikaners, to get those beliefs out of their bodies and minds."

Kleynhans shook his head sadly. "I'm pessimistic because I can't expect the governing party, which introduced those white supremacist policies in a crusade, to shed those policies overnight. The party that implemented those draconian policies cannot be the party that undoes them." Kleynhans sat down wearily and took another sip from his tea. He shook his head again and then folded his long, skinny legs beneath him.

So, I asked, after a sip of tea, was there no hope for change, for peace?

"If it depends on whites to introduce real basic reforms, then nothing will happen in South Africa in a peaceful way." Kleynhans sat back in his chair and closed his eyes. We had been talking for a long time, and he was tired. The late afternoon sun threw an orange glow over his tanned face. "It won't happen," he said again, his eyes opening in slits. "And before I deviate from that view I must see a massive, genuine swing of white sentiment toward the real sharing of political power with blacks. Only then will I change my mind." Then he unfolded his bare legs and walked slowly over to his desk.

He rummaged on his desk for a minute and pulled out a pile of papers. "I want you to take these," he said. "They'll help you understand what it was we went through thirty years ago. They're copies of some of the letters we got in the mail." They were all in Afrikaans.

We walked out of his study and into the warm evening. The cicadas were beginning to chirp, and the sun was dropping slowly. "Thank you," I said. "I've really enjoyed the afternoon."

"Pleasure," Kleynhans said in the South African way, smiling. The sunlight seemed almost to pass through his frail body as he waved goodbye sadly. I watched him walk back into his house, hobbling a little, bent and tired.

When I had the letters translated, one stood out from the others. Most were filled with bile and hatred, but I think he kept that one letter — and gave a copy to me — for a sign of hope and as a comfort.

It was unsigned, like the others, but this one, two short sentences, was from the tender heart. "Ons dank die Heere," it began: "We thank the Lord that there are still Afrikaners who value honesty, truth, and freedom above political ambition. May you, and all who stand by you, be an example to all true Afrikaners."

Herman Charles Bosman, the great South African short story writer, wrote a story called "Seed-Time and Harvest." I read it in the southern autumn of 1986, as the Afrikaners were struggling with their souls and wait-a-bit thorns, and the story seemed to dramatize their dilemma. It is about Jurie Steyn, who goes off to work in a far district during a bad drought. His wife becomes pregnant by another man while he is away. Jurie comes back, raises the boy, Kobus, and the whole district laughs at Jurie as a cuckold.

Near the end of the story, the teller of the tale gets embroiled with Steyn over the placement of some fence posts. Out of mean revenge he tries to prod Steyn into admitting his cuckoldry and Kobus's illegitimacy. Pure spite. "Jurie Steyn and I started walking towards the farmhouse, in front of which I had left my mule-cart," the narrator recalls. "The boy Kobus came to meet us. 'You look tired, Kobus,' Jurie Steyn said. His voice suddenly sounded very soft. And in the dusk I saw the way that Kobus's eyes lit up when he took Jurie Steyn's hand. A singular variety of ideas passed through my mind, then, and I found that I no longer bore Jurie Steyn that same measure of resentment on account of his thoughtless way of acting with my fence-poles. I somehow felt that there were more important things in life."

The story was important to me because I needed to keep reminding myself that there was a tender side to the Afrikaner as well as the vengeful, spiteful side. During that southern autumn I could see that the fate of thirty million people rested on which way the Afrikaner heart reacted — with its tender side or its other. I needed to tell myself that there was more to Afrikanerdom than Dave Kuim — that there *were* tender whites in South Africa.

One such person was a lovely woman who once walked into a stadium filled with angry blacks gathered for a mass funeral and was cheered. "I can't stand bullies," she had once said, explaining why a fifty-five-year-old mother of seven would go into politics. Blacks and whites alike got used to visiting her house in Port Elizabeth and then being asked to spend the night. On the night she died, in January 1986, one of the crustiest, most cynical members of the foreign press corps broke into tears when he came to write the words "Molly Blackburn was killed in a car accident Saturday night, police said." The next day a package arrived at his house. It had been sent by Molly Blackburn, and it contained a sweater the reporter's daughter had left at the Blackburn house the week before.

The Rev. Allan Boesak of the anti-apartheid coalition United Democratic Front (UDF) eulogized Molly Blackburn as someone who tried to "mold out of the hatred and misery and suffering of our people something new, joyful, beautiful." It was probably unprofessional of me — merely human — but I began to hope that Molly Blackburns and Willem Kleynhanses would start to spring from the ground like dragon's teeth. I felt like the psychiatrist who fell in love with the schizophrenic. I cared too much to simply write the country off, but I was powerless to provide the remedy — a transformation that would let loose the people who cared, people with hearts touched by tenderness and pain.

What made matters worse was my slow realization that for every Molly Blackburn there were two or three like Eugene Terre'Blanche, the oxlike former cop who heads the neofascist Afrikaner Weerstandsbeweging (AWB), or Afrikaner Resistance Movement. Terre'Blanche preaches a gospel of Afrikaner supremacy, strict segregation, white rights, and Boer power. His flag looks like the Nazi swastika, and his followers wear brown para-Nazi uniforms.

His meetings, like early Broederbond rallies, are mixtures of religious revival and politics. Terre'Blanche once had trouble filling a room, but by March 1986 he began to attract crowds in the thousands, all chanting "Ah Veeah Beeah!" — Afrikaans for the letters AWB — in scenes reminiscent of Nuremberg in the 1930s. In May 1986 Terre'Blanche joined the leaders of the CP and HNP at an outdoor rally near Pretoria. More than fifteen thousand Afrikaners attended, and Terre'Blanche got the most applause as he attacked the NP and called P. W. Botha a traitor to the Volk.

That same month Terre'Blanche sent out a direct challenge to the NP to show his strength. No NP leader, he said, would be allowed to address a rally in the Transvaal, the NP's traditional stronghold. Roelof F. "Pik" Botha, the foreign minister, announced that he would address a meeting in Pietersburg in the northern Transvaal. The AWB broke up the meeting before it even began, as Terre'Blanche was carried into the hall on the shoulders of a thousand supporters. Botha never arrived. South Africans awoke the next morning to accounts of white police teargassing other whites.

All of us in the foreign press corps were growing increasingly unnerved as 1986 slouched on. For the first time in history, the government was faced with both a black and a white insurgency occurring simultaneously, and it seemed to me and many others that P. W. Botha was going to have to choose which movement to mollify. The tenth anniversary of the Soweto uprising was fast approaching — a date that marked black South Africa's bloody determination to end apartheid. We could see that if the country exploded in a spasm of black violence on June 16, the anniversary, Botha would lose face irreparably with his white constituency. Yet we could also see that if he moved to crush black protest, blacks would only see it as a sign of weakness and increase the level of their protest.

Something would have to give. It seemed unlikely that Botha would tolerate his constituency's sliding further to the right, toward Terre'Blanche and the two right-wing parties. We were expecting a show of *kragdadigheid* — forcefulness. We just weren't sure when it would appear.

We were as skittish as a bunch of racehorses before a derby. All of us were connected to electronic pagers that beeped at all hours of the day and night and flashed out announcements and special messages on small screens. Because an economy of words was needed for those messages, they often came out garbled and sent us dashing for our phones in a panic. One message said that Botha was imposing a state of emergency on Namibia, the former German colony South Africa has governed in defiance of the United Nations since 1966. Nothing of the kind happened.

Another message that sent us all running was an announcement that Winnie Mandela, wife of jailed African National Congress leader Nelson Mandela, was being "held" somewhere downtown. In fact, the announcement was supposed to say that she was going to "hold" a press conference. Every time the local wire bells indicated a "snap" or an "urgent" message, offices along our corridor would empty and gangs of reporters would cluster around the wire for the vital communication. One time the "urgent" concerned the South African national rugby team. Even the false alarms could not lessen our increasing tension.

In the end, Terre'Blanche, Dave Kuim, Jan Leroux, and Hannes Luus won the day. Botha opted to avert an irreparable rift in the Tribe. On June 12 he imposed a nationwide state of emergency, which included the strictest curbs ever imposed on the press, on public meetings, and on political expression for blacks. More than twenty thousand black leaders and "comrades" (pronounced "com-raids") — radical youths in the townships — were rounded up and thrown in jail on no charges in the days and weeks that followed.

Reform, it seemed, was dead. The *broedertwis* within the Tribe mattered more. The Afrikaners were going to stand still. For the first time ever, the NP's leadership had been forced into conformity by the party's rank and file instead of the other way around. For P. W. Botha it was either conform or see his party eventually thrown out of office by the Conservatives. The tables had been turned: P. W. Botha himself had to adapt, or he would have died at least a political death.

When the permanent state of emergency began, I had little choice but to describe what had happened and why. I wrote that P. W. Botha had caved in to pressures from the right wing and that hardening of the lines on the right surely meant that the country was headed for bloody civil war. Eleven days later, when my expulsion order came, I began writing a valedictory.

I sat out in my cold office at home, across the *stoep* from the kitchen, and as I began to write, I could not find it in myself to be bitter at the Afrikaners who were throwing me out of their country. I could lament what they were doing to the country, and I was angry that I had to leave. But I simply could not find it in me to hate them. Then I remembered Nico Smith, and I knew I could not leave the country condemning all Afrikaners, because Nico Smith was probably the most decent man I met in South Africa.

Nico Smith is a big man. I went to visit him one morning, and as we sat in his study drinking coffee and talking, I could see that even sitting on a couch he looked tall. With his thinning brown hair and smoked glasses, the fifty-five-year-old Smith could have passed for a policeman. He even dressed like a cop. I had seen him on other occasions dressed in blinding polyesters and rippling sharkskins, but on that day he wore a soft brown safari suit and a plain brown tie. As he talked he often looked up at the walls, filled with centuries of books on theology.

He is a curiosity in South Africa — a theologian trained at Stellenbosch, Afrikanerdom's Harvard, and a Broederbond member who left the Afrikaner mainstream and became the minister in Mamelodi, one of the two black townships outside Pretoria. In 1984 he petitioned the government for an exemption to the Group Areas Act and for permission to reside in the township. Permission was granted a year later, and in early 1986 Smith and his wife, Ellen, left their comfortable suburban house and moved into the squalor of Mamelodi.

Sitting in my frigid office at home, I recalled the day I went to see Smith. It was the second day of construction on his Mamelodi house, and we took a drive over to take a look. We talked as he moved easily around the foundation, interrupting for an occasional comment to the construction gang, and later when we visited his church and his school.

"I felt we were visitors and not residents in Mamelodi," he explained, his arms crossed and his back hunched. He spoke with a great gentleness, the kind I have always associated with a reading of the Twenty-third Psalm or a Shakespeare sonnet. "It made me feel like a stranger and that people were not accepting us as part of the community. I wanted to identify with the people. I felt it would make my ministry easier."

He explained how the ministry he had chosen was to bring black and white families together at each other's homes for dinner and long evenings of conversation. "The first thing I noticed when I came here from Stellenbosch was how successful they had been in implementing apartheid and creating four different worlds. We, I should say, because I was part of it, too." His voice, still gentle, became sad as well.

He shook his head dolefully and spread his arms, as if embracing all the shabby houses and unpaved streets around us in the township. "I supported it. I'm to blame, too. What nobody

ever realized was that if you separate people you cause alienation, and when you have alienation you have animosity. I am
trying to bring whites and blacks together — for whites to see
blacks as something other than units of labor. For blacks to see
that there are whites who care."

I remembered those words, sitting at my portable computer
and writing my last story, trying to marshal my thoughts. I was
tired and I was angry, but I was searching for a chord — like a
musician trying to find the right combination of keys with six or
eight fingers. I looked out at the *monstro delicioso* and the aloes
in the night and recalled vividly the drive we took over to the
school that Smith and his wife had started for retarded children,
the only one of its kind in the township.

We drew up to his school, and some of his eighty children
came running out onto the bare gravel lawn when they saw
Smith coming. They threw themselves onto his legs and torso,
hugging him. He moved easily among the mongoloid faces and
twisted limbs, smiling down at the children, offering a hand to
be shaken, a finger to be pulled. It was the only time I saw blacks
in South Africa look at a white man with any feeling approaching love.

The children looked up at him, and they smiled as well. I remembered the looks on their faces and how they trusted him.
"You know," he said, a child hanging from one finger, another
from his arm. "Every night I look at the trains pulling into the
station from Pretoria. And I see those hordes of people being
forced to leave the city to live here." His voice dropped below its
gentle sadness, to just above a whisper. "And I say to myself, 'My
God, what have we done? My God, what have we done?' "

I remembered those words, and I began to write, thinking, To
hell with it. Others could accuse me of cockeyed optimism, but
I wasn't going to condemn an entire people as long as there were
still Nico Smiths around to care.

It was late, and the cicadas were grinding softly in the garden.
The rest of the night was quiet, and as I wrote I thought that if

remorse appeared in one Afrikaner, that was at least a sign of hope. If one or two could pry loose the wait-a-bits, then perhaps others could, too. I put aside skepticism and cynicism, two familiar tools for reporters in South Africa, and I wrote not of what had happened but of what I hoped would happen: that somehow, somewhere, the Afrikaners would see the light and share their country with the blacks in peace.

Maybe it was on a whim — months later I still didn't entirely know why I did it — but I grabbed for a well-worn volume on my bookshelf and began to read the Zulu words. After a while I was even humming the tune. *Nkosi sikelel 'i Afrika* — God bless Africa. *Malupakam upondo lwayo* — Raise up her spirit. *Yiva imitandazo yetu* — Hear our prayers. *Usi, sikelele* — And bless us.

Hamba kahle, I whispered to the night. Go well.

Two

THE SOWETO GENERATION

ONE OF THE MOST DIFFICULT ASPECTS of covering South Africa
was trying to keep up with the elusive black leadership. If the
Afrikaners were intent on standing still, the mood and nature of
black opposition to apartheid were just the opposite — in constant motion, a steadily spinning gyro centered in an implacable
opposition to a racist system.

One of apartheid's most elusive opponents was Winnie Mandela, wife of the leader of the outlawed African National Congress, Nelson Mandela, who began serving a sentence of life plus
five years in 1964 on charges of treason and sabotage. In 1985
and 1986, Winnie became the center of the anti-apartheid struggle, and during that time she won a place for herself alongside
her husband as an acknowledged leader of the liberation movement. She became "Mama Afrika." The only trouble was that
Mama Afrika seemed to be everywhere at once.

Banned by government order since 1962 and banished to the
Orange Free State since 1978, Winnie Mandela moved back to
her family home in Soweto in August 1985, in open defiance of
the law. From that time on, covering South Africa became a dicey game of trying to figure out how and when the government
would move against her, trying to keep track of her whereabouts, and memorizing the Johannesburg–Cape Town plane
schedules.

In early 1986, when the country boiled with rumors that P. W.

Botha was going to let Nelson Mandela out of jail and begin negotiations on the sharing of power, the only way to crack the rumors was to stay in touch with Mandela's Johannesburg lawyers and follow Winnie wherever she went. Her trips to and from Cape Town to visit her husband in Pollsmoor prison became a game of fox and hounds. It helped if one had no stomach and could drive fast. One Friday I made it from Johannesburg's northern suburbs to the arrivals lounge at Jan Smuts Airport in fifteen minutes, half the usual time, because Winnie had just returned from Pollsmoor. But, as was often the case, she could report nothing new.

On a Sunday in February 1986, Mark Peters and I thought we would get a jump on the rest of the press corps and bought ourselves seats on Winnie's 8:15 A.M. Jo'burg–Cape Town flight. There was nothing special about her visit, she said in her soft, lilting voice.

No one else seemed to believe her either. Half the foreign press corps met us at D. F. Malan Airport outside Cape Town. Winnie boarded a green BMW and shot off toward Cape Town at seventy-five miles an hour, with fifteen tailgating Mercedes rentals in hot pursuit. We all ground to a smoking halt in front of the downtown Cape Sun Hotel, where Winnie made a courtesy call on a group of visiting diplomats. Then she got back into her BMW and screeched off south, along winding De Waal drive, with the same fifteen tailgating maniacs following. John Rubython, a SIPA photo agency photographer, almost ran me off the road twice in his zeal to get into position behind Winnie's car. When we finally got to the prison, covering the news became a matter of sitting on the road outside the jail doing nothing for two hours under the blinding summer sun. For mental stimulation, I made a list of World Series winners starting in 1985 and going back as far as I could remember.

On another occasion, in Krugersdorp, Winnie left a courthouse in another green BMW and shot off toward a nearby black township. The press corps scattered like drivers at the start of the Indy 500, equipment clanging, a couple of network cameramen falling down, and zoomed off after the green BMW. I was far back in the pack because I'd parked too far away. I had no idea where the motorcade's final destination lay and had to squeeze through five red lights just to keep the tail car in sight.

We got to the township, Kagiso, and word quickly spread that Mama Afrika was in town. There I saw for myself how important this one elusive woman had become to the blacks of South Africa — and what her mere presence did to their spirits.

A crowd gathered outside the small house she had entered. Blacks surged in the front door simply to meet her and shake her hand. Later, an *impi* — battalion — of black youth came stomping down the street, dancing so hard that the ground literally shook. They carried clubs and *sjamboks* — whips — waiting for a police confrontation. "*Siyayah, siyayah,*" they sang — We are going, we are going. *Tsotsi* violence, I thought at first — hooliganism. But no, they had come only to chant and to dance.

The dance looked like a slow motion version of a person running — left leg kicking back, right arm stabbing forward, back hunched over as if against a stiff wind: *Si*-kick-*ya*-kick-*yah*-kick. Gradually it accelerated and became more emphatic until the ground shook and Winnie came out and waved.

The chant continued, evoking something ancient: "*Hih, hih, hih.*" Feet running in place, sometimes knees kicking high. The chant seemed to come from deep inside the children's abdomens, building momentum like a train approaching. No freedom song or chant is ever performed standing still. Everything moves — lungs, feet, arms, chanting, running in place, hopping.

Then the children broke into the angry anthem of black militancy, *Hamba Kahle, Umkhonto we Sizwe* — Go Well, Spear of the Nation. Nelson Mandela was head of Umkhonto we Sizwe when he was arrested, and, jogging in place, the children sang the anthem loudly for his wife. Their voices swelled in volume and intensity when they reached the words *bulala AmaBhunu* — kill the Boers.

For all the fury that surrounds her, I saw how Winnie Mandela remains calm and steady as a rock. She is a beautiful woman, still, at age fifty-two. Wearing kaftans and colored hair ornamentation causes her to stand out in a crowd. She is tall, and to see her walking, especially with her hair in colorfully beaded cornrows, is to see something regal. Her inner confidence or inner peace with herself and with her role as a leader lends authority and weight to her presence.

In person, she radiates a sensuality that a woman friend calls "more than charisma, more of warmth and loving." But it is sensuality nonetheless. She has a way of half closing her eyelids, fluttering them over her large brown eyes, cow eyes, that is warm and inviting. When she talks, she holds her head cocked at an angle, making her audience, large or small, feel closer, intimate. It was said that the Afrikaner policemen assigned to watch her in exile had trouble keeping their strict Afrikaner composure in her presence. So they shortened their duty rotations so as not to be with her overlong.

She radiated sensuality and defiance the first time I met with her in private. I noticed it many other times — in airplanes, cars, airports — but that first time I was struck by her calm self-assurance and poise. And perhaps because of her calmness, the depth of her commitment came through as immutable — as firm in its way as the intransigence of the Afrikaners she was determined to oppose. It was just before Christmas 1985, and she was living in Soweto in open defiance of her government banning order. We met in Johannesburg's Carlton Hotel in a suite I had rented for the afternoon for that purpose. She did not want to meet in Soweto because she feared police intrusion. But I could tell she feared very little else, as she spoke calmly and quietly about her reasons for defying the laws that bound her. Never did she raise her voice. Her words bore the quality of words long reasoned over.

I asked her why she was breaking her ban, and she smiled. "As far as I am concerned I am defying no one." She grinned.

Black South Africans, and especially Xhosas like Winnie Mandela, have a wonderful sing-song quality to their speech. Sentences begin on a low note, rise slightly toward the middle, and then drop again to a low note, often after a slight pause. Winnie sat back on a blue upholstered couch, her arm relaxed on the back; listening to her talk was like hearing the song of a mourning dove, sweet but sad at the same time.

"I am highlighting the inequality of an unjust law," she whispered simply, her head cocked. "The Afrikaner had no right to take away my freedom in the first place. I have been banned since 1962. Those years were the best years of my life, and they took them away from me. They were the best years of my productive life. They were the best years when I could have shown my motherhood toward my children."

She paused then, and the word *motherhood* hung in the air — *mothahooood*. I remembered that this was the woman who had started crèches — preschools — with her own money in Soweto and later in exile in the Orange Free State.

"They were the best years when I could have contributed to my society," she continued, her words crisp and precise. She took her arm off the back of the couch and leaned forward, seeming to crack a whip over every fifth word. "I could barely take my children to school. I have never met, at my age as a grandmother, any of my own children's teachers. I have never known what it is to walk into a classroom as part of a parent-teacher body and determine my own children's education, my own children's futures. I just came to a stage where enough was enough." She paused again, crossed her legs demurely, and extended her hands, palms up, as if presenting the obvious to plain sight.

"Our obedience to these unjust laws has gone on for so long that we, too, were at fault by conforming to them," she explained quietly, slumping back on the couch. She was dressed uncharacteristically in a two-piece, Western-style blue suit. She also wore a long black wig that softened her delicate, high cheekbones and took some of the sharpness off her long chin. It wasn't exactly a disguise — just a gauzy mask to make it easier for her to move around the city without drawing too much attention to herself. The get-up, combined with the drab hotel suite of our clandestine meeting, made me think of the "damned elusive" Scarlet Pimpernel. Her husband, after all, had once been called the Black Pimpernel for his success at eluding the police.

"No human being has rights over another human being," she said softly. "This is a government that determines even how you worship. One of the most humiliating things I found, for instance, was having to apply to go to church. These are ordinary human beings, and they give themselves supernatural powers. In any civilized society those are God's powers alone."

Winnie leaned forward on the couch, seeming to rest her full weight on her clenched fists on the cushions beside her. Though she still spoke softly, the pace of her words began to quicken. "We knocked on the doors of Pretoria year in and year out, and the government never left any doubt that its answer was violence." The final word came out with a hiss.

Gone was the coy, inviting sideways slant of her chin. Her head bobbed rhythmically, straight up and down, for emphasis. "The answer was the killing of the opponents of apartheid, the killing of all the people who make demands for a roundtable conference. This is an immoral and unjust country where an orderly demonstration is treason. The answer is always the same. Violence. And arrest and detention without trial, and people disappearing."

She paused then, and her head resumed its sideways tilt. Her speech slowed again, and she drew out her words so they sounded like a plea. "Noooo mothah, noooo brooootalized mothah who has lost, as we have, soooo many children, would want to see one drop of the blood of our children spilled in the name of ideology, in the name of freeeedom. But we have no choice."

Her pace began to quicken again, and her eyes opened wide.

"It gets worse every day. This very minute little boys eighteen years old are on Casspirs, and they are occupying the townships and shooting our children at random in the streets of Johannesburg and the streets of the eastern Cape. The entire country is under siege. We are under siege by apartheid." And her fist pounded the blue cushions softly.

I asked if there was reason for hope, if she thought her cause could win. She smiled a big, broad smile. Her eyes lit up and her teeth flashed in the dim light. "No doubt at all," she said with a laugh, easing back in her couch. "Absolutely. And if anything, I feel it more than at any other time in the history of our struggle. I feel the pulse of freedom. I feel the hope of the nation. We have never been as near to freedom as we are now today."

We rode down in the elevator together to the Carlton lobby. We got off on the wrong floor and had to take the escalator down to the street level. Faces, white faces, turned to look at the striking figure of Winnie Mandela floating slowly down to the lobby, recognizable even through the wig and the Western suit.

"I can't thank you enough for coming here," I said. "I hope this isn't going to get you into trouble."

"That's all right." She laughed quietly. "They can't do anything more to me that they haven't done to me already." And she walked off through the lobby, proudly and with head erect, through the revolving door and into the summer afternoon drizzle.

Her words hung in my head, and I busily scribbled them down on a piece of note paper, standing distractedly in the middle of the busy hotel lobby. I was discovering that most black South Africans felt the same way — that arrest, imprisonment, and banning were simply part of the normal course of their lives. And walking back to my office through the bustle of black faces on Commissioner Street, I realized that some unalterable collision course had been set. Afrikaner leaders I had spoken to showed little sign of scrapping the apartheid system — and yet here was Mama Africa talking about the pulse of freedom and the hope of the nation. It was like watching two eighteen-wheelers playing chicken on a two-lane country road.

I felt Winnie Mandela's pulse of freedom in three black South Africans I came to know: Seth Mazibuko, Murphison Morobe, Thabo Ndabene, three brothers. Theirs was the story of a generation of black opposition to apartheid and of why that opposition will probably never end. They, too, have felt the hope of the nation through torture, imprisonment, solitary confinement, and hiding. Yet in the end, theirs was also the sad story of a people gone from unity into discord and from a singleness of purpose into fragmentation — the heartbeat of freedom as cardiac arrhythmia.

In May and early June 1986 all of us in the foreign press corps were looking ahead with trepidation to the tenth anniversary of the Soweto uprising on June 16. I wanted to find a way to tell the story of the "Soweto generation" because they were the ones who started the struggle as teenagers and led it still in mid-1986 as young men in their late twenties and early thirties. They were black South Africa's brightest and best.

The story, I figured, would cover the continuum of a decade of black defiance and explain the steady, decade-long escalation of black anger over apartheid. The problem was pinpointing a representative quartet or trio of young blacks, so one afternoon I got together with my chief Soweto stringer, Nhlanhla Mbatha, also known as Lucky. We decided to find three members of the Soweto Eleven, a group of Soweto teenagers who had essentially run Soweto for fifteen months in 1976 and 1977 and who were later tried for terrorism and sedition. The three we settled on were Murphy Morobe, then national spokesman for the anti-apartheid coalition United Democratic Front (UDF), Seth Mazibuko, a youth organizer for the South African Council of Churches (SACC), and Thabo Ndabene, national labor organizer for the Azanian People's Organization (AZAPO).

The three were very different but still very much alike. Thabo

Ndabene, tall and willowy at age twenty-nine, reminded me of Eldridge Cleaver at the same age — the same shade of brown skin, scruffy beard, bushy Afro haircut. Murphy Morobe, stocky and balding at age thirty, had the look of a well-dressed bank assistant. And Seth Mazibuko, twenty-eight, looked like a flyweight wrestler, all wiry and wired. However their looks — and politics — differed, they all shared one thing: an unchanged hatred of the system that governed them.

The hardest to reach was Thabo Ndabene. He had been hiding from the police for six months. Lucky contacted him through an AZAPO intermediary, and we were told to meet him at his office in downtown Johannesburg.

The "office" turned out to be three bare rooms furnished with one desk and three chairs. It was just a message drop. We waited for an hour before he showed up. He had had to make sure there were no police in the area. He walked briskly down the corridor, a tense bounce in his step, eyes always moving behind his smoked gray glasses. He wore a heavy green sweater whose collar came up almost to his ears. "Nhlanhla vouches for you," he said laconically, under hooded eyes. He had a deep bass voice that seemed to come from his navel. "He says you're okay."

"I hope so." I shrugged with a smile. I could see the problem. The radical AZAPO has a natural mistrust of all whites. I tried to smile my best sheepish American smile. "I'd just like to talk for a while."

"So," he said. "You want to talk about Soweto." When spoken by most blacks, the word comes out *So-way-too,* as Johannesburg comes out *Johannesbeeg* and Meadowlands comes out *Meeedowlands.* "Okay. Let's talk about Sowaytoo." And we did, several times over the course of the next week. Later, when I was ordered out of the country, Thabo Ndabene telephoned me, the only one of the three Soweto brothers who did. He wanted to know if I was okay. I was touched that a man on his own like Thabo would ask.

Finding Murphison Morobe was not too difficult. As national

spokesman for the UDF, he stuck close to home base in Johannesburg. I had seen him many other times, at UDF rallies around the country, and he had impressed me as a powerful and eloquent speaker. He spoke with the same calmness and deliberateness as Winnie Mandela, not shouting or haranguing but simply pointing out the logical necessity of unbanning the African National Congress and releasing Nelson Mandela.

The first time we met in private was in Morobe's cramped office in Khotso House, the building in downtown Johannesburg that houses the UDF and several other anti-apartheid groups. Yellow, red, and black UDF sweatshirts were piled in boxes and were hung over chairs. It was 7:30 in the morning, and Morobe was looking a little worn, in contrast to his smart blue wool overcoat, his tweed jacket, and blue wool tie. "You know," he said with a scowl. "I saw that story you did a few weeks ago."

"Which one?" I asked innocently, though I knew he was talking about a story I'd done on the Necklace, the brutal method of killing with tires and gasoline that was used by the radical young blacks called "comrades."

"The Necklace," he said, and we both nodded slowly. "It didn't paint a very positive picture of the struggle."

"You should try talking to Louis Nel," I said, referring to the government's propaganda minister. "He doesn't think I'm painting a very positive picture of the National Party." And we both laughed.

"So you're just trying to make everybody mad, is that it?" And we both laughed again.

"The story I'm doing now, though, Mr. Morobe, is about the long-range struggle, about what got you from point *A* to point zed and all the *P*s, *Q*s, and crossed *T*s in between."

"Okay," he said, "but we're trying to get you foreign people to stop using the word *mob*. Think you can do that?"

"I'll try," I replied. And then we started to talk.

I found Seth Mazibuko in Khotso House too, in the SACC offices. Mark Peters and I were waiting for him in the SACC foyer one afternoon when he literally ran through the front door, waved, skidded around a corner, slammed a door, and ran back the same way he had come. He was a blur of baggy red sweater, purple jeans, and maroon knit cap. Somewhere in the distance we heard a faint "Be right back." We continued our wait, and five minutes later he was back in the door, still running. He came over and stood before us, panting. "Busy day, busy day, busy day," he puffed, like a pint-sized locomotive. "Let's go to my office. Very busy. I hope you won't mind if we're interrupted a few times. I'm very busy, very busy."

"That's okay," I said. "We've got time." And as expected, the door opened every five minutes or so, and kids aged thirteen or fourteen popped their heads in.

"Be right back," he said again after five minutes and then ran down the hallway to the front door.

"What's with this motor mouth?" asked Peters. "Doesn't he ever sit still? Acts like he's running the whole fucking world."

"Give him time." I shrugged. "He'll calm down." He did, but it took a while. It took a while with all of them, as they explained life in Soweto and Alexandra and Crossroads and why they are what they are — young men willing to go to jail rather than submit to legalized underprivileged status in the land of their birth.

Thabo and Murphy and Seth were all born and raised in Soweto — an acronym for South West Townships — the sprawling slum that lies on the other side of the Crown Mines dumps from Johannesburg.

Soweto is a thirty-two-square-mile hodgepodge of single-story brick, mud, and wooden houses, most with corrugated tin roofs. Some of the streets are paved. Most are unpaved ruts, with human excrement, dead animals, and garbage lying in the gutters. There are parks, but most of them are filled with garbage. There are no sidewalks, just paths of red clay winding through the grass, weeds, and scrub. It is a common sight to see women shuffling down those paths, bags of groceries balanced delicately on their heads and *bubbas* — infants — tied to their backs.

One of the things that impressed me about Soweto and other townships was how slowly everybody moved, as if they were all slogging through mud, carrying invisible burdens on their heads and backs. Trains and buses begin ferrying blacks to the northern suburbs and the city's downtown at 3:30 in the morning. For some residents of Soweto, getting to and from work is a forty-mile round trip that begins and ends in the dark. Soweto is a city of trudgers.

Soweto is also apartheid in practice. Between Johannesburg's southern boundary and Diepkloof, the corner of Soweto closest to the city, there is virtually nothing but open veld and mine dumps. There are also, characteristically, only two major entrances to the township. If things got dicey enough, a small number of soldiers could close off the township at its two entrances, and if things got very dicey, the township could be bombed from the air without risking the loss of white lives in the distant city.

Soweto, more than other places, lives in a state of siege. The times I was there, mine-proof troop carriers — Casspirs — rumbled over the rutted red clay roads. Once I saw a group of white soldiers playing soccer in the dust outside Orlando Stadium, while their mates looked on from the backs of trucks. Meanwhile, blacks trudged through the streets, oblivious of the soldiers' presence. A Casspir on every block had been a fact of life in Soweto for more than ten years.

"Nothing has changed here," growled Thabo in his deep bass voice, arms crossed and lips scowling. The heavy green sweater was to ward off the chill in his small, unheated "office," and he shivered in the cold from time to time. "Ten years ago, we had a very *kragdadige* [forceful] regime in Pretoria, and this one has been concerned about the way they are viewed abroad. They're sensitive about foreign attitudes, so they've tried to make apartheid acceptable to everyone. It's not possible. Soweto has not changed in ten years. Our lives haven't either."

Soweto is one of the places in South Africa where the first world crosses the third in vivid contrast. One morning I was sitting in my car talking with Seth — it was the only place we could get him to sit still — when we heard a strange noise coming from behind us, a clomp, clomp, clomp. I looked out and saw it was a horse pulling a wagon full of sacks of coal.

"Five rand for a twenty-kilo bag," Seth declared with a shrug, looking out from under his maroon knit cap. "Maybe it lasts a month, if you're careful. And look what it does." And he waved his hand at the putrid air.

Virtually all the homes in Soweto are heated by coal in the winter, and the township lies awash in the thick coal smog from May through September. One June morning I was standing with Murphy on a street corner in Soweto, and I noticed that the light had an eerie, underwater quality. When we had left Johannesburg, we had both worn sunglasses. In Soweto, we didn't need them.

At nightfall Soweto looks as if it's burning to the ground. Cook fires, making the city look like Dickens's London. Seth had a terrible cough most of the time I was with him, and he continually sucked on lozenges as we talked. In Soweto and other black townships, tuberculosis occurs as frequently as the common cold in New York or Los Angeles, and its incidence is on the rise. South African cases of TB grew from forty-seven thousand in 1979 to nearly fifty-five thousand in 1983, and in one township more than six hundred children died of the disease in one month alone. The homelands are becoming vast reservoirs of TB infection. Many infected homeland blacks come to the big cities looking for both work and treatment for their disease, and the TB spreads.

Many children in Soweto and other townships suffer from malnutrition and its advanced form, *kwashiorkor,* their bellies distended and their legs rail thin. But I learned that frequently they do not die of starvation. Their bodies do not have the strength to fight off illness, and so they die instead of TB.

Tuberculosis is a disease associated with stress, poor nutrition, and overcrowding. In South Africa, overcrowding is caused by laws decreeing that eighty percent of the population must live on thirteen percent of the land. Soweto is a city with the population of Philadelphia and Pittsburgh combined; yet to approximate Soweto, residents of those two Pennsylvania cities would have to squeeze themselves into an area the size of Pittsburgh's downtown and live in single-story housing.

In the Diepkloof section of Soweto, families sleep four to a house. Four families: one to each room. One morning Lucky and Seth and I drove through the White City section of Soweto, one of the most overcrowded and impoverished parts of the township. Blacks fleeing their poor homelands had flocked into Soweto looking for work, but there was not enough housing. Local black authorities solved the problem by setting aside a vacant lot the size of a city block and providing stacks of corrugated metal. More than five thousand blacks built tin houses in the camp. We were there on a Monday, which is wash day. We saw perhaps a thousand women doing the family laundry that winter morning. They all shared three cold water faucets, the camp's only source of water.

Poor nutrition in South Africa means that about fifty percent of the school age black children are underweight and that the majority of the preschool age children have stunted growth. Yet South Africa, I learned, produces plenty of food, enough to meet 112 percent of the optimum daily energy requirements of everyone living in the country. One result: the infant mortality rate among blacks is more than six times the infant mortality rate among whites. In one homeland it is fourteen times the white rate.

The single largest killer of blacks in South Africa is infectious and parasitic diseases, which account for twenty-one percent of the deaths among blacks every year. One study of black schoolchildren living in slum housing found that fifty percent had blood in their urine, suggesting the presence of the bilharzia parasite. Bilharzia, in turn, suggests stagnant water. On the chilly winter morning that we drove through White City, we stopped at the intersection where the shooting had begun on June 16, 1976. On one corner of that intersection sat a big pile of wet garbage, discarded tires, and rusting metal, surrounded by deep pools of filmy water. Black children were playing, bare-assed, in and around the garbage. Virtually all of them had runny noses and cold sores around their mouths. The parasites were invisible but omnipresent.

Murphy Morobe described growing up in Soweto as "having to grow up in an environment that stimulated my way of thinking." He was sitting in his small cluttered office in Khotso House, his balding brow wrinkled in thought. He spoke with a high, reedy voice that sounded like a clarinet in high register. "It wasn't just the surroundings," Murphy said with a shrug. It was still early in the morning and the heat in the building had not yet come on. He still wore his blue wool topcoat, tweed jacket, and blue wool tie against the cold. "It was the pass arrests and the raids on permits. With me, it spurred me to seek out more information. I was fortunate in having friends who were political. It led to big fights with my parents, who were not convinced we had to be politically involved. But we stayed after school and at the YMCA and had political discussions. It broadened me."

I asked Murphy when this was, what year.

"I'd say 1968," he remembered, leaning back in his wooden chair with a creak, his hands knotted behind his head. "I was twelve."

Black politics for twelve-year-olds in the 1960s consisted of Black Consciousness. Thabo, Seth, and Murphy all turned to BC, as it became known. BC is often identified with Steve Biko, the black leader who died in police custody in 1977, during the nationwide wave of bannings and arrests that came down fifteen months after the Soweto uprising. To Biko and other BC leaders, South Africa's blacks had looked too long to the white man for help and support in their struggle for equality and liberation. Blacks had to look to themselves for leadership, said Biko. Blacks in South Africa had to take pride in themselves as blacks and fight back.

BC stirred controversy — and was directly at odds with the central beliefs of the African National Congress (ANC) and its leaders Nelson Mandela and Oliver Tambo. The ANC's Freedom Charter, adopted in 1955, called for a nonracial democracy in South Africa that would include whites, albeit with their entrenched privilege lost. The charter also accepted whites into the anti-apartheid struggle. Black Consciousness could accept the ANC's goal of a nonracial state, but in the sometimes fuzzy world of South African politics, BC could not accept the ANC's multiracial approach to establishing the nonracial state. The debate over white participation led to a major split in the liberation struggle in 1959, when Robert Sobukwe left the ANC and formed his Black Consciousness Pan Africanist Congress (PAC). The split in the black ranks was to last until the present day, as Seth, Murphy, and Thabo would later discover.

In the late 1960s, however, BC succeeded in planting the first seeds for what would come to full flower half a decade later in Soweto. BC got kids like Seth and Murphy and Thabo *thinking* about liberation. "BC filled a vacuum for us," Seth remembered, hugging the arms of his baggy red sweater. "It gave us a psychological liberation we never had before." Thabo recalled having a math teacher with strong BC beliefs who would stay after school with him for long hours talking about BC. "Before you can participate in the struggle," Thabo recalled of his early training, "you have to determine what the root cause of the problem is." His deep bass voice paused, and he opened his Eldridge Cleaver eyes wide. He was sitting on a rickety wooden chair in his bare office, leaning back on the hind two legs, his hands clutching the front of the seat, relaxed. "We were talking about a philosophy of complete freedom. That was how we grew into political consciousness."

BC also turned the three Soweto kids into brothers. On several occasions Murphy and Thabo sat up all night talking Black Consciousness. Seth would drop in from time to time and join the discussions. All three became fast friends: Seth Mazibuko the tiny motor mouth, Murphy Morobe the stocky intellectual, Thabo Ndabene the somber judge. The three were so close that even their mothers became close through them. "BC was like that," remembered Seth in his rapid-fire banter, scratching his maroon cap. "It filled a vacuum and brought us all together. That was what we needed."

Seth, Murphy, and Thabo made Soweto's schools the first target of their plan for "psychological liberation." The schools were a natural target because they were psychologically and educationally in the Stone Age. They still are. Education has remained a central issue in the black liberation struggle for the past twenty years because education is crucial to equality, advancement, and dignity. And because for forty years "Bantu education" remained unequal, regressive, and void of dignity.

In black schools in South Africa, some teachers have little more education than the students they teach. The black schools in 1983 had 6,700 teachers with nothing more than eighth grade diplomas and 13,700 teachers with twelfth grade certificates, compared with 101 in white schools. There were 14,800 with junior certificates and no teacher training in black schools, compared with 37 in white schools.

In all, ninety-four percent of the nation's 45,000 black teachers are underqualified. Over the last ten years, half the underqualified teachers have been under the age of thirty. The average age of black students who make it as far as the matriculation year, or final year of high school, is nineteen years and ten months. So close in age are teachers and students that the most often-heard complaints among black high school students have been molestation and rape.

Twenty-three percent of the black population drops out of school before the first grade. Twenty-eight percent drops out after the fourth grade. Seventy percent of South Africa's black population has an education ending at or before the seventh grade.

A study based on the 1980 census found that, excluding the "independent" self-governing homelands of Transkei, Ciskei, Venda, and Bophuthatswana, one third of South Africa's blacks over the age of fifteen were unable to read or write. The percentage would be far higher if the four homelands were included. More than two thirds of the school age population of the Transkei, the impoverished homeland in the eastern Cape, never made it past the fourth grade. Only about ten percent of South Africa's black population gets as far as the final year of high school and has the chance to take the "matric" exam. Only eleven percent of those blacks who actually take the exam pass with a high enough grade to qualify for entrance to a university.

The futility of black education walked into my office one day in early 1986. He was a young black radical from Soweto. What, I asked him, did he want to do after high school? He said he wanted to go to the University of the Witwatersrand, the nation's best English-language university, and then become a teacher. I could only sigh inside. Our conversation was being conducted in Zulu, with Lucky translating. The kid did not know enough English to describe killing, let alone qualify for university.

Pupil-teacher ratios are forty to one in black schools, compared with a ratio of nineteen to one in white schools. The ratio is fifty to one for primary schools in Bophuthatswana, the hodgepodge of a homeland scattered over the Transvaal and the Orange Free State in seven separate pieces. In 1983 South Africa's minister in charge of black education said that there was a shortage of thirty-five hundred classrooms for blacks at the primary level and a shortage of twenty-five hundred at the secondary level. As a result, for the last decade and a half, many black students have attended class under a platoon system, with two teachers teaching two different classes in the same room. In some cases, one teacher conducts the same, abbreviated class twice in one day. "We're in this situation because education has been racially split," a white school principal told Johannesburg's respected weekly, the *Financial Mail,* in early 1986. "There is unequal expenditure on each child. The provision of facilities, like grounds and buildings, is unequal. How can you talk about providing equipment like projectors when black schools often have no electricity? Sometimes there is not even water."

"Man, you're looking at a product of Bantu education," laughed Murphy Morobe, sitting in his office that early morning as the sun began to filter through his one curtained window. His laugh had the same clarinet quality as his speaking voice. "When it all started in seventy-six, I was twenty years old and still in my matric year. There were lots of us like that. Still are. But Bantu education was what got us out there."

Before June 16, 1976, the word *Soweto* meant nothing more than a place. After that day, *Soweto* became synonymous with rebellion and protest and the quest for liberation. The Soweto uprising began as a one-day student march to protest inferior Bantu education and the use of Afrikaans as a medium of instruction in black schools. By the time it ended in mass arrests and bannings fifteen months later, Soweto had become a mass movement. It saw the rise of Winnie Mandela as a political force in her own right. It saw the flowering of the Black Consciousness movement and of Steve Biko, before he died.

Sitting in his cramped little office, Murphy looked wistful, remembering June 16, 1976. "The single most important day in the life of my generation," he stated flatly, his brow unwrinkled. The look on Seth's face, sitting in the back seat of my car, was dreamlike as he looked at the spot where the shooting started. "It was the time when everything began," he whispered, hugging the knees of his purple jeans. "Everything began here." Thabo looked at the bare ceiling in his bare office. "Everything that's happening now is a direct result of what happened then," he said gruffly in his deep bass voice, his green sweater bunched under his neck. "Everything."

* * *

The winter dawn broke cloudy, cold, and filled with coal smoke, Seth remembered ten years later, "suggestive of the day it was going to be." Seth, eighteen at the time, kissed his mother good-bye and walked to Musi High School. At eight o'clock he rang the school bell: a kid summoning a township for the orders of the day.

Insurgent students in the fledgling South African Students Movement (SASM) had chosen June 16, 1976, as their day of action. Seth was an assistant to SASM President Tsietsi Mashin-ini, and as he rang the summoning bell his friend Thabo was in another part of the building, trying to decide whether to take an exam or join the protest. He eventually did both.

Across town their friend Murphy was painting placards for the planned march. One sign read "Down with Afrikaans"; another one goaded the prime minister: "If we must do Afrikaans, Vorster must do Zulu." Murphy carried them into the assembly room at Morris Isaacson High. At the close of assembly, instead of singing the Lord's Prayer as usual, the students sang *Nkosi sikelel 'i Afrika* — God Bless Africa. "I am not a goose bump per-son," Murphy recalled with a shy smile, straightening the knot of his blue tie uneasily. "But that gave me goose bumps. That was the clarion call that sent us marching out." Twenty thousand black students marched on Orlando West High School from four directions. Two of the student columns reached Orlando West, Seth remembered, when a third hove into view. It was fol-lowed by a detachment of police. The police gave an order to disperse. Then they opened fire.

Thirteen-year-old Hector Peterson was the first to die. Blood foaming at his lips and running from his nose, Peterson's dead body was carried away by a young black man. A picture of the dead Peterson circulated around the world. The most haunting aspect of that photograph was Hector Peterson's sister, Antoi-nette. Arms raised, as if warding off bullets. Screaming. "My God," Seth remembered saying to himself when he saw Hector Peterson fall. "They're killing people and I'm supposed to be responsible for them. Go home, everybody. Go home."

No one went home. Ten days of rioting produced nearly two hundred dead. By the time the unrest ended fifteen months later, more than six hundred had died. But for the first time since the Sharpeville shootings of 1960 — the Mandela generation's strike at apartheid — there was a feeling abroad in the land that the system could be beaten. "The majority of students may have had an opinion or two about apartheid before the shootings," Murphy remembered, leaning back in his chair and taking off his heavy coat. "After June 16 they *all* did. That day raised the political consciousness of a generation and mobilized us all."

Running the mobilization was the Soweto Students Representative Council (SSRC), an expanded version of the old SASM, with Thabo, Murphy, and Seth serving on the executive committee under President Tsietsi Mashinini. The SSRC began by taking over Soweto's schools and instituted a system of Black Consciousness "people's education."

"We had this principal at our school," remembered Thabo with a smile, running his right hand through his bushy Eldridge Afro. "He was a real problem. One of the ways we tried to raise political consciousness was by instructing the students to write poetry and paint paintings. We would hang them on the walls of the school. It was an important emotional and political thing to do. One day the principal came and took them all down." Thabo paused, as in disbelief. "He actually took them all down. We fired him. Gave him his walking papers. He was unacceptable to us."

The SSRC was soon running more than the schools. Its first target after the schools was the *shebeen,* or speakeasy, network. Black Consciousness would not tolerate black adults taking their paltry wages and wasting them on alcohol. Booze was a way to forget the grimness of township life, and BC wanted people aware of repression, not trying to forget about it. The SSRC closed the *shebeens.* Police later reported that Christmas 1976 and New Year's 1977 were the most peaceful on record. There were no alcohol-related crimes.

The Urban Bantu Council (UBC) came next. The UBC was

Soweto's black, but white-appointed, self-governing body. Black Consciousness would not accept blacks governed by white-imposed stooges. So the SSRC closed down the council and ran Soweto for the next year.

The SSRC's next target was the white power structure that supported the apartheid system. The SSRC's leaders organized a series of work stay-aways, consumer boycotts, and rent strikes. The first three-day stay-away was announced for early August. Students ripped up portions of track and sabotaged signal boxes to keep the trains from running. They went to the bus depots in force and blocked commuters from boarding their long, blue PUTCO buses. The student tactics worked. The stay-away produced a worker absentee rate of sixty percent in Johannesburg. Later, despite a significant police presence, a second stay-away resulted in a seventy percent absentee rate.

At one point the SSRC tried to organize a march on Johannesburg's main police barracks at John Vorster Square. The police blocked it. The students retaliated a month later by doffing their school uniforms, putting on work clothes, and commuting into town with adult Soweto. They then assembled in front of the barracks and staged their demonstration.

"It was exhilarating," recalled Thabo with a great grin. He crossed his green-sweatered arms and looked at me over his wire glasses, as if to make sure I understood. He pushed his glasses up onto the bridge of his nose and smiled again. "I was excited at the prospect of trying to shut down the system and cripple the white man's economy. It was a useful experience as well. We were all young and eager. But the situation forced us to come to grips with reality. We learned that it is not an easy task to overthrow a government." He shook his head and gave out a short, deep chuckle that made his green sweater shake. "But we were trying." And his voice rose. "Still are. That's why it all started for us then. We got a sense that we could win."

Seth missed the heady days of organizing the boycotts and stay-aways, for he was in jail. He had been arrested on July 2 and taken to what the Afrikaners call *die waar kammer* — the truth room — at Protea Police Station in Soweto.

"They wanted to know where Tsietsi Mashinini was," Seth recalled with a sigh that clearly showed he was entering miles of bad road ahead. Then his squeaky, scratchy voice, a rusty weather vane voice, quickened and resumed its rattle-fast tempo. "Because I was his vice president, they thought I would know. They wanted to know whether the ANC was involved in organizing the march. They wanted to know how we planned the demonstration. I told them I didn't know where Tsietsi was and that no one over the age of twenty-five was involved in planning the demo." His voice, like a 33 rpm record on 45, slowed to 33 again. "But they tortured me anyway.

"It was the worst ten months of my life." The motor mouth was gone, replaced by a slow, lifeless drone. "They made me stand on needles. They sat me there with a tight rubber cloth over my head." Sitting in a small wooden chair in his cramped Khotso House office — several of his teenage charges sitting on the floor around him — Seth clasped his hands together in a double fist. Slowly and unconsciously, as he continued, his hands lowered to between the legs of his purple jeans, clasped tightly.

"The worst thing they did to me was my balls. They tied twine around them while they made me squat." The fast rattle was back in his voice, and Seth leaped out of his chair and began angrily to act out his torture. "They tied the other end of the twine to a brick. Then they made me stand up." He stood, and a grimace covered his face, the cords in his neck sticking out like wire.

"It was awful. But I told them nothing. What could I tell them? I didn't know what they wanted me to tell them." Seth was still standing, leaning over his desk, his eyes accusing. "They nearly killed me once when the interrogation officer slammed me into the wall so hard he broke my arm and then kicked me when I was down on the ground. Stamped on me, really. I was in plaster up to my neck."

Seth had been talking so fast he was out of breath. He stopped for air and then the rusty weather vane started up again, pausing occasionally to collect fresh wind. "Wouldn't you hate a system that did that to you? Wouldn't you hate apartheid if it did that to you ten years ago? Tied up your balls and then made you lift a brick with them? Wouldn't you still hate it today? Surely, I do."

Seth was released from jail in May 1977, but his release came too near the end of the Soweto renaissance to be of any use. Murphy Morobe had been arrested on the last day of 1976, Thabo Ndabene a month later. Seth himself would have only another five months of freedom before the SSRC was banned and all its leaders arrested, in September 1977. All three remained in various jails — Thabo and Seth shared the same cell, tin plate, and bath water — until July 1978, when charges were finally brought against them, and the Soweto Eleven trial began.

They were charged with terrorism and sedition; while all were cleared of terrorism, which is a capital offense in South Africa, they were all found guilty of sedition. Seven of them, including Thabo Ndabene, received five-year suspended sentences. Three — Murphy Morobe, Seth Mazibuko, and Daniel Montsisi, the last president of the SSRC — were sent to South Africa's Alcatraz, Robben Island, a barren rock in the middle of Table Bay off Cape Town. To many of the student leaders, Robben Island became more than just a prison. The Island became known as Mandela U.

"Whoooo-eeee," shrieked Seth, revving up his motors and raising his arms. "In my personal struggle against apartheid I consider the Boer sending me to the Island an honor. What it did for me! What I learned there! How I changed! All because I met Nelson Mandela and talked with him and knew him and learned from him and the others there like Govan Mbeki and Walter Sisulu." The look on his face was close to ecstasy, like a goofy kid recalling getting the autograph of his favorite baseball player.

"I had been brought up to believe — we all had — that Mandela was an animal," Seth explained in his rusty voice, his brow furrowed in puzzled wrinkles below the maroon knit cap. "Our parents taught us: Don't get involved in politics because you'll end up like that animal Mandela. You'll be like that animal. A terrorist was an animal. But how I learned differently!"

Seth leaned back in his chair, the baggy red sweater hanging off his thin frame lazily, and he smiled at the memory. "The Boers brought us in, a bunch of us together on a boat, and I heard this voice, deep and strong, call out, 'Which ones are Seth, Murphy, and Dan?' I looked up and there was Mandela." His voice had a touch of amazement. "Mandela! A while later other inmates arranged for us to be brought in to see Mandela. He wanted to meet with us and find out about the uprising. This was no animal."

Seth's voice was breathless. "He was tall, over six feet. He spoke with this deep but gentle voice. He was big. Strong. Robust." Seth stood up and did his best to make his five-foot frame look a foot taller and many muscles heavier. He pushed out his chest and threw back his shoulders. The sight was absurd, and I almost started giggling because he looked like a five-foot black chicken with glasses. "He had just come back from playing tennis. What an impression he made, sitting there with a towel around his neck, asking us what we had been through and how we had done things. He kept asking, 'Tell me more, tell me more.'" And Seth did his best to make his rusty weather vane voice sound basso.

"Sitting there that night, and on other occasions, taught me so many things." The quick clatter was back in his voice, and his words sounded like a playing card brushing the spokes of a bicycle wheel. He held out his arms as he talked, and his red sweater drooped off him like a loose rag. "Just being near him was enough to make me feel that this was a leader and I must follow him. He never spoke of sectionalism and political fragmentation. He wanted to unite. It was then that I began to question some of my Black Consciousness beliefs. I mean, here was our leader preaching unity and nonracialism and a democratic South Africa. This was different.

"Another man — we called him simply the Old One — really affected me. As BC leaders we wanted to defy everything the white man told us to do. We would not wash. We would not clean our cells. We would not *do* anything. But this old man came to me. He had been sent, I think, by Mandela. He told me that in this struggle we were all prisoners of war. We had to be disciplined and orderly. I looked at how different that was from BC."

Seth paused, out of breath again, and that gave him a chance to reflect. "I had to come to a decision on whether to follow Mandela and the Old One or keep on with Black Consciousness. The Island changed me, because eventually I came to the decision that I had to follow Mandela and nonracialism and not BC."

Being near Mandela proved an inspiration for Murphy Morobe as well. "He was a legend," Murphy explained matter-of-factly, leaning forward on his desk and fiddling with a pencil. "When you meet the person who is acknowledged as the leader of the struggle, you have to be proud to be in the same prison with him; you have to be inspired."

Murphy Morobe completed his drift away from Black Consciousness on Robben Island. "I have great respect for BC because that is where I began politically," he explained, and his face bore the pained expression of a boy telling his girlfriend he was dating other girls. "But I never saw it as a substitute for the banned organizations of the 1960s. Even as we organized, we students, I saw BC as a way to keep the home fires burning for our leaders."

Murphy paused then and scratched his balding brow. "My political consciousness began to develop beyond the mere conscientizing of BC." He shrugged, his broad, tweed-covered shoulders rising to his ears. "It began to see more and grapple more with questions of strategy and significant strategy. In the end I could not see any significant strategies in Black Consciousness. My political development was a logical development to a higher consciousness that began with BC and then began to change in detention and then change more on the Island. We have to work toward a nonracial democracy. BC rejects that idea. So I reject them." He waved his right hand dismissively, as if explaining why a full house beats three of a kind.

At the close of the Soweto Eleven trial in 1979, Thabo Ndabene was told that if he was ever found at a demonstration he would be arrested and thrown in jail. It didn't take long. In 1981 he was arrested during a demonstration and sent to Moderbee prison, east of Johannesburg, for eighteen months. He was released and then jailed again in 1984 for another eighteen months. Thabo's prison experiences only deepened his Black Consciousness beliefs.

"We talked together of Black Consciousness and our ideals," he remembered vaguely, tucking his chin into the neck of his thick green sweater. Prison for Thabo in the 1980s was the same as it had been when he shared a cell with Seth before their trial. There was no experience of Nelson Mandela, no major landmark of change. It was all the same, and his tone of voice was almost bored. "We talked of how the oppressed, the blacks of South Africa, must take control from the oppressor. We talked of our different experiences at the hands of the white man and of how we would one day run the country ourselves." Thabo shrugged.

"We talked of *when* we were going to be liberated, not *if*," he remembered with a laugh, shaking his head at the obsessive enthusiasm of youth. "We were talking in terms of ten years. We were mad, of course, but we were young. We still thought, in prison, that we had control of the country." Thabo paused and laughed ruefully again, shaking his head. His glasses fell to the tip of his nose. "We were wrong, but thinking that kind of thing when you're in prison keeps the resolve there in your mind. It strengthened me. They thought, these Boers, that by sticking us in prison they would break us. They only made us stronger."

Thabo's tone of voice — so offhanded — seemed odd at first. But later, walking down Kerk Street back to my own office on that cold June winter day, I understood something about his voice from the mudlike walk of the blacks on the street around me. The walk to a free society is a long and hard one, and Thabo's offhand tone merely underscored a black South African reality: the quest for liberation had become so deeply ingrained in so many that it was second nature to them now. I saw that to ask black South Africans to cease looking for freedom would be to ask them to give up a part of themselves. That was how far things had gone.

Once out of jail, the three young men were not the same band of brothers who ran Soweto for fifteen months. Murphy Morobe left the Island in 1983 and joined the United Democratic Front (UDF). He became its national spokesman in 1986. Thabo Ndabene got out of jail and went to work for the Azanian People's Organization (AZAPO) as national organizer and labor secretary. Seth Mazibuko flirted briefly with AZAPO after his release from Robben Island, but many of the things that bothered his friend Murphy about BC — such as lack of grand strategies — began to bother Seth as well. He went to work as a youth organizer for the South African Council of Churches in 1984. Seth and Murphy and Thabo saw less of each other, growing apart over politics.

Yet in 1983 and 1984 something happened that galvanized them all. The Afrikaners called it reform. The blacks called it exclusion. In 1983 P. W. Botha asked white South Africans to go to the polls and vote on whether to change South Africa's constitution. It was a yes-no referendum on whether to give South Africa's Colored and Indian populations their own houses in Parliament in Cape Town. The whites passed the referendum in November 1983, and the first Indian and Colored elections were set for August 1984.

Black South Africans like Seth, Murphy, and Thabo saw the

tricameral Parliament referendum as a ham-handed attempt by the Afrikaners to split the nonwhite population and pre-empt part of it into the white camp. They also saw that if thirteen percent of the nonwhite population voted in Afrikaner-sponsored elections, South Africa's nonwhites would be perceived as giving apartheid at least a left-handed endorsement. The election campaign was marked by great bitterness, and every major anti-apartheid organization urged Indian and Colored voters to boycott polls on election day. When the results were tallied, only 83,000 voters, sixteen percent of those eligible, had gone to the polls in the Indian election. Only 273,000 people, eighteen percent of those eligible, cast ballots for the Colored House of Delegates. In the Cape peninsula, where the Colored population is most heavily concentrated, the voter turnout was eleven percent.

With such shallow backing it would have been difficult for the Indian and Colored houses to claim any legitimacy to begin with. Subsequent events proved the elections cruel hoaxes. The government handed down the emergency regulations of 1985 and 1986 without even consulting the Indian and Colored chambers. When P. W. Botha called an election in January 1987 to rally support behind the beleaguered NP, he made the elections for whites only. He apparently realized that if Indians and Coloreds were also polled, vote totals could end up even lower than the embarrassing 1984 totals: support unraveling, not rallying. His plea that Colored and Indian voters were "not ready" for another election was hardly an endorsement of the new constitution in any case. In addition, Colored and Indian politicians count for nothing nationally. When the nation's leading Colored politician, the Rev. Allen Hendrickse, defied Port Elizabeth's whites-only beach policy in early 1987 to protest the continuing state of emergency, he was threatened with expulsion from the Cabinet unless he apologized for his actions. He apologized. Politician to bootlicker overnight.

The most significant aspect of the new constitution — and all later "reforms" — was that they both raised and dashed the expectations of South Africa's blacks, the eighty-seven percent of the nonwhite population *not* represented in Cape Town. It raised their hopes because the tricameral Parliament gave the appearance that old forms were falling away. And it dashed them because the reform contained no "dispensation" — political arrangement — for black Africans. South Africa's black anger began to mount until it finally exploded.

The pattern of raised and dashed expectations continued as the program to "reform" apartheid went forward. Away went the Prohibition of Mixed Marriages Act and the rest of the "love laws." A black now could marry a white; but the couple could not live together because the Group Areas Act still forbade blacks and whites from living together. The United Democratic Front was allowed to form, something that never would have been allowed under the *kragdadige* regimes of the past. The UDF encompassed six hundred anti-apartheid groups, and it flourished as the most respected voice for liberation in the country. Yet it had no real clout because the Afrikaners refused to meet with it in the only forum that could bring about significant change — a legislative forum.

Blacks were promised their South African citizenship back, after having had it taken away and replaced with meaningless citizenship in the tribal homelands. Yet blacks still had to vote in those homelands — for leaders and legislators who were little more than Afrikaner-appointed stooges. Blacks were given the right to own land in their townships, yet many remained too poor to buy the land. The pass laws were revoked amid much fanfare, but the pass that blacks had been forced to carry was replaced by an identity card that served the same purpose of restricting their movement around the country. Reform would contain a program of "orderly urbanization" for blacks, but residents of some townships found that that meant a fleet of bulldozers and a forced removal to already overcrowded townships sometimes fifteen miles farther away from their workplaces.

"Qualified" black leaders were offered seats in a National Statutory Council. Yet many blacks saw their only qualified leaders as the ones serving life sentences in Pollsmoor prison. P. W. Botha said he would release Nelson Mandela "unconditionally" if he forswore violence. I once asked Louis Nel, the deputy minister for information, how an unconditional release could involve a condition. With familiar Afrikaner Flat Earth Society logic, he replied that rejecting violence was not a condition since "all civilized societies reject violence." Half-baked reforms and broken promises left South Africa's blacks confused, frustrated, and angry.

Blacks like Seth, Murphy, and Thabo saw reform as a duplicitous attempt to put a better face on apartheid while doing little to change the basic structure and condition of black South African life. "Nothing has changed here," Seth said one day as we drove thorough the Orlando West section of Soweto. He spread his arms wide to encompass the squalor of the township. "Nothing has changed except that they have sugar-coated apartheid. The situation has actually worsened because while they have been so beautifully decorating the outside of the cake, inside it has remained rotten. Do you think that things have changed when all that has happened in the last ten years is that now the government says it will sell me my two-room house in Soweto — a house I can't afford to buy?"

Frustrated by raised and lowered expectations, with no voice in Cape Town, with conditions around them unchanged, black South Africans took to the streets. The date was September 1984, right after the election for the tricameral Parliament. More than two years of protest began, with police fighting angry black mobs from one end of the country to the other. "The changes were simply inadequate," explained Murphy, leaning forward over his desk and scratching his head. He paused and fiddled with his blue tie. "The government was trying to make apartheid more comfortable for us while seeking to prolong white privilege. That's what the crisis has been all about here. It was a direct challenge to us."

In Mamelodi in November 1985, nearly the whole township marched on the township offices to protest a rent increase. The South African Defense Forces (SADF) arrived and told the crowd to disperse. Either the order was not heard or the crowd chose to ignore it. The soldiers opened fire. Twenty-seven blacks, most of them old women, were killed. Residents later claimed that many of the dead were shot in the back, fleeing the police. I went to the funeral for twelve of those blacks a week later. A young father carried the coffin of his two-year-old child in one arm. His other was raised in a black power salute. The coffins were draped in the banned colors of the ANC, and the crowd displayed open anger and defiance.

In mid-1985 the government imposed a limited state of emergency in thirty-seven magisterial districts around the country. Seth Mazibuko was arrested once again and spent the last six months of 1985 in jail. Schools continued in a state of open revolt; one student protest, in Athlone near Cape Town, showed not only how black anger had increased but also how white opposition to that anger had taken on a new and gruesome tinge. Colored students in Athlone formed a gauntlet one day in October and stoned every passing vehicle driven by a white. Soon they focused on a yellow truck loaded with heavy wooden packing cases. The children, aged between ten and eighteen, surged around the truck, threw their rocks, and broke the windshield. Then half a dozen riot police, armed with heavy-caliber shotguns, rose from within the packing cases. They began to fire, pump action, from pointblank range. Within minutes the street was littered with dead and wounded children. Three died. Leaping from their "Trojan horse," the police ran after some of those who had been able to flee. Police kicked in doors and dragged the fugitives out, some of them still bleeding from shotgun wounds.

The violence continued for the rest of that week. Photographer Mark Peters was there to cover for me — I had to be in Pretoria to report on a hanging — and he later wrote about what he saw in Athlone: "It was about 10:30 in the morning, and I saw two of the students preparing a petrol bomb in the nearby school grounds. Suddenly the police arrived in a Casspir, and one of them opened fire with a shotgun. The crowd fled, but one youth dropped to the ground. The police leaped out of the Casspir, picked up the wounded boy and threw him into the back of the troop carrier. Then the mother of the shot boy arrived. And she was desperate and she was weeping and shouting in grief. At one point she literally hopped up and down on one leg, holding out her hands to the police officer in charge and pleading: 'Please Master, please. Give me my son, pleeeeeease, Master.' "

Alexandra, another township north of Johannesburg, burst into flames one night in early 1986, and before four days of rioting ended, eighty blacks were dead. A white colleague of mine took his rented BMW into Alex, as the township is known, on the first night of rioting. He returned home in a car with no windows and with a rock the size of a football in the front seat beside him. So high was the level of unbridled anger in the township that even a black colleague thought better of going in and stayed away.

It was frightening to watch the street violence and killings spiraling in an ever widening gyre. The harder the police and the army cracked down, the greater became black resistance and anger. Funeral celebrations enveloped the townships and accounted for most of the increased violence. Blacks would die fighting the police. Friends and whole townships would honor the dead at mass funerals. After the funerals, fighting would often break out between mourners and the police. And more would die. And more funerals would be held. And then still more would die. The funerals became more than simple burials. "They're not funerals," one white analyst mused. "They're celebrations of martyrdom."

Acts of defiance seemed to escalate with every passing week. The Congress of South African Trade Unions (COSATU) was formed in November 1985, with half a million members, the vast majority black. Its new president, Elijah Barayi, called for the imposition of worldwide punitive sanctions and gave P. W. Botha six months to scrap the pass laws.

The ANC began planting land mines in the northern Transvaal. Several white farmers and their families were killed when their cars and trucks detonated the mines. Two days before Christmas 1985 a bomb exploded in a crowded shopping center near Durban. Seven whites were killed, three of them children under the age of sixteen, and forty-six others were injured. A month later, a bomb exploded in the toilet of divisional police headquarters in downtown Johannesburg, injuring two policemen and two civilians. Even though no lives were lost, the ANC had struck a white nerve: an ANC cadre had managed to sneak a bomb into one of the most secure police barracks in the country.

A corner had been turned. The mood of blacks had gone so far beyond Soweto and 1976 — and the violence was getting so close to whites — that many of us in the foreign press began to wonder not if, but when, the big crackdown would come.

What made matters worse was that the fighting in Soweto, Alexandra, and other townships was not simply between black protesters and white police. It was fast becoming apparent that there were blacks who hated other blacks as much as, if not more than, they hated their white oppressors. I slowly realized what had happened as these black hatreds played themselves out on the streets of Soweto and other townships: apartheid had succeeded. Probably beyond all Afrikaner expectations, it had managed to divide everybody.

And I saw something else, the emergence of the greatest sadness of South Africa: that the black search for liberation suffers as much by its own hand as by the hand of the oppressor.

Lucky, my Soweto stringer, told me of some radical young comrades who one day forced a black woman to drink a liter bottle of bleach as punishment for breaking their consumer boycott. The woman was certainly not pro-apartheid; she was simply content to accept change less fast than her punishers. Young comrades enforced a "black Christmas" boycott in 1985 by searching shopping bags and dumping anything bought at a white-owned store into the street — everything from milk and bread to new shoes, underwear, and Christmas presents.

During 1986 conservative black Witdoeke — White Hats, so named for the white bandanas they wore for identification in battle — waged open war with radical black youths in the Crossroads shantytown outside Cape Town. The Witdoeke tired of getting picked on by the comrades, so they fought back with machetes, hammers, pipes, and clubs. The same year saw black police in Soweto fighting against the young comrades — for the same reasons that the Witdoeke arose. Followers of AZAPO were fighting pitched battles with members of the UDF in the middle of Soweto. Black police were fighting Sotho protesters in the homeland of KwaNdebele. Zulus were fighting Xhosas in the province of Natal. The Xhosas were moving east and north into fertile Natal province, which encompasses Zululand, to escape the unemployment and poverty in their Ciskei and Transkei homelands in the eastern Cape. The Zulus resented their coming because the Zulus had enough unemployment of their own and didn't want to share the meager economic pie with anyone, regardless of tribe.

Another factor in the Zulu-Xhosa conflict was Chief Mangosuthu Gatsha Buthelezi, nominal leader of the nation's six million Zulus as chief minister of KwaZulu and head of the largely Zulu political organization Inkatha. Buthelezi had been openly at odds with the ANC for a decade and with the UDF since its formation over leadership of the anti-apartheid struggle. By mid-1986 there was persuasive evidence that the government was furnishing arms to Buthelezi, who opposes sanctions and other ANC/UDF policies, and that Zulu *impis* were being sicced on UDF rallies and gatherings. There was something of a turf war to the Zulu-ANC conflict as well. Buthelezi, whose power base lies around Durban, all but declared Natal off limits for the UDF in early 1986. Later, when Buthelezi made several government-sanctioned trips into Soweto, which is UDF territory, his appearances only fanned the flames of hatred toward Inkatha in the township. The violence became worse.

The troubles in KwaNdebele, an amalgam of fifteen expropriated Afrikaner farms in the northern Transvaal, started when Pretoria told the homeland's leaders to annex a rich neighboring area. The neighboring area contained Sotho tribes who opposed annexation for two reasons. They did not want to become part of a meaningless self-governing homeland, and they especially did not want to become part of a self-governing homeland that was due to become "independent" a year later.

The differences between the UDF and AZAPO were all political. In April and May 1986 the streets of the Orlando and Diepkloof neighborhoods in Soweto were impassable after dark. It had nothing to do with Casspirs or curfews but with a continuous night war being waged between the UDF and AZAPO. People awoke in the mornings to find black bodies in their front yards. Differences over politics had turned into an old-fashioned turf war, continually feeding on itself. Bands of AZAPO youth from the Orlando East section of Soweto led forays into UDF-dominated Diepkloof, and Diepkloof retaliated night after night until the permanent state of emergency was imposed, in part, to put a stop to the internecine Soweto warfare. And then it began again.

Murphy Morobe watched the cycle of violence — particularly blacks turning on other blacks — and the developments scared him because he saw how far things had progressed beyond the controlled militancy of 1976. "We learned the truth the hard way — at the point of a gun," he explained, sitting in his office while the sounds of an awakening Johannesburg began to filter up through the closed window. His balding brow creased, and he worried over his words.

"We received a baptism by fire, and we were able to control

ourselves," he said painfully. "What's happened in the last two
years is that people have been so affected by the intensity of
events that they present themselves as 'We are about to be free.'
They have a false sense of the immediacy of victory."

He paused and shook his head again. I could see that this was
all painful for the bankerly Morobe. "The impact has been a
widespread attitude of militancy. It is real radicalism." He
paused again, reflecting, concerned. "Some blacks are deeply
politicized and are engaging the system for political reasons. But
one development keeps outstripping another, and we're in a situation now where militancy has outstripped political consciousness." It was raw militancy as random rage — the emergence of
a politics of hatred that was fast tearing the country apart.

Seth Mazibuko could see it too. "Our lives as black South Africans have not changed at all in the last ten years under apartheid," he said one afternoon, looking down at De Villiers Street
from his office window, his thin and red-sweatered shoulders
sagging. "In fact, our lives have worsened because apartheid has
managed to divide us one black from the other. Apartheid has
succeeded at what it set out to do. It has succeeded in dividing
us not simply as people but as black people as well. It is going to
take us some time to work out a unity again, a unity like we had
following June 16, 1976."

Tiny Seth was saddened to see that the AZAPO-UDF war and
the emerging politics of hatred had turned a small band of Soweto brothers into bitter enemies. Seth, who shared a prison cell,
a plate, and even his bath water with Thabo Ndabene, no longer
spoke to his old cellmate. Murphy Morobe, who once stayed up
through all hours of the night talking Black Consciousness and
politics with his friend Thabo, got into the habit of crossing the
street and nodding frostily whenever he saw his old friend.
Apartheid had succeeded even with them.

The last time I saw Thabo, he was relaxed and open about his
hatred of whites and those blacks who cooperate with whites.
"You see, I view my position as having remained with the main-

stream," he explained. It was a cold afternoon in early June, and he was bundled into a brown suede jacket. His deep voice bore the traces of a cold because he had spent the last several nights in the open, on the run not just from the police but also, now, from the UDF.

"It is the others who have moved away from the mainstream," he said, his voice a deep rumble. "BC was founded on the concept that as a black man in this country you are on your own. I have maintained that attitude. Some people have decided that it is possible to take a nonracial approach to the struggle. I do not believe that is possible."

He paused, and when he started up again, his voice began to grate. "We know that any organization the white man joins he must dominate. That is his nature. He has dominated everything else in this country for three hundred years, so he will continue to try. Those who are the oppressed are the only ones who can overturn the system and bring change. It can be no other way. Any black who thinks it can be another way is wrong."

For his part, Murphy regarded the hostility that has embraced the struggle and his Soweto Eleven brothers as merely emblematic of the times. "That's how politics works," he said with a shrug of his tweed shoulders, and his clarinet voice changed. Gone was any life in his voice, and the words came out hard, like bricks. "These things have to work themselves out. In the struggle there are no permanent friends, and sentimental attachments are of no consequence in it." His face took on a blank look, impassive. "For clarity of purpose one cannot have sentimental ties because they affect where the purpose lies."

"I have nothing against Murphy personally," said Thabo laconically, leaning back in his wooden chair in his bare office. "The only problems I have are with his politics. So we speak very little. It's tragic to lose a friend. But there is nothing one can do."

The enmities surfaced, however, a few days later. I had asked the three to gather one morning at Morris Isaacson High School in Soweto. The purpose of the meeting was for Mark Peters to take a picture of them together, as they had once been, as friends. Seth arrived. Murphy drove up, worked the scene, and then drove away to hide his car before walking back to us. "I don't feel safe here," he whispered, ducking behind a building. He and Seth did more hopping than a pair of cheerleaders. They were both very nervous waiting for Thabo to turn up.

He never did. First he said it was a fender bender that kept him from coming. Later he confided that he had stayed away because he didn't have a pistol.

The emergency began on a starless, chilly night. Only a pale crescent of moon glimmered through the coal smoke in the skies over Soweto. Otherwise the midnight sky was washed in darkness. It was the beginning of a new day — 00:01 on Thursday the twelfth of June, 1986. Under the smoky moon, bright yellow police vans prowled Soweto's streets. They also crawled through the streets of Mamelodi and Atteridgeville, of Guguletu and Zwide, and of all South Africa's segregated black townships. They wound through the garbage and excrement and dead dogs, under the coal smoke, to preassigned houses and preassigned front doors, looking for Murphy, Thabo, Seth, and thousands more. Before the sweep ended two months later, there were more than twenty thousand arrests. South Africa's permanent state of emergency had begun.

The Afrikaner brought his *kragdadige* might down on all forms of black protest, dissent, and opposition to apartheid. The emergency regulations that went into effect that day were the farthest reaching in a long history of regulations designed to crush black hopes. A few days later Louis Nel, the deputy minister of information, dressed down a reporter in public for calling the new laws draconian. But the word was not harsh enough.

Police were instructed to arrest anyone, without need of a warrant, whose detention was considered necessary for the maintenance of public order. The police were given the power to search anyone and anything in the republic without a warrant. The new regulations made it illegal for the press to print the names of persons detained and to print or record any "subversive" statements. It also became illegal to utter or display a subversive statement. "Subversive" was defined as anything that advocated protest meetings, demonstrations, processions, boycotts, or strikes.

It became against the law to advocate sanctions or disinvestment. It became against the law to "weaken or undermine the confidence of the public" in the government. It became against the law even to "aggravate feelings of hostility."

It saddened me greatly, during my last two weeks in South Africa, to see that beginning of a long night of the soul. It all seemed so utterly futile. I knew that black hopes and black militancy would not be easily broken. I could not see Winnie Mandela simply giving up because new laws had been imposed. Nor could I see Murphy, Seth, Thabo, and others of their generation agreeing to lie down after more than a decade of constant struggle against a system they hated and were determined to destroy.

Murphy Morobe was not at home when the police came to arrest him. I tried to reach him repeatedly by phone at the UDF and at home, and one day I caught only a glimpse of him. He went underground, and the last I heard, many months after the emergency began, was that he had succeeded in staying out of the hands of the police. He still occasionally issues statements from underground to the foreign press.

I also tried reaching Seth Mazibuko. Some said he was arrested early in the emergency, but I also heard that he had avoided arrest and was hiding out in Soweto.

I thought of him in September 1986 when I heard about Father Smangaliso Mkhatshwa, secretary general of the South African Catholic Bishops Conference. I had heard Mkhatshwa speak many times, and I remembered him fondly as the tall, strikingly handsome priest who always appeared at rallies in a long gray cassock and commanded the respect of the comrades simply with his physical presence. Father Mkhatshwa was arrested on June 12, and after someone saw what was being done to him, a lawsuit was filed on his behalf. In an affidavit, Mkhatshwa described how he was handcuffed and blindfolded with his trousers and underpants pulled down around his ankles. He was made to stand in the same spot for thirty hours while police questioned him. Twice police discharged a pistol just behind his ear. A "creepy creature or instrument" crawled over his buttocks and legs, "invariably ending up biting my genitals. When I cringed with pain, they would laugh."

When Thabo Ndabene called me after my expulsion order came, the country was already ten days into the permanent emergency. I asked him what he was going to do. He laughed. "It's not as if I haven't been through this before." He chuckled, his deep bass voice still showing the effects of his cold. "They have my office surrounded so I surely don't go there. I'll just do what I did before. It's a matter of sleeping at a different house every night. The struggle continues. They couldn't stop us after Soweto, and they won't stop us now."

Two days before I left the country, I was standing on the corner of Pritchard and Harrison streets in downtown Johannesburg waiting for the light to change, when I saw a familiar black face across the street, also waiting to cross.

I did a double take. I knew he was on the run from the police, and I could not believe he would be out on the street in broad daylight. I stared, barely recognizing the heavily disguised figure in sunglasses, scarf, hat, and heavy coat. He met my stare and smiled. I smiled back and laughed.

He laughed, too, as the light changed, and then he skipped diagonally off across the street. We passed within ten yards of each other: he still smiling and I shaking my head at his midday audacity. He threw back his head in laughter and raised an arm in a brief, barely visible black power salute. Then he darted behind a moving bus and disappeared.

Go well, Murphison Morobe.

Three

COMRADES

THE ONLY TIME I was really scared in the nine months I spent in South Africa was on March 5, 1986, when all of Alexandra township and a good part of Soweto turned out for the burial of seventeen of the eighty people killed in the four days of rioting that shook Alexandra in February. The government banned photographers and reporters from attending the funeral, so I had to sneak into the township through a back entrance.

Alex, which lies to the north and east of Johannesburg, is one of the sorriest and grimmest slums in South Africa. It is unique among South African townships in that it abuts white residential areas, a black spot that was allowed to stay during the forced removals of the 1950s and 1960s. In the 1980s Alex became an overcrowded and festering sore, a city with the population of Dayton, Ohio, squeezed into mostly single-story housing in an area smaller than Manhattan's Upper East Side. It lies out of sight of most of Johannesburg's tony northern suburbs, its western boundary just on the other side of a ridge, the rest of the township falling quickly east into a three-sided *kloof*, or ravine.

Alex burned for five months in 1986, its people fed up with the overcrowding, the filth, and the police. I was always horrified by the place. There seemed to be even more raw garbage in Alex than in Soweto, and more raw sewage as well. Alex was especially grim in summer, when the thunderstorms came in torrents at about 4:30 nearly every afternoon, thunderbolts crashing straight to the ground because of the high mineral content of the Witwatersrand. In Johannesburg the rain washed into storm sewers, but in Alex there are no storm drains, only rutted unpaved streets. Blacks living at the bottom and sides of the ravine were deluged nightly with the entire township's rainfall, along with the township's entire supply of mud, garbage and sewage. It was no accident that in 1986 the most violent part of Alexandra was the eastern, or downhill, section.

I should never have gone in alone that day. But my wife was out of town on a trip and I had to get my son packed off for school in a hurry and arrange day care for the afternoon. So when Mark Peters called offering me a lift into the township, I told him I was running late and would meet him inside the soccer stadium, where the mass funeral was to be held. I knew Alex pretty well and knew that there would probably be an unguarded back entrance at the far northwest corner. Police Casspirs blocked the main entrances as I drove by them. I reached the back entrance, which lay atop the northern ridge, and from there I could see almost the whole township below me. The Georgia-red clay streets looked deserted, and in the far distance to the south I could see the soccer stadium filling with people.

I rolled down the filthy hill to the bottom of the *kloof*, my VW racking and pitching on the ruts. Garbage filled the gutters on my left and right, and when I got to the bottom of the *kloof* the car slogged through three inches of standing water. Muck. I snorted, remembering the words of my colleague Tony Robinson of London's *Financial Times,* spoken once about Alex in his broad Midlands cockney: " 'ad lunch wif a few bankers. Told 'em 'ey maight wanna put a few bob in 'ere." No evidence of any recent improvements, I muttered to myself, not in the last twenty-five years.

Then I began to hear the noise. It started quietly at first, off to the north, and grew in volume. The ground began to shake. My car crept up to the intersection and I looked to the left.

Five thousand black children were stamping up the hill to the stadium, and it was not so much the sight of them that made my spine tingle, but their chant. It was deep-voiced, fierce, and elemental. "*Ih, ih hih, ih hih. . . . Ih, ih hih, ih hih. . . . Ih, ih hih, ih hih. . . .*"

There was something very Zulu to it, although by no means were all of the children, who call themselves comrades — "comraids" — Zulus. I was scared stiff. The Zulu quality of the chant was what got to me. Probably that same Zulu quality got to the British at Isandhlwana in 1879, when the Zulus became the only spear-carrying native warriors in the history of the British Empire to defeat a fully armed and prepared English army. "*Ih, ih hih, ih hih. . . . Ih, ih hih, ih hih. . . . Ih, ih hih, ih hih. . . .*"

The chant was not fast, just steady, like a locomotive, and loud. And what made the ground shake was the children's stamping march keeping time with the chant, ten thousand bare feet hitting the clay earth in unison. "*Ih, ih hih, ih hih. . . . Ih, ih hih, ih hih. . . . Ih ih hih, ih hih. . . .*"

They were churning up a long column of dust, and they were coming right at me. *Skollies* — thugs? I sweated. *Tsotsi* ending?

I looked in my rearview mirror, and more were coming, another phalanx, stomping and churning up dust and waving the ANC flag. And they were singing *bulala AmaBhunu* — kill the Boers.

"Oh, shit," I muttered.

One of my main problems in covering black South Africa was that I looked like an AmaBhunu. Even though I'd lost about thirty pounds since my arrival in the country, I was still a six foot two former football player who weighed two hundred pounds and had thinning blond hair and a mustache. To make matters worse, my metal-framed sunglasses had years before lost their bridge, making them look less aviator and more square — less American and more Afrikaner. They had also lost some of their polarized coating and looked more smoky and menacing. Afrikaner. Nine out of ten times when I boarded South African Airways flights the stewards addressed me in Afrikaans.

The first thing I did was take off the damn sunglasses and put on my regular specs in the harsh summer light. Then I rolled down my window so the comrades could see I was wearing a coat and tie and not a police uniform. It was a tip I learned from Alan Cowell of the *New York Times,* a former Oxford oarsman who also stands over six feet and weighs two hundred pounds. He gave me one invaluable pointer for former footballers and oarsman in townships: do everything you can to be mistaken for a member of the liberal opposition Progressive Federal Party and not a policeman. So I stuck my blue blazer sleeve and striped shirt casually out the window and squinted tearfully into the blinding sunlight.

Children six and eight years old passed by the car, and they looked at me as if they wanted me dead. If looks could have killed, I would have been dead five thousand times over that morning. I had never seen such hatred in my life. It was the narrow-eyed, blank-look hatred, the kind that is beyond anger and well into the realm of condemnation. I could feel my face burning. I swiped the palm of my left hand across the VW's imitation leather steering wheel, leaving it glistening with sweat.

Then I remembered another Cowell tip, and I started saying "Sawubona" — Zulu for "hello" — to everyone passing by. "Sawubona," smile, "Sawubona," smile. After a while, my cheeks were sore. Then I tried the Xhosa variation: "Sokubona," smile.

The looks of condemnation lessened slightly. At least the mob was moving, I said to myself. Nobody was stopping and calling for a Uniroyal and a can of petrol. The crowd of comrades kept moving, like a herd of elephant past a baobab tree. Then I looked in the rearview mirror and heaved a sigh of relief.

It was my ticket out — the Black Sash, the anti-apartheid white women's group, in convoy, taking up the rear of the march. I'd never been so happy to see a group of grandmothers in my life. I let them pass and then followed them slowly through the crowd and into the stadium parking lot. I parked in the shade of a scrub oak and sauntered slowly into the jammed stadium with the ladies of the Black Sash.

Inside the soccer stadium I could still feel the raw rage of the comrades. At one point I wandered away from the main press area because in my rush to keep up with the Black Sash I had left my sun hat in the car. The harsh summer sun was so bright — Johannesburg is six thousand feet above sea level — that my sunburn was starting to blister. Even though the angry burn made me look less like an AmaBhunu and more like an Anglo *rooienek,* it hurt like hell. I went to get my hat and when I returned, access to the press area was blocked off.

I couldn't get back in, so I stood listening to the speeches in another part of the stadium. I saw the hate looks again, the condemnation looks, from ten-year-olds. The looks said they wanted me dead. On the spot. Several comrades came up to me and asked to see my identification. Then they told me it would be a good idea if I moved back into the main press area. I moved, and things felt better.

Probably the most significant political development that took place in South Africa during my time there was the political rise of the young comrades of the townships. They became the leading force behind black politics in South Africa, and they mobilized an entire population into a movement to overthrow the white regime in Pretoria, just as the Soweto youth had mobilized their generation into open defiance ten years before.

In Xhosa they call themselves *amadla kufa,* the defiers of death. During my time there it became axiomatic that to defy the defiers of death was to risk death or political oblivion. They literally have no fear of death, and, I came to learn, they will stop at nothing to achieve total liberation. Nothing will stand in their way, including other blacks.

Like many in the West, I originally approached the black liberation struggle in South Africa using the American civil rights movement of the 1960s as a model. I saw an oppressed black people trying to overcome the unjust and cruel ways of a white regime, and I figured that when I arrived in South Africa it would be easy to distinguish the good guys from the bad guys.

I discovered something very different. I learned that to see the struggle in the context of the American civil rights movement was to see only a small part of the struggle: the struggle was very complicated, and it was very cruel.

I didn't realize how cruel until April 1986, when I met a kid who called himself Killer. I had wanted for some time to write a story on the Necklace, even though I knew the story would not win me any points with black leadership. But I felt it was an important story, principally because to my mind the Necklace was one phenomenon that set the South African struggle apart from its American counterpart.

So one Friday afternoon I sat down with Lucky, my chief Soweto stringer, and told him what I had in mind. Did he know any kids who had necklaced anybody?

"Begyouse?" he said, using the township patois for "I beg your pardon?" His big brown eyes opened wide behind his tortoise-shell specs, and his brow wrinkled. Lucky was a thin, spindly Zulu of twenty-three who always walked around with a locked briefcase in his hand and a slightly bemused look on his face. He would often come into my office, which contained a big desk, a moribund fern, three chairs, and a wall-sized map of Africa, sit down in one of the empty chairs, and throw his feet up on the desk. There he would read the *Star* or critique my files or look at the map of Africa. He had been gazing at the Sudan when I shocked him out of his reverie. "Begyouse?"

"Do you know anybody who's necklaced anybody?"

He shifted his gaze to Tanzania and laughed. Then he thought for a while and looked at the dying fern. "Why you ask?" He chuckled in his thin, reedy voice.

I told him I wanted to do a story on the Necklace and wanted to talk to some comrades who had taken part in a necklacing. I'd guarantee anonymity, I said, and use just first names and ages. No photos. Lucky nodded his head thoughtfully, picked up his briefcase, and locked it. He said he'd call me Monday.

The phone rang at ten o'clock Monday, and it was Lucky.

"Hello, Ricky!" he shouted. "Got one! Got two! Wednesday this time okay?" I told him that sounded fine, and he showed up, as promised, with Killer, on Wednesday morning. Killer said he was sixteen, but with his smooth skin, short hair, and hooded eyes he looked more like thirteen or fourteen. He was small and slight, and his high, delicate cheekbones gave him the look of a choirboy. His clothes were rough, dirty, and old — green corduroy pants with holes in the knees, a dirty white T-shirt, and a frayed leather jacket.

He sat on the other side of my desk — he had wanted to meet on neutral ground in the busy bustle of Johannesburg rather than in Soweto — and he talked quietly and softly in Xhosa, while Lucky translated. He often looked shyly at the floor as he described how he got involved in killing Mary Skhosana.

"We knew she was a police informer," Killer explained quietly, looking at the floor and occasionally glancing over to Lucky. "We did not need proof. We just knew. We attacked her three times before we finally got her. The first time was late in 1985. She managed to get away and went to a police station to hide." Killer's voice bore almost no expression. There was no passion in it at all. "Then she went to live with her sons in another part of Soweto. So we burned her house down. We saw her again in January, but she managed to get away. But then on February 10 we saw her at the burial society where she worked." He could have been saying, "We went home, then we packed a lunch, and then we went down to the river and ate it."

"At around 7:30 that night we went to the house where she was staying. There were perhaps two hundred of us. We took her from her house and into the garden. There we tied her hands and feet." His voice, whispery, was as soft as his features. "She was pleading for mercy and crying and screaming. She said she would pay us seven thousand rands if we let her go."

Killer looked up, and his eyes bore expression for the first time. His voice roughened. "We told her we didn't need her money. We needed her life," he spat over at Lucky. "She would always buy and sell her way out because she was in the business of buying and selling people to the police. That was what we told her."

The momentary passion faded from his voice, and it returned to its calm monotone. "We put a tire around her legs and another around her neck and shoulders. Then we forced her to drink petrol. We poured the rest of the petrol into the tires and set her alight."

What was she doing? I asked. Did she scream?

"Oh yes," he replied in the same monotone. "She was screaming. She was screaming very loudly." "Oh yes, the sandwiches were big, and we ate them very quickly," he might have been saying.

Killer paused reflectively. "But I think we had made her drink too much petrol," he mused, quietly, "because she went off."

I looked at Lucky. "What do you mean 'went off'? What the hell does that mean?"

"You know," Lucky said in a pained whisper. "She went off. She went out. The fire went out."

"Jesus. Why?" I asked, shocked and unbelieving. "How could the fire go out?"

"There was not enough petrol to burn her," Killer explained quietly in his monotone. "We had made her drink too much. Another tin of petrol was fetched, and it took about an hour. Although she was partly burned she was still alive."

"What was she doing?" I asked, my flesh starting to crawl as I imagined a partly burned body lying in a Soweto street for an hour, two hundred comrades standing around while one of them went to get more gas. "Was she screaming then, too?"

"Oh yes, surely," Killer replied, looking down at the floor again, shyly. "She was screaming, yes, and pleading for mercy then, too. The other tin of petrol came and we poured it on her. Then we lit her again and she burned. She was killed."

But why? I asked. Why this woman?

The monotone disappeared from Killer's voice, suddenly. His

eyes began to light up, and he spoke with a harsh forcefulness — bearing down on the natural tongue clicks of the Xhosa
language so that each of them was a small explosion. "Most of
the residents in our area, in Diepkloof, were tired of this
woman," Killer said, his hands on his knees, leaning forward
aggressively. "She participated in the arrest and killing of a number of people in the struggle. She was working for the system
and had to be eliminated because of that. There was nothing else
we could have done but to eliminate her. The police and the
town councilors and the police informers are the ones who spark
what *you* call black-on-black violence." There was a bitterness in
his voice, an accusation. "They are all extensions of the system
and deserve to be killed."

But, I said, this was so cruel. Wasn't this too horrible a way to
die?

"Yes," he replied, defiantly, his hand banging my desk hard
enough for the morning papers to slide onto the fern. "It surely
is a horrible way to die. But those who commit horrible crimes
deserve to die horribly."

Killer left a short time later, and I sat in my office with Lucky,
numb. The tone of the boy's voice, the lack of caring, the lack
of a sense of human life had knocked me cold. But, I was beginning to realize, that is what happens in a country where people
are not regarded as human beings. They lose their humanity.
"That was just a boy!" I shouted in exasperation at Lucky. "That
was just a fucking boy, an infant, for God's sake!"

Lucky shook his head with a shallow smile. "You wanted to
talk with Necklace people." He shrugged. "You got Necklace
people."

"Yeah, but are they all like that?"

"What?" Lucky shrugged again. "That what? That young or
that hating or that cruel?" And his question seemed to hang in
the air, like an answer.

In the fall of 1986 the women of the Black Sash revealed that
forty percent of the twenty thousand blacks arrested during the

permanent state of emergency were aged eighteen and under. The response from the West was indignation. But I could see that it could be no other way. The average age of South Africa's black population of twenty-five million is eighteen. South Africa's black youth would be important for their numbers alone, and they become more significant when the politics of hatred is added to the raw numbers.

I found that perhaps the most frightening aspect of the comrades' hatred is that it is not particularly pro-anything, except an exhilarating but vague notion of liberation. It is anti-everything: antigovernment, anti-adult, anti-West, and anti-authority. A colleague of mine in Port Elizabeth explained it one night: "You must understand that the comrades' hatred goes beyond hatred of whites or simple hatred of the government," he said. "It is hatred of anyone who *has* anything, because they have nothing."

One rally outside Khotso House in Johannesburg in late May 1986 oozed with raw hatred. The comrades always sang and chanted and danced during those rallies. That day they sang a responsive litany, where one side chanted names of heroes and villains of the struggle and the other responded with approval or disapproval. That chant was a harsh melody of "O-li-vah Tahm-bo . . . *Eesojah!* (He is a soldier), Nel-son Man-day-lah . . . *Eesojah,*" "Pee-Vee Botha . . . *Voertsak!* (Fuck off) . . . Louie La-Gran-gee . . . *Voertsak!*" It grew louder and louder and echoed off the stone facades of the buildings on De Villiers Street until the air resonated with the vibrations of a hysterical crowd in a packed stadium.

I was watching one kid as the chant rose and rose. His name was Scarface Toni Fuck You Montana — the words were written in ragged ink on the back of his ragged suede jacket. Scarface Toni could not have been more than ten. He was scrawny, about four and a half feet tall, decked out in dirty cotton pants and torn, dirty sneakers. Under his jacket he wore a thin cotton T-shirt, and the only thing that seemed to protect him from the cold was a purple knit cap pulled over his bushy Afro and down almost to his eyes.

I watched him glance across the street, where a yellow Ford Cortina was idling at the corner. Two policemen were sitting in it. The look on Scarface Toni's face turned to stone. I watched as he reached down and picked up a piece of the pavement, still peering at the cops in the Cortina. Then he walked halfway across the street, looked at the cops again, and heaved the paving brick through a supermarket plate glass window. As the glass shattered, he turned and made an obscene gesture to the cops in the Cortina.

I learned how the comrades' hatred could extend to anyone associated in any way with the system. In December 1985 a student nurse at Soweto's Baragwanath Hospital was necklaced when she did not join a strike. A week later a twenty-year-old Soweto man was necklaced for holding a party: he was judged in defiance of a "people's ban" on Christmas celebrations.

A Soweto *shebeen* owner named Rambo had his speakeasy repeatedly closed down by the antidrinking comrades. Rambo retaliated by killing several comrades and then fleeing. The comrades kidnaped Rambo's best friend and forced him to reveal the fugitive's whereabouts. Rambo was brought back to Soweto and beheaded. His body was burned and his head paraded around the city's schools for other comrades to see.

My family saw at first hand some of the terrible pain felt by black families who crossed the comrades. My wife came home one afternoon to find our housekeeper, Ann Molefe, crying in the front hall. She had just gotten a phone call from her husband's parents. Her husband, Saul, worked nearby and was on his way home. "They killed Saul's brother," she wept. "They killed him." Saul's brother had just completed a township councilor's training course, and he had been poisoned at work that morning. Why? Township councilors are part of the system.

Saul got home minutes later and stood stunned in the hallway, his thin body shaking with sobs and his arms limp. He was a kind and intelligent man, then working for a friend of ours as a bookkeeper and chief stockman. "He was the best of us," he cried. "He was the best of us all and they killed him. Oh God. Oh God."

And he stood in our front hallway, leaning on the fired brick, away from my wife and son, crying his heart out.

After the autopsy and the funeral I went to Saul Molefe and told him that I knew a black legal aid counselor, a friend of Winnie Mandela's, who might be able to help the family if they wanted to pursue the case. No, he said with a shudder. It would be too dangerous.

Everyone grew to live in fear of the comrades, I discovered. I once spoke with Joe Latakgomo about the comrades and their politics. Latakgomo is editor of the *Sowetan* and lives in one of the townships outside Pretoria. Every night, he told me, his wife goes through the same ritual. She pulls the four children's beds away from the walls and goes to the closet to get blankets. She walks to the kitchen, throws the blankets in the sink, and covers them with water. Then she takes the soaking wet blankets and tacks them over the windows. "Petrol bombs," explained Latakgomo. "You never know where the comrades are and whose house they are going to hit next. The wet blankets keep the fire from starting in the middle of the room."

Yet in all my time there, I remained haunted by the Necklace, for just the sheer hatefulness of the act. After we talked with comrade Killer, I asked Lucky if he could find a necklacer a little older than Killer. He peered at the fern and nodded. "Shu, shu." He smiled, his glasses slipping down to the tip of his nose. And the next day he showed up with Bongani, a twenty-one-year-old comrade who had taken part in the murder of a young man named Kutasi outside Orlando Stadium on May Day.

Bongani was still in his senior year of high school, and he was a tall, sallow-skinned kid with a scraggly beard and a bushy Afro haircut. He wore a heavy wool shirt tucked into a pair of grungy tan khakis, and his eyes remained hooded and dark the whole time we talked.

"We asked him about this car he was driving," Bongani said. He spoke in a deep, animated bass voice, and as we talked I could see that he was trying to make me understand. "It was a Datsun Laurel, the kind the police use. He said it belonged to his uncle. We didn't believe him. Then he was searched. A small tape recorder was found taped to his ankle, and that proved he was an informer." Bongani waggled his finger like a lawyer before a jury.

"We tied his hands and feet and forced him to drink petrol," he continued after a pause. "We put the two tires over him and soaked them in petrol and lit them."

But wait, I interrupted. What was he doing this whole time?

Bongani shrugged, as if it wasn't important. "He was screaming for mercy and crying and saying that he would never do it again and that he didn't know what he was doing and that he was sorry. We strung the tape recorder around his neck. We killed him."

Was it all necessary? I asked. It seemed so brutal, so horrible.

"It is a general agreement among the comrades that all police informers get the same treatment," Bongani explained. He was speaking slowly and deliberately. His tone of voice was soft, matter-of-fact. He just explained, as if telling me why the square root of 144 is 12. "They have to be killed without exception.

"If other would-be informers see today what could happen to them tomorrow, then they won't take the job, you see." I was beginning to get the sick sense that South Africa was a country where anyone, black or white, could explain away anything, no matter how violent or cruel.

Bongani's deep voice began to rise, and he spread his arms. "We surely believe it deters other would-be informers because their consciences will always say, 'One day if they get hold of me I could die that way.' Those that don't heed our invitation deserve to be killed. The town councilors deserve the same treatment because they are no more than extensions of repressive laws. And we will continue to use the Necklace until the last day of repression and exploitation of the black man in South Africa." He leaned forward in his chair and glowered at me.

But why? I asked. Why the Necklace? Why not just shoot someone or hang him? Why this way?

Bongani sat back in his chair and folded his arms over his

chest. His brow furrowed, making him look like a doctor about to deliver a prognosis. "Necklacing is very final," he said, his voice deep again. "If you shoot someone or stab someone, he can still run to hospital. If you hit somebody with a *panga* — machete — it's the same way. With the Necklace you can be sure the person is dead."

I don't think I would have been as bothered by Bongani and Killer and others if it had not been for the way they talked. It was as if all the life had been drained out of them. They seemed like zombies. I think it was the cruelest thing I saw about apartheid — that the hatred in the children was actually a numbness to life and that apartheid had made them that way by making their lives empty.

As the southern autumn rolled on, with Alexandra in flames much of the time and Crossroads, outside Cape Town, in a state of civil war, I was becoming nearly obsessed with the politics of hatred, and I needed to know more. I'd drive home at night saying Why, why, why over and over again.

This went far beyond what the Soweto generation had intended in 1976. The Soweto uprising had called for unity and for challenging the system. The current actions seemed to be an expression of sheer brutality, or, as Murphy Morobe had put it, of blind militancy outstripping politics. I needed to talk to more of these comrades, and I asked another of my stringers — one who had special contacts with the ANC and its affiliated organizations — if he could contact a leader of a banned student organization for me: the Congress of South African Students (COSAS) or the Soweto Students Congress (SOSCO). I had spoken to the rank and file; I needed to meet a leader. My contact eventually put me in touch with Vusi Mabaso, a leader of COSAS when it was banned in August 1985.

Vusi was a handsome look-alike for Billy Dee Williams — close to six feet tall, with the athletic, stocky appearance of a football halfback. His jet black hair was set back in waves, and his teeth, like the whites of his eyes, were big and shone bright. His jeans were pressed and well fitting, and his rippling blue shirt, with three buttons undone, revealed a strong, hairless chest. When he walked into my office, he strode with grace and confidence. I could see that he was a leader — someone to be followed.

We started talking, and I asked him about the logic behind intimidation. He smiled and leaned forward on the other end of my desk, ticking off the fingers of his left hand with his right, like a chemistry professor explaining the periodic table. "If people gave one hundred percent support to the boycotts and stayaways, then Botha would be forced to change," he said, and his voice had a mellow tenor quality, like a French horn. "The problem is getting people organized and together. We ask them: 'Do you understand?' And those that don't? What do you expect? We punish them. If you defy the will of the nation, then the nation will punish you. We are teaching the people that they have to have self-discipline."

Self-discipline is one thing, but some of the punishments seemed pretty severe, I said. In the Soweto Christmas boycott women had been stripped to their underwear in forced searches, while others had been forced to drink bleach, laundry detergent, cooking oil, and lye soap.

"The people need to be mobilized and they don't understand that things are changing fast," Vusi explained, some belligerence tinging the French horn. Yet it was still a mellow tenor, and it worried over the words he wanted to emphasize. "During their time there was no COSAS. It is our duty to educate them, share our ideas with them, and talk to them. And if they don't listen, then we punish them. They have to be re-educated."

He paused and sat back in his chair, looking oddly at the dying fern and crossing his arms. "Those who can't be re-educated or refuse to be, we necklace." It was matter-of-fact. Two minus two equals zero. "Those people have to be necklaced because they don't listen to reason. It is dangerous to have someone living around you who is with the government."

We talked for a good while longer. He told about killing people in the same way most people talk about killing chickens for dinner. But Vusi's words reminded me of what Nico Smith, the Mamelodi minister, had told me — that these children had never been treated as people, so why should they see other people as people? They obviously did not, and as Vusi talked on, I found myself wanting to get closer to his reasons. He was starting to lose himself in political rhetoric, and I wanted him to go beyond the fancy political dogma. The best way to get the truth, I figured, would be to provoke him a little.

But, I asked innocently, why get involved in the first place?

He looked at me, stunned. I had gotten the kind of feeling out of him that I'd hoped to get. He leaned forward on the edge of his chair and his eyes narrowed. His nostrils flared, and he let me have it.

"I'm twenty-one years old and I still haven't taken my matric exam," he shouted, his hand pounding the desk. "You want to know why? I've been eligible to take it the last three years. But I couldn't take the exam." His hand pounded the desk again, and his eyes closed in frustration. "I've been in jail the last three Decembers. That's why." And his eyes opened wide, so that the whites of his eyes looked enormous, and his nostrils flared. He looked like a bull about to make a charge.

"This is a country where if you're white you start school at the age of five," he spat, hitting the desk again. "If you're black you start at the age of seven, and the schools teach you absolutely nothing." He was standing now, leaning over my desk like an angry teacher bawling out a stupid student. "People my age who are white are right now, right now, finishing university." He paused again, and his panting breath showed how angry he was. "And I haven't even finished high school." It was a scream, and his rich black face turned purple.

"This is a society run for the benefit of the white middle class." The shout had left his voice now, and he was talking through clenched teeth, furious. "They say it's a democracy, but it's not, because if it was then everything would be equal. You think things are equal when if I don't take my matric again this year, they won't let me back into school again?" I nodded, blushing, because what he said was true, that twenty-two is the cutoff age for black high schools. "You think things are equal when I can't get a high school diploma and I'm twenty-one years old? Fuck you!" And he sat down again, glaring.

"And what about jobs?" he spat, punching his fist across the desk at me. "White people get jobs, and black people get no jobs. What are my chances for a job? Huh? And what do you think it's like living in Sow-way-too these days? Huh?" He was leaning on my desk again. "Right now the police want to kill me because I won't turn informer for them. That's right. They want to shoot me because I told them to fuck off.

"We want things to be equal." Vusi's angry voice was pleading, drawing out the words. "We want to form a government of the people, by the people, and for the people. Does that sound familiar to you, American? It should, to you and your president, who supports the Boers. Fuck you!" And he sat down again, a disgusted look on his face.

"What we have here is a dictatorship that doesn't want to listen to the demands of the people. These haven't been reforms we've seen in these last three years. They're nothing but castles in the air." He waved his hands over his head, looking up at the wall-sized map of Africa. "They're not reforms, just promises the government has no intention of fulfilling." He pushed his hands at me, as if dismissing me.

"There is no alternative but to follow what the ANC has told us all: submit or fight." Vusi stood up and leaned over my desk. I noticed that his knuckles had turned pink. His voice lowered. "I am going to fight."

And he did fight. I kept up with Vusi, through my ANC stringer. He took the fight back to Soweto, where he continued a widespread comrade campaign of fingering black policemen and town councilors for expulsion from the township. He built himself a reputation as one of the most dedicated cop haters in the township. Two months later there were virtually no black policemen living at their homes in Soweto. They had all been driven out by Vusi and other comrades.

I had seen the looks of hatred and now had heard the words of hatred. So it did not surprise me when the politics of hatred took over the townships.

I was out of town during some of the worst Alexandra rioting in mid-February 1986, so I was forced to do some reconstructive surgery for a story on the riots. I went over to the Wynburg industrial zone, which borders Alex, looking for eyewitness accounts of the riots. I knew a man who worked at a big BMW dealership in Wynburg. I asked him if any of the black mechanics in the shop had been involved in the riots. He rolled his eyes and told me to wait right where I was. "Wait until you hear this," he said. "We tried to find this guy for three days. Wait there." He left and then came back with Peter, a thirty-year-old mechanic. We sat in a corner of the garage area, and Peter told me his story.

At 4:30 on the previous Sunday morning, Peter was shouted out of a light sleep. A thick pall of smoke hung over the township as dozens of cars and scores of tire barricades burned. "Open your doors or we'll burn down your house," voices yelled, and a shower of rocks fell on the corrugated tin roof of the house. Peter hustled his wife, two children, and twenty-three-year-old sister-in-law into a corner of the house and then opened the door.

Peter spoke in a high sing-song, sitting on a busted wooden chair. He wore the blue overalls common to black laborers, and from time to time he wiped his greased hands on the blue cotton fabric. His high forehead furrowed occasionally, and his milky white eyes squinted often. As he described the previous four days, his voice shook with fear.

Ten youths came charging into his house that dim morning. They were between the ages of about fifteen and twenty-two. They began chanting "Viva comrades viva! Viva comrades viva!" and threatened Peter and his family with machetes, *sjamboks* —

whips — and clubs and made them chant along. Then they grabbed Peter's sister-in-law, Sarah, and shoved her out into the street.

They put her to work helping to drag the half-burned hulk of a car from in front of the house out to a main street to set it on fire again. But a police Casspir rumbled close by, and the comrades shoved Sarah back in the house, where they threatened the rest of the family with their weapons if they made even a sound. Soon the comrades were out the door again, Sarah in tow, and Peter didn't see her until he found her in another part of the township three days later.

Along with several other captives, Sarah had been put to work digging a giant trench in the middle of a street. They finished the trench, and the comrades covered it with camouflage — a township elephant trap. "My wife's sister dug the hole," Peter explained timidly. There was also disbelief in his voice as he continued. "Then she was hidden away. Soon a Casspir came along. It swerved to try to miss the hole, but it tipped over. Then the comrades came out of hiding and petrol-bombed the Casspir and the soldiers in it. It was nearly destroyed. Then they ran away. It wasn't until the next day that I found my wife's sister. She was terrified. I took her out into the country. Alexandra is not a safe place anymore. It is very dangerous here now."

I heard another story that day, about a white man who drove four of his black laborers into the township, even though the comrades had sent out word that no blacks were to report for work. The man's pickup truck was surrounded by a gang of bottle-wielding comrades, who jumped the four workers and began to beat them with *sjamboks*. Then they firebombed the driver of the pickup. "He was driving, trying to get away," recalled a friend who told me the story. "And at the same time he was trying to throw the petrol bombs out of the cab. He said there were two or three. He got one from under the seat and threw it out the window. But the others exploded. He lost control of the truck and drove through three houses."

That pickup truck driver had been hit with a kind of napalm

invented in the township by the comrades. At the end of 1985 I
had begun to notice black children, ten or twelve years old, with
pink bicycle inner tubes draped around their necks and shoulders. I saw them especially in Alexandra. The inner tubes are
not for Necklaces. The comrades, I learned, were cutting the
tubes into thin strips and placing them in bottles of gas, where
the rubber dissolved, producing crude napalm. When the bottle
is ignited and the bomb explodes, burning globs of partly dissolved rubber stick to the skin and eat into it, blistering it to
blackness.

One day Lucky told me about how the comrades had come to
control even the school systems in the townships. We were sitting
in my office, and Lucky, as usual, was poring over the newspapers. He had told me long before that his father was a principal
in one of the Soweto schools, and I asked him how things were
going. He looked up and broke into a broad grin. For some reason, whenever he waded into the gruesome details of black politics, Lucky would always break into a huge grin and say, "Man,
you're never going to believe this!"

"Man, you're never going to believe this," he said with a grin.
"Last night the comrades came to our house. Bam, they knocked
on the door. My father went to answer the door and asked what
they wanted. They ordered my father to open up the school because they needed it for a meeting."

"So what did he do?" I asked.

"Begyouse? Oh, he opened the school." Lucky laughed. "Of
course he opened it. What else was he going to do? They threatened to kill him if he didn't."

I found it all very eerie because the comrades' violence was
doing more than consuming the townships. It was eerie because
you couldn't see it. But the fact was that the comrades were taking over the tone and direction of black politics and were sending the country spinning toward an emergency. I saw that, by
April 1986, any black leader who wanted to maintain any kind
of credibility with the comrades had to radicalize his or her
politics.

It was curious — and frightening — to watch. After Winnie Mandela was unbanned through a government foul-up in early 1986, she became less of a *cause célèbre* and quickly began to fade from view. She fought back onto the front pages — and abreast with the comrades — by telling a gathering that blacks would achieve liberation within a year with matches, tires, and petrol. Never before had a leading black figure made a public endorsement of the Necklace.

In May I went to see a youth organizer at the South African Council of Churches, a friend of Seth Mazibuko's named Diliza Machoba. He spoke of trying to harness the comrades. "We older leaders are trying to point out that blind action is no good and that action and reflection must go together," he said. Four days later I picked up the morning paper to find that Diliza Machoba was dead. He had been taken from his car in Soweto and beaten to death by black youths.

Bishop Desmond Tutu went to Alex and addressed a stadium full of comrades. He was booed for the first time ever. A month later he changed his position on sanctions, saying — also for the first time ever — that he favored across-the-board punitive sanctions imposed by the West. A week later I asked Vusi Mabaso what he thought of Tutu. "Tutu is okay," he replied. "He is understanding us now." The emphasis was on the word *now*.

I went to see Desmond Tutu after that, to talk to him about the comrades. He is well known in the West as the winner of the 1984 Nobel Peace Prize, but I saw firsthand that he really is an exceptionally religious man. He began our interview with a prayer. We were sitting in his Johannesburg church, and Tutu was his usual dapper self — a dark business suit over his crimson clerical shirt, his salt-and-pepper hair neatly brushed. I asked what he thought of black youth in the townships, and he sighed.

"I've never been as scared in my life as when I intervened between the police and some young people at a funeral in Daveyton last August," Tutu remembered in his familiar rapid-fire voice, his eyes opening wide. "It was quite clear there was going to be a confrontation: the young people were determined to

walk to the cemetery. The police were equally determined to up-
hold the law, which said that at funerals there were to be no
walkers. And it was quite clear to me that those children didn't
care whether the police were going to shoot. And that is their
mood." His eyes opened even wider, until I thought they were
going to pop out of his skull. "They are *going* to get this liberation, come hell or high water. And if that means that some of
them are going to die or that many of them are going to die, all
they say is 'The tree of liberation is going to be watered with our
blood.' "

He began to shake his head slowly and sadly. He was sitting
backward on a chair, his arms draped over the back, almost in a
posture of prayer. "I have warned that those of us who keep
talking peaceful change are having our credibility eroded because we don't have anything to show for it. The young people's
reaction is understandable." His already high voice rose even
higher, and he shook his head again. "I have said before that if
I was young I would have rejected Desmond Tutu long ago.
Their views have to be taken quite seriously. You would be very
foolhardy if you were to do anything that would alienate their
support."

It seemed like the understatement of the year, and I asked
Tutu if radical black youth weren't taking politics into another
dimension. He snorted. "They are not just a challenge to established leaders but to all other blacks in South Africa: when are
you going to stand up and have a little more courage?" He sat
up straight in his chair and waved his fist. "They have shown us
up," and he snorted again, a one-note laugh. "We have got to
hand it to them. They have gone into situations where death was
staring them in the face. And because they believe very strongly
in the cause for which they are struggling, they would have
died."

Did that mean, though, that they had advanced the struggle?
I asked. I was still bothered by the raw hatred of the kids in the
townships. I wondered whether hatred could blend with politics
in any significant way.

"We used to be scared of the police," Tutu said, spreading his arms wide, his voice rising in pitch, with amazement. "If your parents wanted to scare you they'd say, 'Watch out. The police are going to get you.' But that doesn't scare *our* children." The voice was pleading. "They think of detention as part of the ordinary run of things. Today if you don't get into trouble with the police there is something wrong with you."

Tutu paused, thinking. He looked at the floor of the church and then lifted his eyes. "They have accelerated things," he said, opening his palms, fingers down as if presenting a finished work. "They have got us saying, 'Hey, there are things worth dying for, actually.' "

I could see that Desmond Tutu meant it. His sincerity was in his hands and in his thrown-back shoulders. The comrades had convinced Desmond Tutu, an Anglican bishop, that there were things worth dying for. His words were not an endorsement of violence. They stopped two eyelashes short of that. But I could see how far things had gone. It was more, I realized, than Tutu moving his political stance closer to that of the comrades, although that was part of it. Beyond that, it was the idea that some of the comrades' wild-eyed radicalism had infected a church leader. It may have started, I said to myself, leaving his church, with Desmond Tutu trying to board the caboose before the freedom train left him at the station. But, Lord, he was right up there in the passenger wagons now.

The odd thing, I saw, was that South Africa would probably be a more peaceful place if all blacks shared the comrades' wild-eyed liberation fever. But many did not, and South Africa was a more violent place for it. Many blacks resented the Necklace and the general harassment they underwent at the hands of the comrades. Police, township councilors, liquor store owners, and homeland officials did not take kindly to being thrown out of their homes, stores, and offices. Many decided to fight back. The young comrades' hatred may have been accelerating the struggle. But it was setting the struggle back at the same time.

Lucky told me how the comrades' arrogance made them easy targets for retaliation. We were driving through Soweto one morning, talking about how police and others were fighting back against the comrades, and I asked Lucky who was getting it bad that week.

"The fight-pickers, mostly," he said in his usual nonchalant way.

"What the hell is a fight-picker?" I asked.

"It's like this," he said, sitting in the passenger seat of the bureau car. "I'll go into a *shebeen* in Soweto, and some student will pick a fight with me over a beer. For fun. 'Hey that's my beer. Give it to me.' And man, some of these fight-pickers are bastards. 'Give me the fucking beer or I'll beat the shit out of you.' " And Lucky started to bob and weave in the front seat of the car.

"The whole idea is to make me hit him." Lucky chuckled, holding his hands out wide. "Okay, so I hit him," and he punched the dashboard. "Then he goes and gets some other students, and together they come back to the *shebeen.* Then they beat the living shit out of me. This is for fun. It's how they get their kicks."

But, I asked him, what's the purpose?

"Hey man," he explained. "These guys just don't like anything or anyone not in a school uniform. So the fight-pickers go around the *shebeens* looking for fights with anyone over the age of twenty-one." He shrugged and grinned.

"Now what is happening? People are getting back at the students and starting to beat the shit out of them instead," Lucky explained, leaning back against the car door and waving his hands. "One of the real bad fight-pickers lives next door to us. Two nights ago at around 9:30 I heard a van pull up and stop in front of his house. I looked out to see what was going on." He slapped his knee and laughed.

"Man, you're never going to believe this," he said with his grin. "I saw these two guys, black guys, go up to the house. They looked in the windows and made sure the fight-picker was there.

Then they snuck around to the front door, and bam, they smashed in the door." Lucky slapped his hands together in a sharp clap.

"Jesus, you would have thought the world was coming to an end in there." He laughed. "They must have hit him with everything. Such screaming. I don't know how the guy ever survived, but he got away. Came running out the front door, his clothes all ripped and blood pouring out of his nose, the two other guys chasing after him with clubs." Lucky stopped and raised his right hand over his head, holding an imaginary truncheon. "Haven't seen him since, though," he said. "Not safe for him to come back."

The black police in Soweto started their revenge attacks by hiring a gang, the Kabasas, who were looking for revenge on the comrades for their own reasons. The Kabasas were car thieves — "BMW specialists," as Lucky called them. The only BMW plant in the world outside of Germany is in the eastern Cape, and the Kabasas lost their market when the comrades declared war on the Bavarian automaker: BMW was using cheap black labor to make parts at below cost in P.E. and sending the parts back to Germany for installation in cars bound for the European market. By early 1986 it was no longer safe to drive a BMW in the townships, and nobody wanted to buy stolen BMWs from the Kabasas anymore. They were as angry at the comrades as the police were, so the police armed the Kabasas with pistols, rifles, *sjamboks,* billy clubs, and tear gas and told them to go after the comrades.

They did, and for two months Soweto was bloody. The Kabasas, often wearing dark clothes and balaclava helmets, roamed the streets of Diepkloof and Orlando after sunset, torching and teargassing the homes of the student radicals. In one four-day period in the middle of May, at least twenty comrades were killed on the streets and in their homes.

There was no stopping the killing. One morning, about two weeks after the incident with the fight-picker, Lucky walked into my office and slumped down in his chair, looking stunned. I asked him what was up, and he shook his head. "We are living in the middle of a fucking civil war," he practically screamed, opening his arms and eyes wide. "I mean, it's no longer news to wake up in the morning and see a Goddamned body in the front yard. There was one out there this morning, a kid, about fifteen, with his head split open by a *panga* [machete]." He shuddered at the memory. "Bleaah. It's not safe to go out after 7:30 at night. I mean, we're bolting the doors. We open them for no one until it gets light outside again."

Many residents of Soweto said the police were doing more than simply arming the Kabasas and were actually joining the Kabasas on their forays — one of the reasons they hid their faces in balaclavas. It is likely that the police were heavily involved because the attackers always knew exactly where to find the comrades and their houses. One thing that seemed to point to direct police involvement in the revenge attacks was the presence of whites in the raids — probably white police.

The night the attackers came to kill Vusi Mabaso, he was not at home. The whole family would probably be dead if his mother had not been up studying. At two in the morning Vusi's mother heard a noise outside. She switched off all the indoor lights and waited in silence. She heard another noise and flicked on the outdoor spotlight. The next thing she knew, a barrage of rocks and automatic rifle fire flew through the air and shattered every window in the house. She ran into the bathroom, the only room in the house without a window, screaming. Vusi's father awoke to find himself and his bed soaked in gasoline.

The firing stopped, and Mrs. Mabaso ran back into the living room. There she saw a man reaching through one of the windows and pouring gasoline onto the rug and furniture. His face was blackened with pitch, but she could see clearly that the hands holding the can of gas were white hands.

"Ek sien jou," she shouted in Afrikaans. "En jy is 'n Boer" — I see you and you are a Boer. The man retreated, firing an army-issue automatic rifle from his hip, and jumped into a waiting van, which sped away.

The police — black and white — were clearly behind the revenge attacks on the comrades in Crossroads, outside Cape Town. The police armed and backed conservative black elders known as Witdoeke, or White Hats, for the white scarves they wore around their brows for identification in battle. Like the black police in Soweto, the Witdoeke were angered by the comrades' bullying tactics and wanted to fight back. Crossroads burned for a month, beginning in the second half of May 1986, and gangs of Witdoeke and comrades fought from one end of the township to the other. Nowhere in the squatter camp was free of fighting. Freelance cameraman George de'Ath was killed when a band of Witdoeke surprised him and several other photographers filming a group of comrades. Greg English, an AP photographer who also did occasional work for us, came back from Crossroads looking as if he had just been through a war: chain-smoking, his eyes hollow, his skin pasty.

As the fighting wore on, the army surrounded the squatter camp but did nothing to stop the fighting. At times the Witdoeke fled behind lines of police Casspirs for protection, and they got all the protection they wanted. After all, the Witdoeke were doing a job the government wanted done — killing comrades. And they were strengthening apartheid — dividing one black from the other.

But as the fighting wore on, the comrades showed few signs of surrendering. One night in May 1986, as the country inched closer and closer to emergency, Lucky and Mark Peters and I were gathering material for a long story we wanted to write on these comrades. Mark was across the hall at his light table, choosing slides, and Lucky and I were in my office, huddled close to the plastic heater that was killing the potted fern. I riffled through a pile of papers, looking for the text of my interview with Desmond Tutu, because I wanted Lucky's opinion on something the bishop had said.

I found the passage I wanted and showed it to Lucky. Did he, I asked, think Tutu was right?

Lucky hunched over the folded page and read the short paragraph I had circled. "These young people are prepared to see even a scorched earth. They will have a scorched earth — if that is what is going to bring them freedom. About that they are quite determined. They are going to be free."

Lucky nodded and then nodded again. "Yeah," he said. "Tutu's right. The only problem is the Boers have a scorched earth policy of their own." And he laughed the grim laugh I had gotten so used to.

He left then, headed back to Soweto so he could get home and lock himself in his house until dawn. I sat in my office, thinking how for years to come the Afrikaners were going to have to deal with their creation, a Frankenstein that will never go away, a kind of collective Scarface Toni Fuck You Montana.

Mark Peters stormed into my office just then, grinning his gap-toothed grin. He never simply walked anywhere but usually loped and stormed through doors with a shout of "Eh Rick!" He loped into my office that night, carrying a slide and a magnifier, booming: "I got it! I got the picture we need."

I had asked him to go back through his slides to see if he could find a couple of pictures for the photo department in New York. I wanted a photo that would show the fierceness of black youth and their commitment to continuing the struggle. Peters strode over to my side of the desk, threw down the slide, and handed me the magnifier. "That does it," he stated surely.

The slide showed a dozen black kids in the eastern Cape. They were all about ten or twelve years old. They were skinny and dirty and ragged. Many of them were dressed just in shorts and filthy T-shirts. They were all smiling and laughing, and they held a sign: "They Cannot Kill Us All."

I put down the magnifier. "Ship it," I said.

Four

THE ENGLISH MINORITY

MY LAST FULL WEEK in South Africa was a nightmare. One of my son's black classmates, Gare, was staying with us because of the violence we all expected to erupt in Soweto on June 16. Our interracial school had asked parents who lived nearby to board Soweto students for a few days, and all went well until Gare, like any five-year-old, started to pine for his mother. He wanted to talk to her on the phone. Not possible. The government had cut all phone lines to Soweto. Gare, who has epilepsy, sat on my desk in my cold office crying. I was glad Mark Peters was there, for he cradled Gare in his big Rhodesian arms, whispering to him softly in Shona and Sindebele, until we dried his tears and got him playing again.

The government threw up roadblocks to Soweto and imposed strict censorship regulations on the press. Gathering news became nearly impossible. The only legal source for news became the government's Bureau of Information, whose daily briefings consisted mostly of government minions denying eyewitness reports of police violence.* I was just glad when the week ended

---

*At one briefing a reporter asked if a colleague had been detained and, if so, whether his paper could report on the incident. The reply, from Brig. Leon Mellet, a former crime reporter who moonlighted as die Ruider in Swart (the Rider in Black) in photographic comic books: "I would like to get one thing clear. We don't want this as a forum now to issue incidents of any kind whatsoever and to try and make that as a legal platform for information. I'm not going to allow that. I'm sorry. And you cannot report on your own questions."

and Sunday arrived. We had been invited to a *braai* — barbecue — at the home of our friends Richard and Vivian Jones, a fun-loving dentist and his wife. We took off for the Joneses with a mixture of relief and anticipation.

It turned out that most of the other guests that afternoon were Richard's dental partners and their wives. Most of the dentists were considerably more dour than Richard, and their wives even more so. We all chatted as Richard sweated over the burning coals, and the talk turned to politics, as it invariably did at every *braai* I ever attended. I was seated at one end of the long table outdoors with one of the dentists' wives. She seemed like a kind, middle-aged woman, one of many Jewish liberals around Johannesburg. Yet as we talked, I began to squirm. My nightmare week was not over.

The dentist's wife asked me what I thought about the emergency, and I told her that I knew Soweto was in a state of siege, with armored Casspirs on every block, and that the government seemed intent on using every bit of its *kragdadigheid* — forcefulness — to stifle black protest. I didn't think, I said, that the government would be able to succeed because antigovernment feeling among blacks seemed to be running too high to extinguish.

She nodded understandingly and smoothed the pleats of her bright yellow sun dress. Then she said that she was in favor of the state of emergency. I sat back, curious, and asked why.

She said she had heard from her maids and from the attendants at her husband's office that they were happy with the emergency. The presence of the troops meant that young radical comrades were no longer harassing her maids as they went to and from work in the northern suburbs. "If they're happy with it, then I think it's good," she said, nodding her carefully coiffed head.

"It's put a stop to the necklacing and the killings," she continued, her voice the genteel upper-crust English of Anglo South Africa. "Those blacks were killing each other, and it had to be put to an end. Blacks in this country hate each other. Would you like to see this country turned over to a bunch of people like that, who will start killing each other and Lord knows whom else when it's turned over to them? Would you really like to see that happen?"

I told her I would not, of course, but that it might help to try to forge some degree of black unity.

"Impossible," she blurted in a Hermione Gingold voice. "What you outsiders don't understand is that this is a tribal country and that the tribes don't get along. They hate each other and will kill each other."

I was beginning to get very weary. I had heard this argument so many times before — usually from Afrikaners — that it made my flesh crawl. I plodded on. I mentioned that most of the trouble in Soweto was not ancient tribal conflict but 1980s politics — UDF against AZAPO. Besides, I said, the UDF coalition seemed to cut across all tribal lines.

"That's different," she said. "Those are township blacks. The situation in the townships is different. The tribes hate each other. I had a Zulu maid once who did nothing but fight with my Xhosa maid."

It was the Flat Earth Society again. I knew that there was no getting her to change her mind, but I kept at it. What can be done to erase black disunity? I asked. Perhaps releasing Nelson Mandela might be the answer. He carries weight with all black groups. Perhaps they will listen to him.

"Never," she replied with a harrumph and paused to light a cigarette. "Mandela is a Communist. Don't you understand that? Do you want us to turn this country over to Communists?"

I was beginning to get the same feeling I often had after talking to other South African whites, and the feeling, raw frustration, was welling up in my throat like vomit. This intelligent woman had only two sources of information: her maids and NP propaganda. She knew nothing. Nor, it seemed, did she want to know anything. When I told her that the phones to Soweto had been cut off, she refused to believe me. When I told her about the idiocy of the press briefings, she said she thought the government was right to quash irresponsible rumors. And when I told her about the thousands of arrests, she said they were probably necessary.

I had to get away from her. An image passed before my eyes, of Malcolm McDowell in *A Clockwork Orange* doing a face-down into his spaghetti. Richard Jones was going to have to fish me out of his wife's salmon mousse if I didn't move.

I saw my son getting into a dispute over a cricket bat and quickly made an excuse to leave the table. Where would it end? I found myself muttering for about the five hundredth time. And this wasn't an Afrikaner. This was an English speaker — a "liberal." The miserable week would never end.

I straightened out the matter of the cricket bat and took several deep breaths before returning to the table. There we all drank too much wine and too much port by the giant strelitsia, under a warm winter sun that set too soon and sneaked the warmth out of the evening. "I hope I didn't drive you away," the woman said. No, I lied, and we fell back to talking of how hopeless she thought the situation was, how cruel the blacks were to each other, and how powerless she felt.

She reminded me of a man I'd seen only days before. A bomb had exploded in the middle of downtown Johannesburg, and the force of the explosion was so great that it rocked this one man off his feet and shredded his clothes. He stood in the middle of Harrison Street, stunned and bleeding, shouting: "What is happening? What is going on in this country?"

I thought of how long ignorance had been a way of life for South Africa's two million whites of English descent — the Anglos — and how the Anglo contribution to the South African drama had been to watch quietly from the sidelines. They had turned themselves into a giant irrelevancy. It made me sad, that afternoon and many other times, because I had come to South Africa expecting something more from the Anglos. They were supposed to be champions of the anti-apartheid movement. It was one of my greatest disappointments to see that they were merely antigovernment. As Americans, it was natural for us to gravitate toward the Anglo community because we shared many things — chiefly language and schools — and many Anglos became our friends. It is sad to see friends waste themselves. It's like sitting on the back porch watching the neighbors mainline heroin.

I came to see how the Anglos' is a strange and hopeless world. Though the Anglo heart is often in the right place, it often is not big enough to encompass what the blacks want. I saw how Anglo liberals want blacks to have dignity; but I also saw how they fall short of wanting to give blacks complete power. They want to give, but they are unable to give a full measure.

No one can question Helen Suzman's liberal credentials, for example. From 1961 to 1974 she alone constituted the liberal opposition in Parliament, and she remained in the 1980s a tireless opponent of apartheid. Yet she also remained adamantly opposed to the imposition of sanctions against South Africa, saying that sanctions would only cripple the nation's businesses and hurt its blacks. Blacks viewed her position as paternalistic and more heedful of businesses than of blacks.

Liberals like Suzman or like Colin Eglin, leader of the liberal opposition Progressive Federal Party (PFP), favor a nonracial democracy and a "truly representative government with protection for the legitimate rights of minorities," as Suzman wrote in a 1986 *New York Times* essay opposing sanctions. Yet that ideal differs from what most blacks want — namely one man, one vote in a unitary state. In defending his position, Eglin told me once that nowhere in the world was there one man, one vote, not even in the United States.*

---

*White South Africans commonly cite the U.S. Senate as an example of how one man, one vote does not exist in the United States. Wyoming and California, with the smallest and largest populations, respectively, are both accorded two senators. Californians are denied proper representation; hence one man, one vote does not exist. Neither, apparently, does the House of Representatives.

It is ironic that such Anglos as these have been the West's chief source of information on South Africa, because they have not told the whole story. They have omitted their own story.

Anglo portraits of apartheid — by Alan Paton, Nadine Gordimer, Athol Fugard — are all moving, sensitive, and evocative, so we in the West think of the Anglo portraitists as sensitive, tender people. They are. But after living in South Africa, I came to see that they and their works must be examined in the full context of their country: the action and reaction between five million privileged whites and twenty-five million unprivileged blacks.

The Anglos have produced portraits — and portraits alone. They have no prescriptive role in fiction, just as, in reality, Anglo South Africans have played no significant prescriptive role for two generations. The West sees a touching lyricism in the portraits, but the West does not see that it is a lyricism born of hopelessness. The West, for example, does not know that one of Anglo South Africa's most sensitive writers has a drinking problem so severe that he disappears into Johannesburg's alcoholic demimonde for sometimes a week at a time. Nor does the West know much of the activist Anglo family, much respected in the West, one of whose leading members passes the time in a haze of white wine and horse breeding. And few know that one of the most eminent liberal Anglo businessmen is so overcome by hopelessness that he spends the evenings brooding over the speeches of Abraham Lincoln by lamplight and sighing.

Anglo South Africa is every bit the author's alcoholic demimonde, a La-La Land mixture of reality and escape. It is temporary immersion in reality — in the cities, in the workplace — followed by flight to a suburban paradise of swimming pools and bougainvillea to write beautifully or complain bitterly about the cruelty of the Afrikaner. Anglo South Africa allows itself to see the cruelty of the Afrikaner and the misery of apartheid and then does nothing about it beyond the *grand geste* or symbolic effigy burning.

I learned many things about the Anglos I lived among, and one was that the Anglo liberal's ailment is paralysis. In 1985 Duke University photography expert Alex Harris traveled through South Africa helping twenty photographers put together a haunting look at black life for the Second Carnegie Inquiry into Poverty and Development in South Africa. Harris began to notice that whenever he identified himself as a "liberal," his black South African friends would wince.

He asked what was the matter with calling himself a liberal. "When someone is on the run from the police," he was told, "and goes to the house of a liberal and asks to hide there, the liberal turns him away. A supporter of the struggle lets him in."

I saw the liberal Anglo's debilitating paralysis displayed one noontime in Johannesburg in April 1986. Robert Tucker, the managing director of one of South Africa's largest savings and loan associations, hosted a lunch to introduce Desmond Tutu and some other black leaders to several of South Africa's leading white businessmen. I was invited along almost by chance and was seated next to Tutu.

The lunch was full of derision for the government from all quarters, white as well as black. After things were well along and the tide of antigovernment feeling was running high, Tucker decided the time was right to ask the pivotal question. "So tell us, Father," he asked Tutu, "what can we concerned liberal businessmen do to help you in your struggle?"

Tutu answered without a pause. "Stop paying taxes," he said, measuring each word and looking Tucker straight in the eye. "Stop supporting this cruel and immoral regime with your money. That is what you can do."

Tucker turned a bright shade of pink. Silence enveloped the room. After a moment Tucker cleared his throat and changed the subject. Withholding taxes in the interest of ending apartheid was simply not a Rubicon the liberal businessmen could cross. Nor, I learned, can many other "concerned liberal" Anglos cross that Rubicon or even less treacherous streams.

I found that the Anglo's paralysis — the writer in his booze, the businessman in his dark nights of brooding — is caused by a conflict between reality and ability. The reality is that the Anglo South African did as much as the Afrikaner to create a segregated society. Like many in the West, before I got to South Africa I momentarily forgot that *Cry, the Beloved Country* was published in 1948 and described a South Africa before apartheid. The laws that made Alan Paton's black protagonists reside apart and walk apart were not written by the present-day National Party, I remembered. It had not yet come to power. Those earlier laws were written by the Anglos.*

And the Anglos' ability to change that society, I learned, was constrained by an unwillingness to dismantle the seductive system that had long guaranteed them privilege. By early 1986 as many as thirty National Party backbenchers were ready to bolt the NP for the liberal — and Anglo-dominated — Progressive Federal Party. They had grown impatient with P. W. Botha's slow pace of reform and wanted to play a more active role in speeding it along. But they did not bolt to the PFP, and one of the reasons they gave was that they considered themselves more liberal than most of the PFP members they would be joining.

Perhaps because the Anglos talked like the English and sounded even more English than the English, I expected them to *be* English. But, I discovered, they were as much a part of the continent of Africa as the Afrikaners were.

In the years after 1948, the concept of "liberal opposition" came to mean little more than opposition to the cruelties done by National Party doctrine. It was an opposition based on conscience

---

*Among the pre-1948 laws, the Mines and Works Act of 1911 created job reservation. The Land Act of 1913 defined 7.3 percent of the nation's land area as the only places where blacks could live and own land. The Sea Shore Act of 1935 segregated the beaches. The Black (Urban Areas) Consolidation Act of 1945 denied blacks permanent urban rights in white-designated areas. It was not a far leap from United Party segregation to National Party apartheid.

and humanity and genuine concern over black dignity and human rights. But with few exceptions, never has the idea of "liberal opposition" been able to take the extra step and address the larger question of what a liberal white minority can do to fashion genuine political rights for blacks.

The Anglo business community, which sets the pace for Anglo South Africa, did not drop its opposition to the legal right of blacks to form trade unions until 1978, two years after the Soweto riots. Business leaders in the mining industry worked hard to maintain the status quo, even while paying lip service to reform. In early 1986 black workers at the Impala platinum mine in Bophuthatswana struck over pay and working conditions. Management responded by refusing to bargain. It fired all twenty-three thousand striking workers.

In mid-1985 the black National Union of Mineworkers (NUM) vowed to close down the mining industry in a series of nationwide strikes. Industry leaders did not initiate a discussion with the union's leaders over the issues, which included the state of emergency then in effect. Instead, industry leaders went to the government and asked its help in breaking the strike. The strike failed.

Mining industry leaders were as good as silent on the question of whether to modify job reservation, the practice that limits black miners to the most menial jobs. Negotiations on the subject among the government, the white union, and management went nowhere partly because of union intransigence but also because of management's unwillingness to offend the powerful white union. One of the saddest and most confusing cruelties of South Africa is that Anglo liberals count among their champions of reform Harry Oppenheimer and Gavin Relly, past and present chairmen of the Anglo American Corporation of South Africa, the nation's huge mining and industrial conglomerate. Meanwhile, blacks working in Anglo American mines are still not allowed to hold blasting certificates. After a while it came as little wonder to me that blacks rejected the argument that "sanctions will hurt blacks." Blacks look at business and see seventy-five years of exploitation.

A 1983 opinion survey conducted by the Human Sciences Research Council found just how much comfort South Africa's Anglos took in apartheid. Many English-speaking whites favored retention of some of the basic "pillars" of apartheid, though in fewer numbers than Afrikaners. Forty-three percent of the Anglos surveyed favored the continued existence of the Prohibition of Mixed Marriages Act and forty-two percent wanted the Group Areas Act kept in force. Fifty-five percent wanted separate education to continue, and fifty-one percent favored the Reservation of Separate Amenities Act of 1953 — separate bathrooms. Sixty percent were in favor of keeping separate homelands for blacks, and sixty-four percent felt that blacks should continue to have their vote only in those homelands.

I ceased to wonder why Helen Suzman was the only liberal voice in Parliament for thirteen years or why even today the PFP has little political influence.

Everything was very comfortable for English-speaking South African whites — and there seemed no reason to want to change things — until 1985, when Anglos saw their lives, businesses, and livelihoods threatened by apartheid and the angry black revolt against it.

In the early 1980s, South Africa's economy entered a period of prolonged recession brought on by a severe and lingering drought in the subcontinent and by the falling price of gold and other strategic metals on world markets. The government saw the clear political dangers of recession and the unemployment, black and white, that a prolonged recession would bring. Jobs were needed, as were loans to create them. Since interest rates were running as high as eighteen percent on Johannesburg markets, in 1983 the South African Reserve Bank urged South African businesses to seek less expensive loans on foreign markets. Many did, and by September 1985, with the country under a state of emergency and more than a thousand blacks dead in a year of fighting, South African businesses had piled up $27.3 billion in foreign debt.

Seeing South Africa's violence, foreign banks began to worry about the safety of their South African investments, and in early September 1985, whispers began to spread throughout Johannesburg. The quiet whispers soon turned to shouts of outrage. The Chase Manhattan Bank had ordered its South African subsidiary to close down and to extend no further loans in South Africa. Furthermore, it was refusing to extend all existing loans.

A full-fledged banking panic began. Twenty-eight other major banks followed Chase out the door, telling their South African clients that there would be no new loans and that the clients had to begin repaying existing loans immediately. South Africa faced a capital drain of unimagined proportions. Then the government panicked. The minister of finance ordered all foreign debt repayments frozen. More than 130 foreign creditor banks, major and minor, were told they would not receive payment on their debts until a proper — and unhurried — repayment schedule was arrived at. In addition, the Reserve Bank restructured the currency in such a way that any rands leaving South Africa as the result of foreign sale of local subsidiaries — disinvestment — were of a new, lower worth. Restrictions were placed on how much money could be taken out of the country by South African citizens.

Foreign exchange markets always react the same way to actions like those — with shouts of "banana republic." In the first week of September 1985, the rand fell to its lowest level ever — 35 U.S. cents, down from $1.30 in 1980. South Africa's Anglo businessmen saw their assets crumble to a fraction of their former worth.

The debt freeze was sent to a Swiss mediator, Fritz Leutwiler, for resolution. He quickly declared that unless the South African government showed a clear commitment to ending apartheid and ending the violence, repayment terms on the foreign debt would be harsh. South African businesses saw that the debt had to be repaid; otherwise they would have to discount all hopes of future access to foreign capital markets. They looked at the future and saw not only the possibility of no future growth but also the possibility of negative growth. Failure.

It was only then — with the rand at 35 U.S. cents, foreign markets closed, and prosperity threatened as never before — that the Anglos began to speak. Gavin Relly and several other liberal Anglo businessmen flew to Zambia and met the leadership of the ANC. More than ninety of South Africa's best-known business leaders took out a full-page advertisement in the country's largest English-language Sunday newspaper, calling for an acceleration of the reform process, the abolition of statutory race discrimination, negotiation with acknowledged black leaders, and the granting of full citizenship to all blacks. Everybody who was anybody in the Anglo business community signed the ad. The Federated Chamber of Industries, which represents ten thousand South African industries, convened and resolved to become more active in backing reforms. The FCI's chief executive called for "power sharing at the highest level."

For a while it looked as if the business activity was accomplishing something. In November 1985 P. W. Botha offered blacks a place on the President's Council. In January 1986 he offered blacks representation on a National Statutory Council. The Anglo demands had been met and progress was being made, many thought. And then reality hit. Botha's proposals were rejected immediately by blacks because they meant a sharing of power without the whites actually losing it. And, significantly, no further major demands followed from the Anglos. Six months after the first flurry of demands for reform, it was as if they had never been made. And I could see why. The next logical demand would be for black representation at all levels, and that kind of reform would put privilege at risk. The bottom line, I saw, was that there were limits to Anglo activism. The activism had nowhere further to go. The Anglos returned to their pool decks and martinis.

* * *

No one described the Anglo's paralysis better than Vincent Crapanzano in his excellent 1985 book *Waiting: The Whites of South Africa*. Crapanzano, a professor of anthropology and comparative literature at Queens College in New York, brought to his study of a small Cape Province town an eye for the inner soul of the white South African. "In the very ordinary act of waiting," he wrote, "particularly of waiting in fear, men and women lose what John Keats called 'negative capability,' the capability of so negating their identity as to be imaginatively open to the complex and never very certain reality around them. Instead, they close off; they create a kind of psychological apartheid, an apartness that in the case of South Africa is institutionally reinforced."

My wife and I had a friend, Leslie Brown, who told us a story of psychological apartheid. Years ago, when she was a little girl, Leslie and her elderly white nanny took a trip from Johannesburg to the family's vacation home, and they stopped at a country rest stop. Leslie wandered off into the bushes. She heard sounds of a struggle and peered through the bracken to see a white policeman beating a black man to death. She stared in horrified fascination as the white constable beat the black senseless with his truncheon and then began kicking him. Leslie ran off to find her nanny and brought her back into the bushes and showed her what was happening. The policeman was still beating the black's inert body. The nanny dragged Leslie away. Then she told Leslie the killing had never happened.

"I was told to forget about it," Leslie recalled, her voice a disbelieving shrill even years later. She is a lovely and kind woman with two broken marriages and two wonderful young boys, whom she loves deeply. "It never happened. I cannot believe she did that. She wouldn't allow me to tell my parents. Later I did, though, after the nightmares which I couldn't stand. The terrible thing about this country is that we've *always* been told to repress things."

Repression of realities, Anglo style, is above all else a frenzied immersion in privilege and luxury. I found it hard to watch, because nobody likes to watch futility — rearranging the furniture while the house burns down.

In November 1985, three women we knew put together a black-tie party, sending out invitations to well over four hundred people for a hundred-rand-per-couple benefit for the Johannesburg Twilight Children, a fund for black street kids. Through all the planning stages it was unclear who came first, the kids or the bash. The answer came later. The women held the party, complete with a band, an open bar, a porcine buffet, and dancing until four in the morning. There was virtually no money left over for the fund.

One night my wife and I went to the opening of an art exhibit, and I sensed a palpable frenzy in the people there to have fun and enjoy and be merry. They were very forced and nervous — beyond the way small talk over canapés and crudités tends to be forced. A man almost knocked me over with his Rolls-Royce in his hurry to get into the party and the champagne. Inside, the laughter was too loud. The women's laughter, especially, was too shrill to be natural. People drank too much champagne too fast. The talk was of parties and planning safaris into the bush. One woman was going on about what fun the next trip would be, even though I knew that she had grown to hate them — a friend had made a serious pass at her husband on the last one.

They all made plans to move on to the next cocktail party and then to another and then dinner. It felt like an evening at Jay Gatsby's mansion. People were being frantically merry and gay, not because they were merry or gay but because they were frantic.

The upper-middle-class white life in South Africa is the good life, and very comfortable. We saw for ourselves the seductive beauty of white life amid the jacarandas and sweet honeysuckle smell of the yesterday, today, and tomorrow blossoms. Pleasure is immediate, and anything remotely unpleasant is just that: remote. The *braai* is where Anglo South Africans do a good part of their waiting and repressing. The *braais* begin around noon and last until everyone gives out. Nannies often supervise the kids around the pool, and uniformed black servants appear with mountains of food. The men play tennis and the women gossip. A big table is set outdoors — the daytime weather in Johannesburg is nearly perfect year-round, or so it seemed — and everyone crowds round and eats a lot of *boerevors* sausage and charred red meat and drinks a lot of wine. I often got the feeling, sitting around those *braai* tables, that a township could be in flames a mile away and no one would know about it. Or care.

I enjoy a party as much as anyone and can handle a glass of aged port, or two, or more, with the relish of anyone who enjoys a long evening of talk and debate and good company. But in South Africa what set my nerves on edge at Sunday afternoon *braais* was that the parties went far beyond conviviality. They entered a zone of excess, often, it seemed, for the simple sake of excess. Why invite three couples when the house and the table can accommodate ten? Why cook a kilo of *boerevors* when you can cook three? Why buy a case of wine when you can buy four? Why go home when the flowers smell so sweet, the breeze feels so warm, and the sky looks so blue? It seemed a stolen life — hedonism on the sly: hiding from the cruel realities of South African life behind a gauzy mask of self-indulgence.

One thing I found curious at many *braais* was how people reacted when they found I was a foreign journalist. Scowls. Harrumphs. Pursed lips. I suppose I represented something "outside" — the realities those people dealt with for six days a week and were trying to escape on the seventh. So I was an unwelcome intruder in paradise, a Banquo's ghost disrupting dinner.

One man whom I saw at many *braais* and other social occasions obviously considered foreign journalists on the same plane with worms and the Chase Manhattan Bank. I must have been introduced to him a dozen times, but I think I blocked out his name because he was such a son of a bitch.

"You're ruining our country for us, you know," he shouted one warm January Sunday noontime, sounding as potted as the fern behind him. "You and the rest of the press. You just want to get out there and get pictures of the police *sjamboking* blacks to titillate American audiences. Why don't you just leave us alone and let us solve our own problems?"

I told him that there was a great deal of interest in South Africa worldwide, especially among banks and American investors. "Banks," he spat, moving his large stomach toward me aggressively. "Like our good friend Chase. What do they care? What do they care if this country falls apart now? They've got no stake in it now. You and the banks. You made the banks leave. Responsible for all our problems." As the afternoon wore on he got drunker and drunker, and finally his wife had to take him home.

The Anglos looked to me like anyone waiting for the end of an empire. Alcohol, especially beer and wine, is cheap and plentiful. Hard liquor is inexpensive by American standards. People drink a lot, and the Health and Welfare Department's allotment for alcohol rehabilitation for whites is higher than its allotment for black child welfare.

I noticed repression and psychological apartheid in something as simple and everyday as going to the theater. The Market Theater, the best in Johannesburg, sits in an area more deserted than the Detroit waterfront after dark, and about as attractive. It was the invisible hand of apartheid in action. The white theatergoer could go downtown from the northern suburbs, see a play, and make believe that blacks never lived.

There is repression and hiding even in Anglo humor, which masks reality by making fun of it. Just as the tide of black defiance was reaching its height at the end of 1985 a joke began making the rounds of Johannesburg's living rooms: Have you heard about the South African version of the game Trivial Pursuit? There are no answers. Some jokes dealt with the Necklace. What is a bicycle tire? A last warning. What is a *combi* — van — with six tires on top? Circuit court. What does UDF stand for? Uniroyal, Dunlop, and Firestone. How many people can you kill with one tire? Three hundred and sixty-five if it's a Goodyear.

I suppose what disturbed me most about Anglo behavior — the steady immersion in *braais,* humor, booze — was that it bred an overall insensitivity to life. One of the saddest things we saw in South Africa was how the lifestyle and the insensitivity it produced came to consume an American friend, an intelligent woman from the far west with a postgraduate degree. Mary's days were taken up with leaving the two young kids at home and shopping and planning trips and planning dinner parties and bitching constantly with the maid. Her youngest daughter, aged two, would never call for her mother. She would call for the maid. Mary never understood why we always asked our housekeeper, Ann, to bring her children out to our house from Soweto on weekends to escape the township and play in tranquil surroundings. One Sunday we had a number of friends and their kids over, and my wife went out to close the gate to the street. There were kids out there, she told Mary, and she didn't want them in the street. Mary looked out the window. "Oh," she said, "they're only black kids."

Some Anglo behavior was brought to life in J. M. Coetzee's short novel *Waiting for the Barbarians.* The story is about a magistrate posted to a far rural district, where he waits in the wilderness for the inevitable coming of unnamed barbarians. He finds release from the unbearable tension of waiting through a sexual relationship with a young barbarian woman. Bed hopping has become a common practice in Anglo South Africa, though it is seldom talked about in that Calvinist society. Nobody ever came up to my wife or me at a *braai* or a dinner and said, "Do you like apples? Want to fuck?" But social occasions in the homes of Anglos in their thirties and forties were more intense mating dances than they were dinner parties and *braais.* I sensed in the eyes of many women I met a pleading, really, a wanting to be warmed.

There were times we almost needed a scorecard to figure out which peach was shacking up with whom, which weebit was carrying on behind whose back, and when they managed to get together. It was almost painful to watch one woman friend, at dinners and *braais,* stealing time with her boyfriend while her husband tried to prepare whatever meal we were having. My wife and I would drive home after those social occasions, sometimes arguing not over advances made to either of us but over advances made to others.

"You mean you saw them in the pantry?"

"They were just kissing . . . "

"But her husband was . . . "

"Then they disappeared?"

"I've talked to her about it and she says she can't give him up . . . "

"What is this, a soap opera?"

Some Anglo men actually boasted in the open about how many women they'd had and of how many more they intended to have. The man who hated journalists was particularly good at that. In the men the behavior always seemed to me crass and cruel. In the women it was sad because they were the ones who initiated the mating dances and because their actions seemed born of desperation. Perhaps that was because for South Africa's women a future without privilege seems especially cold, and they are grasping for all the warmth they can get while they can still get it. The future seems cold because South African women are some of the most pampered on the face of the earth. Their society, intensely male chauvinist, has produced a woman who has little role beyond being an attractive bauble.

A woman cannot have signing rights on a bank account unless she furnishes the bank manager with a power of attorney signed by her husband. Shortly after we moved into our house, my wife went to rent a VCR. The store would not accept her check without a note from me authorizing the transaction. When my wife applied for overdraft protection at her bank, she was told by a sympathetic branch manager — a Canadian — not to bother: she would have to provide a letter from me stating that I was responsible for her financial security and a copy of our marriage license to prove she was married. Too humiliating. Married women have no rights of their own.

Women also pamper themselves in ways that make them less than whole people. White South African women do not perform many tasks that most American women, even some of the most well-to-do, perform. They don't have to prepare meals because the black cook makes them. They don't have to clean house because the maid does it. They don't have to take care of the kids because the maid does that too. They don't have to take out the garbage because the gardener does it. And in meeting many South African women, I got the distinct impression that even if they did have to take out the garbage they would put on makeup to do it. South African society simply expects a woman to look pretty and act refined. It is typical to see bevies of smartly dressed women clustered at mid-morning in the various coffee shops in the northern suburbs. There they chat and drink espresso and Perrier and browse through the fashion magazines like *Fairlady* and *Sarie*. Many of them drip with jewelry. One woman frequented the Hyde Park shopping center, one of the hubs for Johannesburg's *beau monde*. She would come there three times a day. Between each visit she would go home and change her clothes.

Formal dinner parties — private black-tie gatherings of eight or ten are common — still end with the British colonial custom of the hostess's command. She rises, and the other women rise and go elsewhere to "freshen up." My wife told me that freshening up amounted to little more than milling around idly in some far corner of the house waiting to rejoin the men. The men, in the meantime, are in the dining room drinking port and smoking cigars before they move outside to pee in the bushes.*

---

*The host gives the cue by saying, "Shall we go water the garden?" The first time I was present for this ritual, I tagged along, wondering what was up, and then blanched when I saw what I was expected to do. Not out of modesty but of mechanics. The second time I was part of the ritual I had the foresight to leave my glass of port behind.

Most Anglo women lead wasted lives, and many are not allowed to go beyond certain previously set boundaries. Our Anglo friend Leslie Brown was a professional businesswoman, an unusual role for a woman in South Africa. Her company sold imported cosmetics, but it failed because the low value of the rand forced the price of imports sky-high, and her market dried up. She came to see us after her business was forced to fold, and she sat on our patio, despondent. She had tried to succeed in that man's world, she said. She had wanted to be a lawyer. But her father would not allow her to go to law school. A woman's place, she explained bitterly, was at home.

The Anglos themselves repress many things, but many others are repressed for them by the government. The National Party, through the state-owned South African Broadcasting Corporation (SABC) television and radio network, has created a climate of ignorance in white South Africa. On occasions when I visited the home of an Anglo South African, my host would say something like "You're a foreign journalist. You can tell me what's happening in my own country. What's going on?" Often it was very jovial and offhand and accompanied by much laughter. But I also found it very sad because those people really did *not* know what was happening in their own country and were ashamed. They repressed their shame by laughing at it, like repressing the horror of the Necklace by making jokes about it.

One night in December 1985 while watching the SABC television news, I decided to time it. I knew it had been a busy day, filled with riots in the eastern Cape and Winnie Mandela defying her ban. A provincial court had just ruled in favor of twelve blacks accused of treason, and they had been set free. The first five minutes of the twenty-five-minute broadcast described road conditions for vacationers driving from Johannesburg to the Durban seafront for the Christmas holidays. Next came four and a half minutes on a decision not to allow the English national rugby team to play in South Africa. Halfway into the broadcast, the announcer took fifteen seconds to say that there had been "unrest" in the eastern Cape. A few other stories followed, and the broadcast ended with the usual five minutes of sports reports.

The SABC chooses its footage carefully because it wants to give white South Africans an impression that all is well. A common sight on the SABC news is Chris Heunis, the minister for constitutional planning and development, meeting with various black leaders in their townships: an orderly future is being planned. Another common shot is P. W. Botha meeting with leaders of the homelands: the homeland leaders are legitimate, and Botha is paving the way to a peaceful future.

The SABC's favorite black is Gatsha Buthelezi, for the Zulu leader opposes sanctions and has been at bitter odds with the ANC for ten years. Whites come away from watching Buthelezi on the news believing that "responsible" black leaders oppose sanctions and that most blacks support Pretoria's war against the ANC.

Scenes of township violence seldom appear on South African TV screens because the government does not want whites to know how deeply blacks hate the system, to the point of fighting it to the very end with petrol bombs, rocks, and bricks. The only exceptions are when the violence is black on black. The SABC shows blacks killing other blacks because those scenes reinforce white beliefs that blacks are incapable of governing themselves, that they hate each other, and that the country would fall into ruin if the white man's restraining hand were ever withdrawn.

Indeed, a good deal of the violence since 1984 has been black on black, and one of the reasons for Anglo paralysis is that television viewers have been fed a steady diet of the Witdoeke slashing comrades with machetes, Zulus maiming Xhosas with axes, and comrades beating and burning other blacks to death. So maybe I was being foolish to be surprised when the white woman at the *braai* quoted her maids and National Party propaganda. The propaganda certainly was working.

The SABC has also tried less subtle propaganda. In early 1986 the network began running a show called *Siyafunda!* — We Are Learning! — in the time slot before the news. It was a fifteen-minute language lesson in Zulu for English-speaking whites. I watched a few lessons because I was curious to see what the SABC was trying to accomplish. I got the point during the gas station lesson. In the age of making apartheid more comfortable for blacks, the government seemed to think blacks would be more comfortable hearing the words "Fill 'er up" and "Pass the coffee" in Zulu rather than in English.

The SABC and other South African media love to highlight racial unrest in other countries, especially the United States. Antibusing protests are a favorite, and South Africans consider themselves experts on the subject. The minister of education, F. W. de Klerk, once shouted me down during a press briefing when I challenged his assertion that busing was illegal in the United States. He was adamant that busing was a plan that had failed and therefore had been made against the law.*

The SABC has reciprocal agreements with the American and British television networks, and at one time the agreements led to a small but curious twist in government workings. The foreign networks' news bureaus use SABC satellite facilities to transmit their stories overseas, and the SABC in return gets access to the foreign networks' entertainment programming. During the first days of the state of emergency in June 1986, I met with *Newsweek*'s lawyer, David Hoffe, to discuss how serious the press curbs were and who was likely to be targeted by the Bureau of Information. I asked him if he knew anything about a rumored hit list and whether *Newsweek,* the *New York Times,* and CBS were on

*Any attention to race or ethnic differences in other countries is apartheid by another name to white South Africans. A favorite argument is what they consider apartheid as practiced in the United States (native Americans), Canada (Eskimos), Australia (Aborigines), New Zealand (Maoris), and Belgium (Walloons). The farthest reach, though, is their use of the Swiss canton system as a precedent for the homelands.

it. Hoffe said that he had heard of the list but that it was unlikely the government would expel a network like CBS. The SABC would lose all its CBS entertainment programming. If "Dallas" and "The A-Team" were suddenly yanked from the screen, South Africa's whites would realize that something was wrong.

South Africa's English-language press is largely antigovernment and anti-apartheid, but the press has suffered so long from economic recession, mismanagement, and government regulations that it cannot fully play the role a free press needs to play: informing its readers of what is happening.

The leading antigovernment daily in Johannesburg, *Business Day,* generally runs to only fourteen or sixteen pages and is dominated by business news. As a rule its editorials vacillate between criticizing the government and criticizing proponents of sanctions, neatly reflecting the Anglo dilemma. Johannesburg's other English-language morning daily, the *Citizen,* is a forty-page tabloid that supports the government editorially and reports the news selectively.

The *Sunday Times,* the largest-circulation English-language paper in the country, was forced by advertising losses and recession to reduce its staff to a mere dozen, and the paper diminished its coverage to the British royal family, female flesh, sports, and the speeches of Gavin Relly.

Facing advertising losses and staff cuts, many newspapers were forced to rely more on the South African Press Association (SAPA) wire. And even though the SAPA tickers chatter from nine in the morning until past midnight, the wire carries very little significant news. I would often learn more from the Associated Press weekend duty person or the BBC World Service bulletins on the short wave.

Even before the June 1986 press restrictions went into effect, South African newspapers had to limit what they could tell readers. It has always been illegal, for example, to quote banned persons — the Mandelas, Oliver Tambo, and most other leaders of the African National Congress. In 1983 Harvey Tyson, editor of the Johannesburg *Star,* was arrested and charged with violating the Internal Security Act because his newspaper had quoted Oliver Tambo as saying he could not be legally quoted.

Even so, government policy on the quoting of banned persons vacillates with the times. In January 1986 Oliver Tambo held a press conference in Lusaka, the capital of Zambia, to say that the ANC's plan to escalate its attacks against targets inside South Africa would surely result in the deaths of many white South Africans. Not only did the government allow these remarks to be quoted, but it also extended the expired work permits of several foreign journalists so we could cover the press conference in Zambia and get back into South Africa to file.

A year later another government action was designed to achieve the same goal of selective news coverage. If the issue had not been so serious, Pretoria's ham-handedness would have appeared laughable. In early January 1987 the government banned all pro-ANC advertisements and all public statements of support for the banned organization. Two weeks later Oliver Tambo met with U.S. Secretary of State George Shultz in Washington in a cordial meeting that covered a broad range of issues. The South African government did an abrupt about-face and allowed some of Tambo's Washington remarks into print — only the ones concerning white deaths at the hands of the ANC.

Following the press curbs of June 1986, whites were unable to learn anything accurate about what was happening in or to their country. At Christmas 1986 my wife and I, in the States, received a letter from our friend Leslie Brown, in Johannesburg, asking us to send her news of what was happening in South Africa. She knew nothing. "I feel like the cheated wife here," she wrote. "That I will be the last to know — if ever."

Some Anglos responded to their country's degeneration by joining the "chicken run" — emigration to Australia, Canada, Brazil, or Britain. In 1985 the number of people permanently leaving the country increased almost forty percent over the number leaving the year before. Most of those who leave permanently are professional people — doctors, lawyers, dentists — and the number of professionals leaving in 1985 jumped nearly fifty percent over the number leaving the previous year. Our friend Richard Jones, the dentist, was thinking of setting up practice in the United States. It seemed every time I saw Richard, he would ask, "So Rick, what's Miami like?" or "How about Denver? Do you know if they need dentists there?" Once we were leaving the ballet and out of the blue he turned and said, "Los Angeles?"

Emigration for middle-class whites is hampered by money problems. The government has imposed restrictions on the amount of money a family can take out of the country, and the fall in the value of the rand has cut the worth of 1980 assets by sixty percent. Yet some Anglos have gotten around the withdrawal restrictions by turning cash into solid assets and shipping them out when they leave. The most imaginative circumventions involved Anglos buying large yachts or airplanes and sailing or flying them to Australia in a neat reversal of the original immigration patterns: South Africa as a two-generation stopover on the way down under.

"The saddest part of the chicken run," a Johannesburg doctor once said to me, "is that it's the moderates who are leaving, and the ones staying behind are the hardliners." Those who remain are faced with a choice: shall they continue to fritter away their time, waiting in their sybaritic La-La Land, or shall they try to solve the country's problems and, if so, how? The old role of the liberal — harassing the National Party from the other side of the aisle in Parliament — has proved to be at the very least not too constructive and at the most a waste of time. Some moderates and liberals think a new role has to be found.

Two such thinkers are Frederick van Zyl Slabbert and Alex Boraine. They were leaders of the Progressive Federal Party until both resigned their seats in Parliament in disgust and frustration in February 1986. Slabbert said at the time that he considered Parliament irrelevant, and Boraine later said he resigned because he considered Parliament "clearly discredited in the eyes of the oppressed majority" and because "it was very clear to me that if I wanted to be of any service to my country I would have to establish a distance between myself and that discredited institution."

I called Boraine on the first day of the permanent emergency to ask what, if anything, Anglo liberals could do to pull the country out of the morass. He said that anything useful would have to happen outside Parliament. Parliament is discredited, Boraine said, because the new constitution excludes blacks from any representation, and therefore blacks view it — and all in it — as a mere tool of the NP. Boraine remembered the response from blacks after he resigned as "embarrassingly warm — because they don't want someone standing up there for them. They want to stand there themselves." And in the months that followed, Boraine began to formulate a new role for himself.

"I'm slowly evolving a plan," he said. Boraine is a tall, handsome man, and the rich sound of his voice was deep and concerned. "It is to play a support role for black leadership, and I think that is all that any white liberal *can* do. It is playing a support role by trying to convince white South Africans that the status quo is unacceptable. It is trying to convince them that there is a future after apartheid." The tone of his voice, over the phone line from Cape Town, was pleading, intense. "It is trying to convince them that the ANC and the UDF do *not* want to drive them into the sea. And it is trying to convince them, make them understand, that it is in their own self-interest to move away from the old way of doing things and to move toward the progressive forces like the UDF."

I had the feeling, talking to Boraine, that this was something new. It also sounded reasonable, and because it was so reasonable, I thought, the idea would probably go nowhere. I told Boraine my thoughts.

"The idea is to build bridges — bridges between the black leadership and the whites," Boraine pleaded, his voice desperate, as if he were trying to convince not just me but five million other people. "It is a very uncomfortable role and a very difficult role to play. But it has to be played. It has to be shouted from the rooftops that whites must identify with the people who are someday going to call the shots here. That is what the ANC advised when I talked with them in Lusaka after I resigned. Help whites understand, they said. Help them to understand that we want them to become a part of the new South Africa, a democratic and nonracial South Africa, where all they will lose is their privilege, simply because full citizenship will mean that everyone has the vote."

Boraine paused, and his voice seemed to grow weary, as if he were describing the mechanics of cleaning the Augean stables. "If whites can come to terms with that, and go beyond that, then maybe they can become part of the process of change here — if they can be convinced that they will count for something."

Whether privileged Anglos have the mental and emotional ability to become part of the process of change is still open to question. Their privilege is so great and so long guarded that it seems more likely that they will choose to remain paralyzed in their fantasy land. And there they are likely to remain until the revolution takes them by surprise, unaware of who Nelson Mandela was and of what he might have been able to do to save their country.

Five

THE FIRST ACCUSED: NELSON MANDELA

SHORTLY AFTER I ARRIVED in Johannesburg I was invited, along with several other journalists, to have lunch with John Maree, chairman of ESCOM, the state-owned utility, at his offices at Megawatt Park, ESCOM headquarters. Like other mainstream Afrikaners at that time, Maree was anxious to improve South Africa's image with the foreign press, and he hired a public relations consultant to help with the task. The consultant, Richard Foxton, was an exuberant former *Newsweek* advertising and circulation man who once sold two thousand *Newsweek* subscriptions to the sultan of Oman in a single afternoon. He went about his PR job with equal panache. Foxy was forever calling us up and arranging lunches with his various clients, and they were usually amiable and pleasant occasions.

The usual suspects were there for lunch with Maree — Tony Robinson of the *Financial Times,* Eric Marsden of the *Sunday Times,* Christopher "Sneaky" Munnion of the *Daily Telegraph* — along with Hugh Murray, editor and publisher of *Leadership* magazine, and me.

Leadership is a glossy, well-respected monthly magazine that Murray puts out virtually by himself from his offices in Cape Town. Murray, as dapper and clean-cut as his magazine, had organized Gavin Relly's business trip to Zambia to meet with Oliver Tambo and other leaders of the banned African National Congress in September 1985.

Maree, the handsome Sean Connery type who had on another occasion drilled me so deeply on the Boer War, seemed skeptical about the trip and asked Murray, in a rather offhand way, what the trip had accomplished. Murray said he thought the trip was very important just for opening a dialogue. The two of them fenced amiably for about five minutes — all "Johnny" and "Huey" — until Murray suggested that the time had come for Pretoria to "grasp the nettle of the ANC" and begin negotiating with the banned organization.

"Impossible," said Maree, thumping his knife onto the cheese plate I was holding for him, so that I almost dropped it. His brow furrowed and a dark look came into his eyes. "The ANC is a Communist organization, and there is no use talking to Communists." I broke in, saying that a lesson could be learned from my own country's dealings with the national liberation movement in Vietnam in the 1940s and 1950s. The United States had rejected Ho Chi Minh as a Communist early on, I said, only to pay for it dearly twenty years later. Wasn't there some value, I asked, in talking to an organization that included Communists but that was also at heart a nationalist organization?

Maree looked at me with something that approached pity. I was clearly an addled teenager who had just given a stupid answer in Latin class. "But Ricky," he said, sounding like Claude Rains addressing Bogart in *Casablanca*. "But Ricky, you don't understand about this organization. They call themselves a liberation movement, but they're just trying to hide the fact that they're all Communists."

I said I didn't think Nelson Mandela was a Communist, and Maree snorted. The room descended into silence and tension. Foxy began to fidget. This was not what was supposed to happen at his lunches. He turned to Sneaky Munnion.

"I say, Chris," Foxy said to the jockey-sized Englishman. "You've been in Southern Africa a long time. What do you think of this? How long has it been, anyway, fifteen?"

"Seventeen years," Munnion answered solemnly. "And when

I started I was six foot six and weighed two hundred fifty pounds."

The room, and the tension, dissolved into laughter. Everyone laughed heartily, including Maree, and Foxton breathed easier. But Maree remained dark and brooding over coffee. The Communists had spoiled his lunch.

I met many white South Africans who shared Maree's prejudice about the ANC. I also learned how the government steadily and heavily plays on that prejudice. The National Party wants white South Africans to remain convinced that the ANC is a Communist organization linked to an international ring of terrorism. At one point the NP's propaganda arm issued a pamphlet called "Dealing with the ANC." With purple prose and McCarthyesque innuendo, it portrayed the ANC as an all-Communist organization doing the dirty work assigned it by Moscow.

David Welsh, a political scientist at the University of Cape Town, told me he would have given the pamphlet a failing grade if it had been handed to him as a paper, but that didn't stop the SABC and the pro-government press from splashing the report all over the airwaves and the front pages.

I learned that the African National Congress, founded in 1912, two years before the National Party, actually is a national liberation movement — with perhaps as many as fifteen Communists on its thirty-man Executive Committee — but nonetheless an organization dedicated to African nationalism. I learned that by reading Nelson Mandela. For any reporter who wanted to have a prayer of covering South Africa well or even adequately, a working knowledge of the story of Nelson Mandela was an absolute necessity. We all had to carry around in our heads a working biography of the man because the government seemed inclined to release him from jail at a moment's notice. I found I had to commit Mandela to memory in the same way I'd once memorized the Persian alphabet and lists of Latin prepositions that took the ablative case. All of us lived in a state of dread that the phone might ring at three in the morning and an ominous disembodied voice say: "Foreign desk. AP reports Mandela's released. We'll need a thousand words in two hours."

Nelson Rohlihlahla Mandela was born the son of a chief of the Tembu tribe in the Transkei in 1918. His father died in 1930, and the twelve-year-old Mandela went to live with his uncle, the Paramount Chief of the Tembus. Mandela quickly rejected the course open to him — hereditary ascension to a leading role in the tribe — and went off to university instead. He attended the black university at Fort Hare, at that time the premier black college in the country, but he was expelled in 1940, along with his friend Oliver Tambo, for leading a student strike.

Mandela moved to Johannesburg and found work as a policeman in one of the English-owned mines. He earned money on the side as a heavyweight boxer and then entered the University of Witwatersrand, where he studied law. He never finished the course — he dropped out in 1942 — but he passed his bar exam and set up Johannesburg's first black law practice, in partnership with Tambo. Together they also joined the African National Congress in 1944.

The ANC was pledged to nonviolence in those days, and Mandela became active in leading protest demonstrations against apartheid. In 1952 he was deputy national president of the ANC and such a thorn in the side of the government that it banned him. In 1955 Mandela and other ANC leaders framed the Freedom Charter, which remains the ANC's blueprint for South African society: a democratic, nonracial state with equal rights for all races and one man, one vote.

In 1956 Mandela was arrested and charged, along with 155 other blacks, with high treason — furthering the aims of a subversive organization, the Communist Party, which had been banned in 1950. The Treason Trial, as it was known, turned into a trial of the Freedom Charter. It lasted for five years, until charges against all 156 defendants were dropped. The Freedom Charter was, in effect, pronounced clean.

Mandela remained active in the anti-apartheid movement

during the prolonged trial and met his wife, Winnie, in 1957. They were married a year later — he was forty and she was twenty-four — but they have spent only two years of married life together since then.

The turning point for Mandela, and for his generation of black South Africans, came in March 1960 when police in Sharpeville fired on a peaceful protest demonstration and killed sixty-nine unarmed black protesters. A nationwide black protest against apartheid followed, during which the government banned the ANC. Its leaders went underground — Oliver Tambo fled the country — and the ANC's leaders vowed to change the tone and direction of their struggle. They formed Umkhonto we Sizwe, the Spear of the Nation, and pledged the ANC and Umkhonto to violence.

Mandela was made leader of Umkhonto we Sizwe and went underground. He earned the nickname the Black Pimpernel for his success at eluding the police, and he traveled freely both inside and outside the country. He was a free man until August 1962, when he was arrested outside Durban — with the help, it later came to light, of the CIA.

Mandela was found guilty of leaving the country without a valid passport and inciting people to strike. He has been in jail ever since. The year was 1962, when Harold Macmillan was prime minister of Great Britain, John Kennedy had more than a year to live, and the Princess of Wales was still in diapers.

The most recent photograph of Nelson Mandela is more than twenty years old, and it is all the world has as a guide to what he looks like. Mandela was a big man — over six feet — and in 1964 he still had the physique of a heavyweight boxer. Photographs of him in the early 1960s show him towering over groups of other blacks, his shoulders slightly hunched as if he were trying not to appear so large. Yet his stance also gave him a look of earnestness, sincerity. His head in those photographs looks huge. The pictures also show that, in speaking, Mandela would often gesture with his right hand, his fingers and thumb drawn together as if holding a pointer. He wore his hair close-cropped and parted over his left ear, and photographs show that his eyes had a slightly hooded look. He dressed impeccably in a dark business suit, and the impression he made — one can see it in his words alone — was of great forcefulness and great authority.

In October 1963 Mandela was brought out of Pretoria Central Prison and made to stand trial for treason and sabotage with eight other defendants in the Rivonia Trial, so called for the Johannesburg suburb where most of the ANC leaders were arrested. The trial lasted through the next year, and Mandela opened the defense himself. The date was April 20, 1964. Nelson Mandela stood before a judge in Johannesburg and explained the ANC and its aims to the court. A reading of the words he spoke in defense of the ANC indicates that he was speaking in a moderate tone of voice — not shouting, but simply forthright, direct. He spoke in a deep, baritone voice, the kind that demands attention simply for its gravity.

His views seem not to have changed in over twenty years. What he told a Johannesburg court in 1964 about Communists in the ANC was identical to what he told Olusegun Obasanjo and Malcolm Fraser of the British Commonwealth's Eminent Persons Group in 1986. I think when the final history of South Africa is written, Nelson Mandela's 1964 defense speech will rank comparably to the *Federalist* papers or Lincoln's second inaugural address in American history: a statement of ideals and a living vision of a dreamed society.

"I am the First Accused," he told the court, and I imagine a clipped, deep voice filling the room as it fell into empty silence.

> I have done whatever I did, both as an individual and as a leader of my people, because of my experience in South Africa and my own proudly felt African background, and not because of what any outsider might have said.
>
> In my youth in the Transkei I listened to the elders of my tribe telling stories of the old days. Amongst the tales they related to me were those of wars fought by our ancestors in defence of the

fatherland. . . . I hoped then that life might offer me the opportunity to serve my people and make my own humble contribution
to their freedom struggle. This is what has motivated me in all
that I have done in relation to the charges made against me in
this case.

Having said this, I must deal . . . with the question of violence.
Some of the things so far told to the Court are true and some are
untrue. I do not, however, deny that I planned sabotage. I did
not plan it in a spirit of recklessness, nor because I have any love
of violence. I planned it as a result of a calm and sober assessment
of the political situation that had arisen after many years of tyr-
anny, exploitation, and oppression of my people by the Whites.

As I read these words one night in 1985, I was torn between
their simple eloquence and the dread of hearing a man pro-
nouncing his own death sentence. And he followed with more.

I admit immediately that I was one of the persons who helped
to form Umkhonto we Sizwe, and that I played a prominent role
in its affairs until I was arrested in August 1962. . . .

. . . I, and the others who started the organization, did so for
two reasons. Firstly, we believed that as a result of Government
policy, violence by the African people had become inevitable, and
that unless responsible leadership was given to [channel] and control the feelings of our people, there would be outbreaks of terrorism which would produce an intensity of bitterness and hostility between the various races of this country which is not
produced even by war. Secondly, we felt that without violence
there would be no way open to the African people to succeed in
their struggle against the principle of white supremacy. All lawful
modes of expressing opposition to this principle had been closed
by legislation, and we were placed in a position in which we had
either to accept a permanent state of inferiority, or to defy the
Government. We chose to defy the law. We first broke the law in
a way which avoided any recourse to violence; when this form was
legislated against, and then the Government resorted to a show
of force to crush opposition to its policies, only then did we decide
to answer violence with violence.

As I read these words they conjured up scenes in the townships that I had seen only weeks and days before. Blacks in 1985

were still using essentially the same argument I had just read, that state violence was pushing blacks to violence. So little had changed in twenty-one years, I thought, as I read over Mandela's continuing defense and his admission that the ANC had planned acts of sabotage and had opted for a long-term strategy of guerrilla warfare. Then he arrived at the issue of Communists in the ANC.

> I joined the ANC in 1944, and in my younger days I held the view that the policy of admitting communists to the ANC, and the close co-operation which existed at times on specific issues between the ANC and the Communist Party, would lead to a watering down of the concept of African Nationalism. At that stage I was a member of the African National Congress Youth League, and was one of a group which moved for the expulsion of communists from the ANC. This proposal was heavily defeated. Amongst those who voted against the proposal were some of the most conservative sections of African political opinion. They defended the policy on the ground that from its inception the ANC was formed and built up, not as a political party with one school of political thought, but as a Parliament of the African people, accommodating people of various political convictions, all united by the common goal of national liberation. I was eventually won over to this point of view and I have upheld it ever since.
>
> It is perhaps difficult for white South Africans, with an ingrained prejudice against communism, to understand why experienced African politicians so readily accept communists as their friends. But to us the reason is obvious. Theoretical differences amongst those fighting against oppression is a luxury we cannot afford at this stage. What is more, for many decades communists were the only political group in South Africa who were prepared to treat Africans as human beings and their equals; who were prepared to eat with us; talk with us, live with us, and work with us. They were the only political group which was prepared to work with the Africans for the attainment of political rights and a stake in society. Because of this, there are many Africans who, today, tend to equate freedom with communism. They are supported in this belief by a legislature which brands all exponents of democratic government and African freedom as communists and bans many of them (who are not communists) under the Suppression of Communism Act.

I put down the volume I was reading from and looked out at the night. So little had changed. Only a few weeks before, I had attended a mass funeral in a nearby township and had seen the hammer and sickle flag of the Soviet Union waving at the end of a long pole held by a young comrade. Afterward I had asked the man I considered probably the most thoughtful and intelligent man in the country, John Kane-Berman, about the depth of the comrades' commitment to communism. Kane-Berman is the former Rhodes scholar who runs the South African Institute of Race Relations in Johannesburg, the liberal think tank that monitors the progress and degeneration of the country under apartheid. I had gone to see him in his small, cluttered office on Plein Street, and, coat off and tie undone, the bearded Kane-Berman talked about communism in South Africa. "The commitment is not very deep," he scoffed, scratching his salt-and-pepper beard. "What you've got is a situation where youth hates apartheid and wants to get rid of it and the government that prolongs it — and a government that hates Communists and wants to get rid of them. Black youths see a government entrenching apartheid and hating communism, and they therefore reckon that there must be something good about communism if the government, which supports apartheid, is so dead set against it. So they say they are Communists and wave hammer and sickle flags."

I looked out at the hot night and remembered those words. The same forces were at work that night as were at work when Mandela took the stand. I picked up the volume and read on.

It is not only in internal politics that we count communists as amongst those who support our cause. In the international field, communist countries have always come to our aid. In the United Nations and other Councils of the world the communist *bloc* has supported the Afro-Asian struggle against colonialism and often seems to be more sympathetic to our plight than some of the Western powers. Although there is a universal condemnation of apartheid, the communist *bloc* speaks out against it with a louder voice than most of the white world. In these circumstances, it would take a brash young politician, such as I was in 1949, to proclaim that the Communists are our enemies.

I turn now to my own position. I have denied that I am a communist, and I think that in the circumstances I am obliged to state exactly what my political beliefs are.

I have always regarded myself, in the first place, as an African patriot. . . .

. . . I am attracted by the idea of a classless society, an attraction which springs in part from Marxist reading and, in part, from my admiration of the structure and organization of early African societies in this country. The land, then the main means of production, belonged to the tribe. There were no rich or poor and there was no exploitation.

It is true . . . that I have been influenced by Marxist thought. But this is also true of many of the leaders of the new independent States [such as] Gandhi, Nehru, Nkrumah, and Nasser. . . . We all accept the need for some form of socialism to enable our people to catch up with the advanced countries of this world and to overcome their legacy of extreme poverty. But this does not mean we are Marxists.

Indeed, for my own part, I believe that it is open to debate whether the Communist Party has any specific role to play at this particular stage of our political struggle. The basic task at the present moment is the removal of race discrimination and the attainment of democratic rights on the basis of the Freedom Charter. In so far as that Party furthers this task, I welcome its assistance. I realize that it is one of the means by which people of all races can be drawn into our struggle.

I paused again, impressed by the forcefulness and honesty of Mandela's argument. It reminded me, in tone, of Martin Luther's own self-defense before the Diet of Worms in 1520: "I cannot; I shall not; I will not recant. Here I stand." I read on, and I imagined a still and hushed courtroom filled with a precise baritone.

From my reading of Marxist literature and from conversations with Marxists, I have gained the impression that communists regard the parliamentary system of the West as undemocratic and reactionary. But, on the contrary, I am an admirer of such a system.

The Magna Charta, the Petition of Rights, and the Bill of Rights are documents which are held in veneration by democrats throughout the world.

I have great respect for British political institutions, and for the country's system of justice. I regard the British Parliament as the most democratic institution in the world, and the independence and impartiality of its judiciary never fail to arouse my admiration.

The American Congress, that country's doctrine of separation of powers, as well as the independence of its judiciary, arouses in me similar sentiments.

I have been influenced in my thinking by both West and East. All this has led me to feel that in my search for a political formula, I should be absolutely impartial and objective. I should tie myself to no particular system of society other than of socialism. I must leave myself free to borrow the best from the West and from the East. . . .

There are certain Exhibits which suggest that we received financial support from abroad. . . .

Our political struggle has always been financed from internal sources — from funds raised by our own people and by our own supporters. Whenever we had a special campaign or an important political case — for example, the Treason Trial — we received financial assistance from sympathetic individuals and organizations in the Western countries. We had never felt it necessary to go beyond these sources.

But when in 1961 the Umkhonto was formed, and a new phase of struggle introduced, we realized that these events would make a heavy call on our slender resources, and that the scale of our activities would be hampered by the lack of funds. One of my instructions, as I went abroad in January 1962, was to raise funds from the African states.

I must add that, whilst abroad, I had discussions with leaders of political movements in Africa and discovered that almost every single one of them, in areas which had still not attained independence, had received all forms of assistance from the socialist countries, as well as from the West, including that of financial support. I also discovered that some well-known African states, all of them non-communists, and even anti-communists, had received similar assistance. . . .

The Government often answers its critics by saying that Africans in South Africa are economically better off than the inhab-

itants of the other countries in Africa. I do not know whether this
statement is true and doubt whether any comparison can be made
without having regard to the cost-of-living index in such countries. But even if it is true, as far as the African people are concerned it is irrelevant. Our complaint is not that we are poor by
comparison with people in other countries, but that we are poor
by comparison with the white people in our own country, and that
we are prevented by legislation from altering this imbalance.

The lack of human dignity experienced by Africans is the direct result of the policy of white supremacy. White supremacy
implies black inferiority. Legislation designed to preserve white
supremacy entrenches this notion. . . .

. . . Africans want a just share in the whole of South Africa;
they want security and a stake in society.

Above all, we want equal political rights, because without them
our disabilities will be permanent. I know this sounds revolution-
ary to the whites in this country, because the majority of voters
will be Africans. This makes the white man fear democracy.

But this fear cannot be allowed to stand in the way of the only
solution which will guarantee racial harmony and freedom for all.
It is not true that the enfranchisement of all will result in racial
domination. Political division, based on colour, is entirely artificial
and, when it disappears, so will the domination of one colour
group by another. The ANC has spent half a century fighting
against racialism. When it triumphs it will not change that policy.

This then is what the ANC is fighting. Their struggle is a truly
national one. It is a struggle of the African people, inspired by
their own suffering and their own experience. It is a struggle for
the right to live.

During my lifetime I have dedicated myself to this struggle of
the African people. I have fought against white domination, and
I have fought against black domination. I have cherished the ideal
of a democratic and free society in which all persons live together
in harmony and with equal opportunities. It is an ideal which I
hope to live for and to achieve. But if needs be, it is an ideal for
which I am prepared to die.

I finished reading those words, and I put down the volume
and sighed. In their context they were probably some of the saddest words I had ever read, because two months after Mandela

spoke them, he was sentenced to imprisonment for life plus five years. He was sent to Robben Island, where he became simply prisoner number 446/64, his prison identity card reading *Sabotasie; Lewenslank plus 5 jaar.*

Mandela lived on Robben Island until April 1982, when he was transferred to Pollsmoor prison on the Cape Flats. He worked in the Island's limestone quarries for the first ten years of his sentence until doctors, citing Mandela's advancing years, recommended lighter work. He took up gardening in the prison compound and sold his produce for pocket money.

Mandela became an avid and successful tennis player. He was allowed to visit the prison library, and his favorite readings were in history and economics. One visitor in the late 1970s noticed that in Mandela's small cell were copies of *An Economic History of Europe, The Naked Society,* a small English dictionary, and the Bible. Like all prisoners convicted of treason, Mandela was allowed to read newspapers and magazines only if they were heavily censored. And the censorship was rigorous. Mandela told one visitor that an issue of the *Reader's Digest* — hardly a radical publication — had had twenty articles ripped out of it. Mandela was allowed to see his wife and family twice a month, a thirty-minute visit each time. They had to speak to each other through a tube and look at each other through a thick Plexiglas window. A policeman was always present, and the Mandelas were not allowed to talk about politics, prison conditions, or friends on the outside.

Mandela was not allowed to touch his wife and two daughters until after he had been in jail for more than twenty years, in July 1984. His younger daughter, Zindzi, was eighteen months old when Mandela was arrested, and she did not see him again until she was sixteen. She was twenty-two the day she was first allowed to touch him. She crawled into his lap and sat there "like a tiny child," she remembered.

Prison authorities never gave a reason for transferring Mandela to Pollsmoor, but the commonly accepted reason was that they were disturbed by the way Robben Island turned into Mandela U. in the wake of the Soweto riots. The move to Pollsmoor forced him to trade a library of economics and history for a library that contained nothing but paperback westerns and to trade tennis for a small exercise yard on the roof of the prison. Instead of the garden in the prison compound on the Island he tended rooftop tomato pots and dirt-filled oil drum planters at Pollsmoor. He traded his small cell for a dormitory shared with four other prisoners.

Yet prison seemed to change Mandela not at all. P. W. Botha offered to release Mandela — if he renounced violence — in January 1985, but Mandela refused. Botha again offered Mandela release "unconditionally" on the condition that he renounce violence when Mandela entered the hospital for prostate surgery in November of that year. But again Mandela refused. Violence had been ANC policy for twenty-five years, and to renounce it would split the ANC. Mandela could do nothing other than refuse or he would have dealt irreparable damage to the organization he had gone to prison for defending.

"I cherish my own freedom dearly," he said in a statement to his countrymen and read by his daughter Zindzi in February 1985, "but I care even more for your freedom. Too many have died since I went into prison. Too many have suffered for the love of freedom. I owe it to their widows, to their orphans, to their mothers and their fathers who have grieved and wept for them. Not only have I suffered during these long, lonely, wasted years. I am no less life-loving than you are. But I cannot sell the birthright of the people to be free. Only free men can negotiate. Prisoners cannot enter into contracts. Your freedom and mine cannot be separated."

I tried several times to get permission to interview Mandela, but my formal telexes to the Ministry of Justice went unanswered. Others from the outside were allowed to see him, however, almost arbitrarily. Former Senate Watergate special counsel Samuel Dash was allowed to see Mandela in early 1985, and Dash found Mandela robust and strong. Dash also found his politics unaltered.

"If white leaders do not act in good faith toward us," he told Dash, "if they will not meet with us to discuss political equality and if, in effect, they tell us we must remain subjugated by the whites, then there is really no alternative to us other than violence.

"Our program is clear," he added. "It is based on three principles: One: A United South Africa — no artificial 'homelands.' Two: Black representation in the central Parliament — not membership in the kind of apartheid assemblies that have been established for the Coloreds and Asians. Three: One man, one vote."

The British Commonwealth's Eminent Persons Group (EPG) was a seven-member panel commissioned during the Commonwealth meeting in Nassau, the Bahamas, in October 1985. The group was charged with investigating conditions inside South Africa and was asked to "initiate a process of dialogue across lines of color, politics and religion, with a view to establishing a non-racial and representative government." The group was chaired by Malcolm Fraser, former prime minister of Australia, and General Olusegun Obasanjo, former president of Nigeria. As part of the process of beginning a dialogue, either all or part of the EPG met with Mandela three times in 1986.

The group's report was published in mid-1986, and the authors went to great pains to explain how they "resolved to approach these meetings with an open mind," though admitting that in approaching Mandela "it was impossible not to be aware of the mythology surrounding him."

Nevertheless, the group came away from its meetings with Mandela clearly impressed "by his physical authority, by his immaculate appearance, his apparent good health and his commanding presence. In his manner he exuded authority and received the respect of all around him, including his gaolers."

Politically, the Eminent Persons Group was impressed by Mandela's conciliatory attitude to those outside the ANC and by the consistency of his beliefs. "That he is a fervent nationalist cannot be denied," the report concluded. "Of his supposed communism, either now or in the past, we found no trace. In that respect we clearly differ from the Government which has resorted to the most dubious of methods to denigrate his reputation."

In August 1986, Fraser and Obasanjo testified before an informal Senate sanctions hearing in Washington, and Obasanjo was asked about Mandela's Communist ties. Would not Communists within the ANC Executive, he was asked, force Mandela to follow their point of view? I was at that hearing — I had been asked to testify as well — and I found Obasanjo's answer highly believable because it bore the Mandela style.

"Mandela gave me an answer to that," Obasanjo said, smiling cryptically. Obasanjo, clad in flowing white African robes, is the pragmatic former military ruler of Nigeria who handed over power to an elected civilian government in 1979, an unusual occurrence in Africa. He continued: "Mandela said that the ANC was a democratic movement that doesn't ban ideas and people and that all you have to do to be in the ANC is be anti-apartheid. And I asked him the same question that you just asked me. He said, 'How can anyone believe that the Communists could get me to do what they want, when this government — for the twenty-four years it has imprisoned me — has not been able to get me to do what *it* wants?' "

The group also concluded that Mandela "had been driven to the armed struggle with the greatest reluctance" and came away impressed by Mandela's willingness to help. Mandela told the group that while he could not speak for the whole of the ANC, he believed it would be possible to begin negotiations if the government released him and other political prisoners and simultaneously took the army and police out of the townships — while the ANC agreed to a suspension of violence.

In the context of the government's delicate fencing with Mandela over the issue of renouncing violence, that statement represented a major breakthrough. A suspension of violence is certainly not a renunciation, but coming from a man who had held for twenty-five years that violence was necessary, an offer to suspend violence was enormously significant. It was as far as Mandela could go without risking an irreparable rift in the ANC, and it was as close as Pretoria was ever going to get to a renunciation.

Things seemed to hang in the balance for several days. Would the government take the bait? all of us in the foreign press asked ourselves and each other. Would Pretoria take this opportunity? It was a real sign of hope. But I suppose all along we knew what the answer would be. The group's report was sent to the Commonwealth secretary-general on Saturday, June 7, and released to the press on Monday, June 9. Pretoria seemed to answer on Thursday, June 12, when it imposed the permanent state of emergency.

The group's final conclusion rang true during that violent and authoritarian week: "While the government claims to be ready to negotiate, it is in truth not yet prepared to negotiate fundamental change, nor to countenance the creation of genuine democratic structures, nor to face the prospect of the end of white domination and white power in the foreseeable future." Nelson Mandela remained in jail, and the campaign of ANC violence and sabotage, which Mandela had offered to suspend, continued.

The ANC's guidelines for sabotage were laid out before Mandela even entered prison, and the ANC held to them for more than twenty years: the only targets of ANC bombs would be police stations, electrical pylons, and government installations. Civilian targets were off limits.

At least until 1983. In May of that year a car bomb exploded in downtown Pretoria, and nineteen civilians were killed, including eight blacks. In December 1985 a bomb killed five people in a crowded Christmastime shopping center in Amanzimtoti, near Durban, and the ANC began planting land mines in the northern Transvaal along the Limpopo River. Several farmers were killed. ANC policy had changed: the ANC had declared war on

Pretoria, and if the civilian population of South Africa got caught in the crossfire, such was war.

I went to see Oliver Tambo at his exile headquarters in Lusaka, Zambia, in January 1986. The occasion was a ceremony marking the twenty-fifth anniversary of the founding of Umkhonto we Sizwe, and Tambo had agreed to meet the press to explain how he was going to escalate the war against apartheid. Oliver Tambo is a small, dignified-looking man who wears his salt-and-pepper hair long, with his sideburns forming neat muttonchops on his cheeks. His eyes hide behind Coke bottle black-rimmed glasses, the kind the aging Cary Grant wore. But Tambo's ear pieces ride well up on his temples, making him look as if he's been wearing that same pair of specs since he was fourteen. On the day I saw him, he strolled slowly into the crowded room in Lusaka wearing a conservative business suit, smiling shyly, and nodding as he sat in a stuffed red leather armchair.

Winnie Mandela once told me that Oliver Tambo was a deeply Christian man, the one who had remained the last stumbling block to the ANC's embracing violence in 1960. She should know. They are from the same village in the Transkei, and it was through Tambo that a twenty-three-year-old Winnie Madikezela met Nelson Mandela in 1957. On this day nearly thirty years later, Tambo sat in his red stuffed chair, leaning on a table, and he did not look violent enough even to play rugby.

The two-hour press conference began with questions on the Amanzimtoti bombing, which had come only two weeks before. Was the ANC responsible? Had the Executive sanctioned the bombing? Did Tambo know about it in advance? Tambo answered calmly that no, he had not known about it in advance, but he exploded when asked about it for the third time.

"Why must I be cross-examined on the matter of Amanzimtoti?" he shouted, banging the table in front of him. Tambo's eyes opened wide behind his thick glasses, and then he shrugged, holding his hands before him, elbows at his sides. His high-timbred voice softened.

"It is not important." He shrugged again, his words coming out slowly. "The bomb exploded. People were killed. And there are going to be more Amanzimtotis in a time of general conflict." His tone was level, matter-of-fact. "We'd better be ready for it and not be surprised by it. There will be more killings. Some will be regrettable. I didn't rejoice when I heard about the bomb explosion." And then his voice quickened, and his right forefinger jabbed the air. "But let me tell you that there were celebrations — yes, celebrations — in South Africa after that happened."

Tambo took off his glasses and rubbed his eyes with his left hand, and then he began talking again in his slow, high voice. "The armed struggle has so far been confined to the townships," he said, putting his two hands together in the shape of a cup and placing them on the table to his left. As he continued, his tone was quiet and logical. "But those townships are not all of South Africa. The people who died there did so because they want a happy, peaceful South Africa. And we are saying that if South Africans are going to die for their country, let all of them do it." And Tambo spread his arms and laid his fingers on the table, as far apart as they would reach.

"The violence must spread outside the townships," and he drew out his words — "outsiiiide." "Aaaall people must be involved in the attempts to solve the problems of our country." He sat up straight, and his eyes opened wide again behind the glasses. "As far as many South Africans are concerned, this violence is happening only in some black back yard. Aaaall must be made to experience the struggle."

Tambo continued talking in a calm and oddly gentle voice. And as the words came out, there was little threat to the tone — just the same special logic. "In the past we have taken precautions to see that civilians are not injured. But we are moving away from that level of caution." He shrugged. "We are certain that many civilians will be killed."

Like many others, I had approached South Africa assuming

that the ANC had always been the leader in the struggle against apartheid. But I learned otherwise, and that day in Lusaka was part of the lesson. Through his calm, pointed rhetoric, Tambo was following up on a decade-long campaign to cast the ANC as the clear leader. I learned while I was in South Africa that the ANC had lost tremendous face in 1976, when the Soweto uprising caught the organization and its leaders completely by surprise. They didn't know how to react, and for a short time the ANC was even vilified by the insurgent youth of the townships. To begin with, many young blacks followed the Black Consciousness beliefs of the Pan Africanist Congress, then at odds with the ANC. In addition, the ANC's distant exile compounded the youths' mistrust of the banned organization: the ANC leaders were sellouts; they had fled; what business did the ANC have claiming leadership when they, the BC youth of the townships, were the ones laying down their lives for the struggle?

The ANC also had its challengers from within the black community. Chief Mangosuthu Gatsha Buthelezi, nominal leader of six million Zulus as chief minister of KwaZulu and head of the political organization Inkatha, has been almost as strident as Pretoria in his condemnation of the ANC. Buthelezi is handsome and charismatic. He comes off as a figure of authority whether in Western business suits or traditional Zulu war gear, and he is unique in South Africa for being the only major black leader to oppose sanctions. He has also denounced the ANC for its campaign of violence and has all but declared open warfare on the banned organization.

And there seemed to be evidence that the Pretoria government was arming Inkatha on the chance that Buthelezi's Zulus might strike out at the ANC and its affiliates inside South Africa. In January 1987 an *impi* — battalion — of Inkatha supporters ransacked a township outside Durban in search of prominent UDF leaders. Blacks inside the township reported that the attackers fired automatic weapons. Twelve were killed, including several children.

In addition, the ANC had suffered a setback in 1984, when Pretoria signed the Nkomati Accord with Mozambique, a non-aggression pact that pledged Mozambique to closing all ANC bases in return for South Africa's ceasing to support antigovernment guerrillas operating inside Mozambique. But that civil war was so chaotic that the ANC was able to bounce back and smuggle arms and munitions into South Africa over the Mozambican border and other borders.

The ANC slowly fought back into a position of control, in no small part because of the role played by Mandela and others on Robben Island. The ANC also gained face as Chief Buthelezi's vociferous campaign against it continued: Buthelezi's open denunciation of the ANC made him appear, especially in the eyes of many young blacks, as an ally of Pretoria. While at one time Buthelezi had something approaching nationwide support, by the beginning of 1987 he had been reduced to the status of a turncoat, if a well-armed and powerful, regional war lord.

Youth in the 1980s began to flee the townships for ANC bases in other African countries, where they received guerrilla training. ANC leadership anticipated the coming of the tricameral referendum of 1983 and campaigned vigorously against it on the ground and over Radio Freedom from Lusaka. Violence escalated — with the 1984 parliamentary elections — in part because the ANC had condemned the voting. This time, the ANC was prepared. And its strength has continued to increase. More than three years of violence directed largely against police and informers in the townships effectively closed down Pretoria's informer network in Soweto and other townships. Arms and ammunition began to flow freely across the borders.

The land mine blasts along the Limpopo in late 1985 were evidence of that, as were the bombings near Durban and in other white urban areas. At one point police in Guguletu, outside Cape Town, flagged down what they saw was a stolen van. They were greeted by a barrage of Russian-made hand grenades and bullets from Russian-made AK-47 automatic rifles. The

ANC was gaining strength, and Oliver Tambo wanted to under-
score that point the day I saw him in Lusaka as well as to support
his contention that the ANC was sole leader of the struggle. He
asserted these points again, a year afterward, when he called for
"armed attacks against the enemy throughout the country." And
I was not surprised when I saw that he even asked for white
support, saying that whites "should fuse with and become part
of the motive forces of the democratic revolution." That
sounded like a man who felt the strength of numbers behind
him.

And I could see that day in Lusaka that Tambo was trying to
take political advantage even of events he had no control over.
He was clearly bothered by the Amanzimtoti killings — I could
see that in the pained expression that came over his face when
he shouted down the reporter who asked if he had approved the
mission. At one point, late in the press conference, he came back
to it on his own. His shoulders slumped in his dark business suit
in that odd way that brings the jacket collar up around the ears,
and he looked small, shrunken. He seemed to sigh. "South Africa is at war," he said slowly, so slowly he paused over almost
every word, as if looking for the full meaning of each word before saying it. "In that war situation, hundreds have been killed.
They are dead. In massacres perpetrated against innocent civilians." He paused again, thinking. "Now the situation is beginning to drift out of the townships in a not regular manner, and
we are seeing South Africans of all races going to bury their
loved ones." The slow, high voice had the tone of a Sunday
sermon.

"South Africa is beginning to bleed," and he drew out the
word, like a plea. "South Africa is beginning to bleeeed in the
face of the persistence of the apartheid system, and when our
units are faced with this situation all around them, one of them
could say" — and his voice rose — " 'I'll have to face being disciplined. I'll have to do it.' " And Tambo slowly took his hands
from the chair arms and laid them palms up on the table before
him.

"After all," he said, leaning forward, "Botha has complained about black Africans killing black Africans. Perhaps one of our units wanted to make a point." He paused again, and the room silenced. "I can see how it could happen. It means we are beginning to move into very stormy times." Tambo shook his head ominously. "Stormy times."

It seemed to me that violence itself could not be an end — the ANC's historical philosophy seemed to preclude that — and neither could "making South Africa ungovernable," which had been the ANC's call to arms since 1983. There had to be something deeper to the strategy than producing dead bodies and ungovernability. So I set off as best I could to find out where the larger strategy lay.

The consensus I arrived at was that the ANC was working toward negotiations, as strange as that looked at first blush. To negotiate, two sides have to feel they are of sufficient strength so that concessions — part of any negotiation — become significant and move the process of negotiation along. What I gathered from many who had formal contacts with the ANC was that Tambo and other nationalists on the Executive Committee felt that by late 1985 the ANC was not yet violent enough. The violence had to increase dramatically for the suspension of violence to mean something as a condition for negotiations.

The level of violence reached by the ANC in early 1986 was insignificant in light of what it did to South Africa's defense and police forces. It challenged them and altered them very little. South Africa did not need special conscriptions among whites, as Rhodesia had needed in the final years of white rule. People in the West may have gathered — mostly from television — that South Africa's police and armed forces were out in full force patrolling every township and trouble spot in the country. But the truth was that when Tambo delivered his Umkhonto we Sizwe memorial remarks in Lusaka, South Africa's government was employing less than five percent of what one analyst called its "coercive capability." The ANC, in other words, had not yet

challenged the white power structure enough to make it feel it
had to negotiate with the ANC.

So, it seemed, the ANC's level of violence had to escalate.
Bombs began to go off in downtown Johannesburg, Durban,
and Cape Town. In January 1987 a bomb exploded in the OK
Bazaar store in the middle of Johannesburg's busiest business
district. Although it killed no one, the very brazenness of the act
emphasized that the ANC was carrying the armed struggle into
white-dominated areas. It seemed likely that the violence would
continue to increase and become more gruesome, with more and
better Soviet-made arms and ammunition slipping across the national borders in the hands of guerrillas.

One thing that occurred to me — and to many others — was
that the government should simply unban the ANC and make it
a legal political party. Once that happened, the ANC would be
demythicized and would come to bear the burdens common to
all political parties everywhere. It would have to make tactical
and strategic choices just as the NP and PFP have to do. It would
have to define its ideological terms in a very precise and open
manner. Close scrutiny of ideological positions might split the
Communists from the nationalists inside the ANC.

Mark Peters and I even dreamed up a scenario in which an
official of the Prisons Services walks into Nelson Mandela's cell,
escorts him to the front door of Pollsmoor prison, and locks him
out. Mandela's status as a mythic icon has been enhanced and
enforced by his incarceration. Once out of jail, Mandela too
would have to define his positions ideologically. Although he
would probably never become "just another politician," Mandela
would be demythicized upon release. However, Mandela stands
the chance of attracting whites, as well as blacks, into a two-
pronged movement to end apartheid and to construct a democratic, nonracial society to take its place. And that is one reason
the government would probably never do it.

One of the hardest lessons I learned in South Africa was that
just because it made sense for the Afrikaners to do something,

there was no assurance that they would do it. One of the great frustrations of living in South Africa was watching things going wrong because Afrikaner pigheadedness and *kragdadigheid* — forcefulness — always seemed to outweigh long-range sense.

In the mind of the Afrikaner, the ANC and Nelson Mandela and Oliver Tambo are all Communists, and it seemed that the Afrikaners would stop at nothing to resist them for as long as they could. Every escalation in ANC violence would cause an equal and retaliatory escalation by the government. Since escalating violence was a central component in the strategies of both the ANC and the government, the future did not hold much hope for negotiations. The South Africans call it "degenerative collapse," civil war. Violence would beget more violence.

The man who could end it, Nelson Mandela, continued to sit in Pollsmoor prison. Mandela would be able to unite South Africa's blacks — a precondition for any negotiation because unless all blacks take part in future talks, those left out will continue to fight on. The comrades of the townships respect him; conservative blacks respect him; even Buthelezi respects him and has called for his release.

It would make . . .

Never mind.

Six

NOT QUITE OUT OF AFRICA

I was out of africa, and I approached the Christmas season of 1986 with a mixture of dread and nostalgia. December 26 would mark the two-year anniversary of my mother's death from cancer and the six-month anniversary of my last day — and our last lunch — in South Africa. I also looked forward to Christmas Day itself with a kind of grim wariness because we had spent Christmas the year before with friends north of Cape Town, and it had been wonderful.

We had celebrated around the pool at Peter Younghusband's wine farm in Paarl. Younghusband had adopted us from the moment we got off the plane at Jan Smuts Airport. He and Mark Peters met us at arrivals, and then Peter took us all out to lunch. The first time I came to Cape Town he booked me one of the best rooms at the Mount Nelson, Cape Town's finest hotel. When I nearly killed myself in an auto accident outside Pretoria, Peter phoned my wife constantly to comfort her and lend support during my recovery. And he also insisted we spend Christmas 1985 with him and his family at the farm.

A warm sun beat down and a soft wind stirred the grapevines that surrounded us, making a sweet, rustling sound. Eighteen of us sat at Peter's immense dining room table, celebrating Christmas in bathing suits and shorts. Big Pete gave me a bottle of 1953 port, and my small son fell in love with his eleven-year-old daughter. Peter played the part of Father Christmas and gave out all the gifts while sitting in a big armchair by the tree, which we had cut the previous afternoon. We all sat around the pool as the day wore on, until the sun set behind the mountains in an orange explosion. The guavas glittered green in the sun, and the whitewashed walls of the farmhouse glowed pink. It was easy and relaxed, a two-day holiday in the midst of turmoil.

I lay awake in our rented Massachusetts farmhouse on Christmas Eve 1986, remembering how we had awakened the year before to the sweet smell of roses and the groaning of the giant blue gums on Peter's farm. I missed South Africa terribly. I had loved living there and I wanted to be back.

I received a bit of South Africa as a Christmas present, though, and it made the country and its people come alive. My sister-in-law and my best friend gave me copies of Paul Simon's *Graceland* album, which features the American singer and several black South African backup bands. I stood in my father's Boston living room, playing the record and swaying to the South African rhythms. At times I even pumped my arms and lowered my back — because some of the songs had the same beat and intensity as township street demonstrations. It was crazy, doing freedom dances five stories above Commonwealth Avenue in the heart of Boston, but I did it anyway: *"Ih, ih hih, ih hih."*

It made me smile because it brought back so much of the music I had heard in South Africa. Some of the best I had heard in Johannesburg was in the Junction Avenue Theater Company's production of *Sophiatown,* a haunting story about life in that black suburb of Johannesburg in the days before the Afrikaners tore it down in 1955. I remembered the eight-character cast singing a cappella in what sounded like eight-part harmony. The cast had included a gangster named Mingus. He had affected the Richard Widmark character, Styles, in *Street with No Name,* strutting across the stage in a huge overcoat, munching on an apple and sniffing a Benzedrine inhaler to be cool. In Boston I laughed at the memory.

I learned, through *Sophiatown* and in many other ways, how

blacks in South Africa have historically admired Americans, both black and white. Part of the reason for the admiration is that blacks in South Africa have looked at the United States as a place where nonracial democracy works. They have seen white Americans like John Kennedy, Hubert Humphrey, and Jimmy Carter as pioneers in a worldwide fight against racism. Robert Kennedy's 1966 visit to South Africa created the same kind of swelling of the heart in the black townships that Pope John Paul II's first visit to Poland created in Warsaw, Cracow, and Gdansk.

In the 1950s, whole extracts from American movies made their way into township lingo because they sounded so cool: "Take some bucks, go buy you some nice clothes. I like my boys to look smart." "Remember, guys, I'm de brains of dis outfit." People actually talked that way. A rand is still a "buck" on the streets of the townships. After a bunch of gangsters in one movie called each other "Brightboy," everybody in the townships started calling each other "Brightboy." Tight blue trousers were "Bogarts," and the gangsters who wore them were the "Americans." James Cagney and Edward G. Robinson were screen idols in black townships. The music of American jazz greats like Duke Ellington, Louis Armstrong, and Count Basie was a smash in the townships. Some elements of jazz and swing and even Latin American rhythms made their way into South African music, sometimes mingling with traditional rhythms and beats. American was good and American was cool. Black or white, cool was cool and to be imitated.

Cool in the townships was New York Yankees baseball caps — I saw them many times, along with Dallas Cowboys T-shirts. Cool was Philadelphia Phillies baseball caps, even if they were oddly in the colors of the New York Mets. And cool was the barbershop next to my office, which advertised "American-style" wave haircuts to make a black South African look a little more like Chuck Berry and a little less Zulu. Perhaps the coolest of the cool was Mr. T on "The A-Team," the highest rated show in the townships — because he was a tough black guy who brooked no jive and took no crap from anybody, black or white. Mr. T billboards blanketed the townships. Every Thursday night at 7:30 our kitchen door would burst open, and in would charge Ann and Saul Molefe and their children and a nephew for their weekly séance with black pride and "The A-Team."

In less than six years Ronald Reagan destroyed a quarter century of good will toward the United States in black South Africa. So intently did his administration concentrate on stopping the spread of communism that all other considerations fell into second place — so that the United States now appeared to be on the side of a South African government whose police killed more than twenty-three hundred blacks in two years. Congressional passage of a watered-down sanctions bill in the fall of 1986 failed to impress many black South Africans after they saw that the bill had passed over a presidential veto. The appointment of a black ambassador made little impression, either, especially after one black candidate proved unacceptable and a second denounced Reagan's South Africa policy as lacking credibility.

Nor did the withdrawal of General Motors, IBM, and several other American companies make blacks respect the United States to any greater degree. Rather, South Africa's blacks saw in Washington and New York and Detroit self-interest and little sympathy. And there was a large degree of truth in black charges that U.S. corporate disinvestment was merely a smoke screen, that American companies "leaving" South Africa were actually exploiting the apartheid system to a greater degree after "leaving" — through lucrative licensing agreements — than while they were still "in" the country.

It is going to take stronger measures than halfhearted sanctions and disinvestments for the United States to renew a meaningful dialogue with South Africa's blacks. It is also going to take a long time. And in my South African sojourn I learned how vital it is that the United States improve relations with black South Africans — because one day blacks will rule South Africa and the mines that are the West's largest source of diamonds, gold, chromium, platinum, and vanadium.

The day of black control may not come next year or even in this century, but it will come. As I watched South Africa's agony, it pained me to see that American foreign policy seemed to have no understanding of that inevitability. Self-interest would seem to dictate that the United States assure itself of a continued supply of strategic metals and industrial diamonds after the day of liberation comes. Self-interest would also dictate that those minerals be seen in the context of what African liberation movements have done in the last quarter century: they have taken the road to Marxism and socialism in part because they mistrusted tub-thumping, anti-Communist American foreign policy.

Setting aside self-interest, the moral reasons alone are compelling enough to make Americans change the way they treat Pretoria: a United States on fair footing with the black majority might someday be able to step in and broker an agreement that could lead to peace and avoid terrible bloodshed. But the black majority will never enter into any bargaining session where they view the broker with the same mistrust and hostility as they view the white minority. And that, in less than six years, is where the Americans have landed themselves.

The Carter administration, with its emphasis on worldwide human rights, deplored South Africa's apartheid regime and made no secret of it. Yet Carter's policy led to no great advances, and it can even be argued that Carter policy set the anti-apartheid movement back several steps.

Carter, for example, chose Nigeria as his rostrum for one attack on apartheid. That only made Afrikaners take Carter less seriously. In 1977 Vice President Walter Mondale met with South African Prime Minister John Vorster in Vienna. At a press conference after the meeting, Mondale came within an eyelash of recommending one man, one vote in South Africa. At the United Nations, U.S. ambassadors Andrew Young and Donald

McHenry, both black, were constant critics of Pretoria. The result: Vorster called an election in 1978 and ran on an anti-Carter, anti-Young platform. The NP gained fifteen seats in Parliament. Apartheid became more entrenched, not less so, as a result of Carter's South Africa policy.

The Reagan administration's policy was the exact opposite of Carter's in tone and substance, but, oddly, it achieved the same result: apartheid was strengthened, at least in part because of the way Washington treated Pretoria. Reagan's policy was called "constructive engagement," and it was the brain child of Assistant Secretary of State for African Affairs Chester Crocker, a former Africa scholar at Georgetown University's Center for Strategic and International Studies. He laid out his policy in an article in *Foreign Affairs* just after Reagan won the 1980 election. Crocker called for an evenhanded approach toward South Africa and urged Washington to pay as much attention to the plight of the Afrikaner trying to implement reforms as to the plight of the black majority.

Crocker in 1980 presumed that conditions were improving in South Africa. P. W. Botha had recently urged Afrikaners to "adapt or die" and had promised reforms. The townships had quieted down after the wave of bannings and arrests that followed the Soweto uprising in 1976. Crocker's policy urged Americans in the 1980s to be patient with the complicated realities of South Africa and to give Botha the benefit of the doubt in his efforts to change the fabric and behavior of his society. "A tone of empathy is required," Crocker wrote, "not only for the suffering and injustice caused to blacks in a racist system, but also for the awesome dilemma in which Afrikaners and other whites find themselves."

Constructive engagement had several failings. It did not foresee what Botha's reform program would do to black expectations. It did not anticipate that reforms would frustrate blacks by raising and dashing expectations at the same time. It assumed, wrongly, that reforms would bring about peaceful change in South Africa and that blacks would find their lives bettered and made fuller as a result of the reforms. But constructive engagement did not account for what the reforms brought about, which was massive unrest.

Moreover, constructive engagement extended beyond South Africa; it was also a regional policy aimed at halting a perceived spread of communism in Southern Africa. The administration found that it could not cease its "empathy" toward Pretoria without scrapping a policy for the entire region. Since that was something Reagan was unwilling to do, he remained glued to Pretoria like a Salvation Army volunteer to the town drunk while the drunk destroyed every bar in town. Reagan remained unable or unwilling to show that the United States was anything other than Pretoria's staunchest backer, and his administration was seen by blacks as the best friend of a repressive and violent regime.

I found it easy to understand why black South Africans took offense at many of the remarks made by Reagan and by some of his chief policymakers. The remarks may have been calculated to encourage Pretoria toward change, but they had the net effect of pushing South Africa's blacks further away from the United States. Not long after taking office, Reagan told a television interviewer that South Africa was "a country that has stood beside us in every war we've ever fought, a country that strategically is essential to the free world in its production of minerals." Reagan was evidently unaware that John Vorster spent most of World War II in a British prison for his pro-Nazi activities, but South Africa's blacks knew it.

In the summer of 1985, even after a limited state of emergency had been imposed in thirty-seven magisterial districts around South Africa, Reagan told an Atlanta radio station that South Africa had "eliminated the segregation that we once had in our own country — the type of thing where hotels and restaurants and places of entertainment and so forth were segregated — that has all been eliminated. They recognize now interracial marriages and all." Black South Africans were outraged at such statements, for they were widely reported in the black press. One afternoon I was driving through Alexandra with Vusi Mabaso, the comrade student leader, and I asked him what he thought of Ronald Reagan. He looked out the window and gritted his teeth. "Fuck him," Vusi spat. "Reagan's just an imperialist who supports the Boers, and everybody here knows it."

In August 1981 Crocker told an American Legion convention that "it is not our task to choose between black and white" in South Africa. Black South Africans assumed that the United States' not choosing sides was equivalent to U.S. support for the status quo — three million Afrikaners dominating and oppressing twenty-five million blacks.

In 1983, at the time of the South African debate over the tricameral Parliament referendum, Under Secretary of State Lawrence Eagleburger told a convention that it was not the place of the United States to take sides in the debate. But Eagleburger also seemed to praise Botha for the "indisputable fact . . . that the South African government has taken the first step toward extending political rights beyond the white minority." Since virtually all blacks opposed the new Parliament — because it excluded them — Eagleburger's statement was seen as an endorsement of a policy designed, in the eyes of many blacks, to split the nonwhite population and pre-empt part of it — the Indians and Coloreds — into the white camp. Blacks assumed that the Reagan administration was foursquare behind the Afrikaners.

And so did the Afrikaners, which is perhaps the greatest failing of constructive engagement. The Carters were barely back in Plains, for example, when Reagan lifted restrictions on the export of military equipment to South Africa. He also resumed the sale of computers to the police and military and allowed the return of South African military attachés to Washington. After the treatment they had received at the hands of Jimmy Carter and Andrew Young, the Afrikaners could not believe their good fortune. Remarkably, nothing in the way of reforms was asked in return. Showing empathy — presuming it would encourage reform — was the first order of business. Feeling no pressure from Washington to abolish apartheid, P. W. Botha did not need to speed reforms in order to curry favors from Washington. Why curry favor when favors had been given in advance? The Afrikaners did nothing.

Constructive engagement did other irreparable damage as well. The policy so outraged the young comrades of the townships that any black with ties to the United States became immediately suspect in the eyes of the revolution. Since most of those blacks with U.S. ties were moderate black leaders, those leaders lost a degree of control over the struggle because they had lost that same degree of credibility with the comrades.

Desmond Tutu's credibility problems with blacks stemmed in part from his close ties to American church groups and his speaking tours in the United States. His credibility has grown steadily with the amount of time he has spent away from the United States and with his advocacy of sanctions. Many other black leaders began to distance themselves from the United States. When Winnie Mandela's house was firebombed in August 1985, she made a loud point of turning down American funds that were offered to rebuild it. Even so eminent a civil rights leader as Coretta Scott King discovered what a mine field South African politics has become for Americans. She went to South Africa in September 1986 and made the mistake of thinking a person of her stature would have no trouble meeting with P. W. Botha and Winnie Mandela. She had to cancel her meeting with Botha or else Winnie and other black leaders would have refused to see her. Black or white, Americans are suspect.

I went to see Tutu one morning because I wanted to talk with him about relations with the United States. He was seated in his church, dapper as ever in a charcoal business suit and crimson shirt, and he glowered when I asked him about his change of position on sanctions. "Mrs. Thatcher applied sanctions in Argentina," he spat, holding his arms straight out at the side. "President Reagan has done it with Poland, Nicaragua, and Libya. He is not opposed to sanctions per se." Tutu clapped his hands, a bang that reverberated through the church, and opened his large eyes wide. "He is opposed to them only when blacks are involved. Would he be as calm in his reaction if it had been twelve hundred whites who had been killed?" Tutu began to beat the back of the chair he was leaning against. His neck bulged under his white collar and his nostrils flared. "Change your government!" he shouted, and the shout echoed through the church. "Get a government that does care about human rights and that backs the right horse! Force your legislators to take the kind of action that is going to avert a catastrophe in this country."

His voice modulated and then softened. It took on an accusatory note. "Right now as far as the United States is concerned, as long as you say that you are anti-Communist, then whatever else you do does not matter in the eyes of the United States." His eyes became sharp slits. "Whatever outrages you commit do not matter."

Two months into the permanent state of emergency, Reagan made a major speech praising P. W. Botha's reforms and opposing sanctions. I was not surprised when Tutu's response was to tell the West to "go to hell." It wasn't difficult for me to see why Tutu and others were so incensed. Black South Africans didn't find much to praise in a government that was doing its best to stifle all forms of black political expression. Nor did they find anything admirable in a foreign chief of state's praising the government doing it.

The longer I spent in South Africa, the more I came to see that constructive engagement's role as an anti-Communist regional policy doomed it to failure. The Reagan administration thought it could enlist Pretoria's help in bringing peace to a region torn by a decade of civil wars and perceived as drifting into the Soviet sphere. Instead, not only did the Reagan administration succeed in helping to entrench apartheid, it also produced a regional bully intent, it seemed, on killing every Communist south of Lake Tanganyika.

Socialist Portugal's transfer of Mozambique and Angola to Marxist governments in 1975 had only reinforced Pretoria's natural fear of Communists and their ally the ANC. So when Secretary of State Alexander Haig and Chester Crocker both told South African government ministers that the United States wanted to view Southern Africa through the prism of East-West relations and to take a "realistic" approach to South Africa and its region, the Afrikaners could hardly believe their ears. They were being told that their most powerful ally in the West endorsed their strategic view of the region.

P. W. Botha seemed to assume that taking a "realistic" attitude toward the region meant license to invade other countries and search out Communist guerrillas in all of them. In June 1985 the South African Defense Forces (SADF) attacked what was alleged to be an ANC hideout in Gaborone, the capital of Botswana, killing twelve civilians, including one six-year-old. In January 1986 Pretoria effectively closed down the entire nation of Lesotho, the small mountainous country that is completely surrounded by South Africa, and demanded the expulsion of all ANC operatives. When the Lesotho prime minister resisted, Pretoria engineered a military coup, and the new junta threw out the ANC. Lesotho, meanwhile, was reduced in status to little more than a homeland, KwaLesotho.

One May Monday in 1986 SADF planes bombed a suspected ANC hideout in Lusaka, Zambia — 650 miles from Pretoria. The raid coincided with raids on other suspected ANC hideouts in Gaborone and Harare, the capital of Zimbabwe. Whether Chester Crocker wanted it or not, South Africa had taken a U.S. pledge to deal "realistically" with the region as an excuse to establish a hard-handed *pax pretoriana* over Southern Africa.

South Africa used more subtle ways to establish the *pax pretoriana,* principally the threat to neighboring countries of economic strangulation if their relations with the ANC became too

cordial or their words toward Pretoria too critical. The Afrikaners did it with railroads. They had not ignored the assertion of
Cecil Rhodes, the great empire builder of the nineteenth century, that Africa was "railroads and the rest was fairy tales."

The only way that countries as far apart as Zaire and Swaziland can export their goods to world markets is now through
South Africa — because the South Africans have cut all the alternative railway lines to the Indian and Atlantic oceans. The
Benguela line begins in Lusaka, Zambia, juts north into Zaire,
and then runs southwest through all of Angola to Benguela on
the Atlantic. It has not functioned since 1975 because South African–backed rebels in the Angolan civil war have cut it in two.
I stood on the Benguela line once. The tracks were as rusted
and overgrown as a rail spur in a closed steel mill.

The Tan-Zam line, from Lusaka to Dar es Salaam in Tanzania
on the Indian Ocean, was built by the Chinese in the 1960s and
has not run properly since the day it was finished. Since 1975 the
Beira line, from Harare, Zimbabwe, to the Mozambique port city
of Beira, has been under constant attack by South African–
backed guerrillas in Mozambique's civil war. Zimbabwe devotes
twenty-five percent of its army — ten thousand soldiers — to
guarding the line and trying to keep it open. It functions sporadically. The Mozambique civil war has been so widespread that
many Mozambican goods cannot make it to Beira and Maputo,
the nation's port capital. So they exit via South Africa.

As a result of South Africa's sabotaging of the region's rail-
ways, seventy-seven percent of Botswana's exports pass through
South Africa, along with all of Lesotho's, sixty percent of Malawi's, thirty percent of Mozambique's, seventy percent of Swaziland's, sixty-four percent of Zambia's, and ninety-four percent
of Zimbabwe's. Copper and cobalt from mines in Zaire's Shaba
province, which account for eighty-five percent of Zaire's national earnings, have no way out of Africa other than through
Durban — twenty-two hundred miles away. The message is not
lost on the so-called Front Line States of the interior. They have

to do South Africa's bidding regarding the ANC or, they know, Pretoria will shut them down. The crushing blow dealt to Lesotho in January 1986 over the issue of ANC bases could be repeated on the rest of the interior states. And they know it.

In 1983 Pretoria responded to regular verbal attacks from the prime minister of Zimbabwe, Robert Mugabe, by holding twenty-five Zimbabwean locomotives hostage inside South Africa. Only U.S. intervention kept the frail Zimbabwean economy from choking on itself. In 1982, South African–backed guerrillas in Mozambique blew up the pipeline that supplies Zimbabwe with most of its oil. An acute oil shortage lasted for two months, and the Zimbabwean economy was drained of millions of dollars.

One official Western diplomatic estimate has it that if the South Africans were to close just two border posts, at Messina and Mafeking, the flow of trade to the interior states of Africa could be reduced by eighty-five percent. Factories and mines from Gaborone in Botswana to Lubumbashi in Zaire would quickly close, and urban centers would become centers of unemployment. Inflation in the interior states would rise, and the economies of those states would degenerate to the subsistence level.

So the civil wars and the closed rail lines go on, making it easier for the Afrikaners to enforce their anti-ANC *pax pretoriana.* What I found most disturbing about South Africa's empire building was that Pretoria seemed to be doing it with a wink and a nod from Washington. If six years of American empathy made the apartheid system more entrenched than before, six years of viewing the region "realistically" made the apartheid system — and its leaders — more aggressive.

Coming back to the United States, I was troubled by the split level of awareness of things African in the West. I met many people who deplored apartheid — yet thought it was correct for the United States to continue aiding Jonas Savimbi's rebels in the Angolan civil war. Many did not see that in aiding the Union for the Total Independence of Angola (UNITA), the United States was helping South Africa destabilize half a continent and hold it hostage economically. Many who favored the imposition of sanctions on South Africa did not recognize that present U.S. policy on Angola enables South Africa to continue applying the equivalent of reverse sanctions to the rest of the subcontinent.

The Angolan civil war is a convoluted and contradictory war in which the United States *and* South Africa back a Marxist rebel leader, Jonas Savimbi, in his struggle against the Marxist faction that took over the former colony from the Portuguese. It is a war in which the ruling party, the Popular Movement for the Liberation of Angola (MPLA), employs thirty-five thousand Marxist Cuban soldiers to protect the MPLA's oil fields, which are operated by American oil companies. The MPLA's share of the American oil revenues goes to the Soviet Union to pay for aid and materiel that the MPLA gets from Moscow to fight the U.S.-backed rebels. Conservatives in the U.S. Congress want to vote more aid for the rebels; the U.S. State Department wants to negotiate a withdrawal of the Cubans; and U.S. oil companies want the Cubans to stay to protect their fields from the congressionally funded rebels.

In the meantime, the South Africans say that Cuban presence in Angola prevents them from granting independence to Namibia, the former German colony also known as South West Africa, which South Africa has ruled in defiance of the United Nations since 1966. The South Africans say they will release Namibia when the Cubans leave, but they conduct so many cross-border raids from Namibia into Angola as to assure a continued Cuban presence there. And the United States, which does not recognize the ruling MPLA, remains Angola's largest trading partner.

I observed that bleak and stupid war twice, and I also saw how important the United States has become in perpetuating it. One time was in April 1986. Twenty of us journalists had jostled and shaken over seven hundred kilometers in the backs of captured Russian trucks, and we had just reached Munhango, a sleepy Portuguese provincial town that sits astride the Benguela railroad line.

The twenty of us were bedding down as the sun began to set when I heard a noise in the distance. It was a strange, ululating cry, like soldiers charging a defensive position. Since we were only six miles from the front, I wondered whether it was an MPLA strike. "What's that?" I asked our guide in French, the lingua franca of that trip.

"Oh, it happens every night," replied Lt. Col. José Chimbele, looking at his watch. "The men listen to the Voice of America Portuguese Service. Congress is debating aid to UNITA. Something good must have happened today in Washington."

Congress had, indeed, approved more aid. The war went on.

That eight-day Angola trip in April 1986 was one of the strangest weeks I spent in Africa. John D'Oliviera of the *Star* later suggested that for a reunion we pile ourselves into a closed bread truck and arrange for a dozen police horses to kick the sides of the truck for several hours. That would come close to re-creating conditions on that trip.

The twenty of us boarded an ancient DC-3 transport outside Pretoria one Monday noontime, expecting to fly to Mavinga, Jonas Savimbi's main logistics base in southeastern Angola, spend a day getting briefed on the war, and then return Wednesday.

We got to Mavinga and then drove for three nights and three days, stopping only to cook meals and take on diesel fuel, before we found Savimbi in Munhango. Day and night we jostled over the savannah and through dense bush forests, the sides of our trucks smashing into trees and ripping out scrub bush.

Savimbi's purpose in bringing us to Munhango was to give us a tour of "Free Angola." "We wanted you to see how much territory we control," shouted our principal guide, Lt. Col. Willondo Battista, over the roar of the diesel engines. "It's always our headquarters at Jamba and Mavinga you see and write about. This is a war of East-West propaganda, and we want to show you that we control this territory and that it is ours."

Free Angola seemed limitless and empty. From the top of an occasional rise we could see the *bundu* — bush — stretching off in all directions. It was the end of the rainy season, and the trees were filled with dusty light green leaves. The wild grass was tall and corn-silk yellow. Under the bright blue sky it shimmered and shone back into our eyes, making them water. It was a land of harsh and gritty brightness.

The land is poor, the soil sandy and dusty. The twenty of us, split between two trucks, fought constantly over which truck should lead — because those traveling in the rear truck coughed all day in the loose and choking dust of the lead truck. The terrain was also rough. Sometimes potholes and tree roots sent us flying a foot or more into the air, smashing us back down into the truck on bruised kidneys and whiplashed necks. Every time we passed a full running stream we stopped to bathe and fill our water bottles to the very top. First, though, we asked our armed escorts to fire their AK-47s into the water to scare off any "flat dogs" — crocodiles.

During the days, we broiled under the blinding African sun, playing word games and liar's dice, telling jokes, and staring at the endless African veld. At night, since the nearest city of any size was more than six hundred miles away, we could see every star in the southern sky. It all gave us a sense of the vastness and emptiness of a continent. When we tried to sleep, we froze and bitched at each other, trying to sleep like sardines, alternating five on a side, head to toe. "Get your foot out of my face!" seemed to be the watchwords of the night.*

---

*As improbable as it seemed to us later, when we got back to Johannesburg we learned that a male and a female colleague in the other truck had spent their nights in coital abandon. Our all-male truck followed more mundane pursuits. Peter Sharpe of Britain's Independent Television News, Jim Smith of the Associated Press, and I had all grown up around Boston, and we spent

Despite putting water purification tablets in our water and taking other precautions, all of us got very ill at one point or another on the trip. Tempers began to run short. The night I got sick, I ended up yelling at some UNITA colonel about dog and pony shows, whistle stops, bait-and-switch advertising, and cheap propaganda. He probably thought I was insane, especially since the next thing I did was turn around and vomit. My suspicions about propaganda, at least, were confirmed when Savimbi met us after our night on the ground in Munhango.

The Swiss-educated and Mao-trained Savimbi cuts a fine figure in the bush. The word *charisma* might have been invented for him. He wore pressed and clean French fatigues and sported an ivory-handled cane, ivory-handled revolver, silver bracelet, and a death's head ring. Everything about him seemed to glitter, even his teeth. His beard and stocky frame gave him something of an Old Testament look, and the AK-47 hanging lightly from his shoulder made him look the quintessential guerrilla. Very impressive, especially since we were all wearing three days of African dust and were filthy by comparison.

Aside from wanting us to see Free Angola, Savimbi wanted to show us how ten million dollars in American aid was being put to use and to plead for more. Savimbi led us through his emplacements, along the railway, and through the town, a wreck of bombed-out blue and pink pastel buildings. It once must have been a pretty place, but it had been reduced to rubble.

"The commitment I got from America was that this was to be the beginning of a major program," Savimbi said, standing on the town's train station platform, jauntily leaning on his cane. Listening to Savimbi talk was like listening to an American politician. One night I slipped and nearly called him "Senator" as he went on about the 1975 Clark Amendment, which banned

---

one night piecing together the roster of the pre-1967 Boston Bruins hockey team — until we heard a grumpy shout of "I don't give a fuck who Johnny Bucyk was. Shut ya fuckin' gobs and go to sleep."

congressional aid to UNITA and then was repealed in 1985. He spoke quickly and confidently, his English clipped and precise.

"Ten million dollars now is not important, or twenty million. We will get more," he said, flashing his cane about him like a wand. Take away the pressed French fatigues, and Savimbi could have passed for a lobbyist. In fact, at that time he was paying a Washington lobbying firm $600,000 a year to press his case before Congress. The MPLA was employing a rival lobbying firm.

"The Clark Amendment gave Angola to the Russians," he argued, hitting all the right buzz words for American consumption. "And if Angola goes to the Russians, then all of Southern Africa will go to the Russians, and I know Congress doesn't want that to happen. I am confident that we will get our way in Congress. The U.S. administration is willing to help UNITA, and that gives great confidence to us and our soldiers."

I could see that Savimbi was using us the same way a presidential candidate uses a flock of traveling reporters in New Hampshire during primary season. He wanted us to do his PR for him. "The coming of more American aid will have a very positive influence on our struggle," Savimbi said, jutting out his chin and smiling for the cameras. "We will show the MPLA that they cannot win a military victory in this war and that they will have to sit down with us at the negotiating table. That is what we want, and that is what American aid will bring us." Savimbi whacked the side of his fatigues with his cane, his big white teeth shining. "Congress must give us more aid."

I could see conservatives in the U.S. Congress eating up Savimbi's words. They do not want to see Angola "lost" in the manner of Vietnam, and they view Angola through the same glass as they view Nicaragua and Afghanistan. Jonas Savimbi is a "freedom fighter" to them, trying to wrest his country out of the control of the Soviets. But I learned that the war comes to more — or less — than that.

Jonas Savimbi's tribe, the Ovimbundu, is the largest single

tribe in Angola, constituting about forty percent of the population. Yet the Ovimbundu's land — the southeastern third of the country where we spent eight days — is also the poorest and least developed. The civil war began when the Portuguese left Angola in 1975, handing over control to the better-educated, Portuguese-trained Angolans of the north and the Atlantic coast, many of whom had been part of the Portuguese colonial administration. Savimbi and his Ovimbundu were left out, relegated to their sparse and brutal bushlands of the southeast.

On our trip we saw one four-legged animal, a small antelope. Our armed escort shot it for dinner. We saw so much maroela fruit, the elephant's favorite food, that it meant only one thing: no more elephants. We counted perhaps a dozen birds, most of them carrion birds. We saw perhaps twenty civilian camps, small ramshackle affairs, and the children who chased after our trucks were scrawny and ragged. We gave some of them food tins from our UNITA-supplied SADF ration packs, and they fell on them like dogs.

I came to see that the battle between the MPLA and UNITA is less a struggle between Marxists and "freedom fighters" than a struggle between a tribe of historic have-nots and the people who control what little wealth remains in that battle-scarred land. Driving through the dreadful sameness of the southeast, I could not help but see that Savimbi's aim is to secure something better for his people. I wondered, though, whether Congress knew that.

Conservatives in Congress say the Cuban presence in Angola is an example of Soviet adventurism in Africa, yet Soviet designs in Africa have always been vague, I found, in part because the Soviet Union does not view a continent so far away from its borders as a vital part of the world. The whole of Africa as a continent ranks somewhere on the third or fourth tier of Soviet global priorities. North Africa and the Horn rank highest on the continent because they are closest to the Middle Eastern oil fields. Southern Africa, as a region, ranks lower. Conservative

cries of Soviet adventurism in the region may resemble what
Clare Boothe Luce called "globaloney." The conservatives' warn-
ings about creeping Marxism show a basic misunderstanding of
the character of socialism in Africa.

In the postindependence era of the 1960s, many newly liberated African states adopted a system of "African socialism" that
was not quite pure Marxism and not capitalism either. African
socialism was mostly a reaction to a century of colonial rule and
an attempt to reverse colonial economies. During the Khrush-
chev and early Brezhnev years, the Soviets actively wooed the
African socialist states, hoping their economies would gradually
evolve into something closer to real Marxism and that the nations would move firmly into the Eastern camp.

The opposite happened. Regimes in Kenya, Tanzania, Zaire,
and Zambia moved away from African socialism and toward still-
evolving models that are ad hoc mixtures of Marxism and capitalism. Like Nelson Mandela, African leaders have shown a de-
sire to borrow liberally from both East and West in forming their
economies. Even South Africa itself — with its huge public sector work force and government-owned communications, munitions, electricity, and transportation companies — has an economy only slightly less socialist than Romania's. The major
difference between the two is that the Afrikaners call themselves
capitalists.

"Creeping Marxism" in Africa is embodied in various African
leaders who experiment with Marxist models — keeping some,
throwing others out, taking on some capitalist models and ad-
justing them to fit their needs. The only thing that doesn't
change is that they continue to call themselves Marxists or so-
cialists — perhaps to spite conservatives in the United States, to
whom the word *socialist* conjures visions of Berlin Walls, stormed
Winter Palaces, and Hungarian freedom fighters. In reality, the
continent of Africa has moved farther away from the Soviet
sphere economically in the quarter century since independence.
Although in the 1960s the Soviets talked of Africa as a breeding

ground for socialism, by the 1980s the Soviet Union's three largest investments were the Nigerian steel industry, the Moroccan
phosphate industry, and Egypt's Aswan High Dam. All three
host countries are nominally capitalist.

The Soviets have suffered several political reversals in Africa
in the last twenty years. The slide started in 1966, when the Soviet Union lost its patron-client relationship with Ghana. The
same thing happened in the Sudan in 1971, in Egypt in 1972, in
Somalia in 1977, in Equatorial Guinea in 1979, and in Guinea
over a number of years in the early 1980s. The Soviets took an
active role in the Rhodesian bush war, only to see the man they
had backed, Joshua Nkomo, defeated by Robert Mugabe in the
1980 pre-independence elections. In 1984, Mozambique signed
the Nkomati Accord nonaggression pact with South Africa and
then applied for membership in the World Bank and the International Monetary Fund. In Angola, President José Eduardo
dos Santos ousted the most radical Marxists from his cabinet, in
part to appear more moderate to the West.

When we finally got back to Johannesburg I wrote a story that
raised the question of how the Soviets might view an increased
American involvement in the Angolan war. I wrote that the
global credibility of a politically precarious regime in Moscow
would suffer terribly if the Russians were to pull out of Angola
after a history of economic and political reversals on the continent and in the face of increased American aid. It seemed highly
unlikely that Mikhail Gorbachev would agree to send home
thirty-five thousand Cuban troops from Angola as long as conservatives in Congress shouted for more aid to Savimbi. The war
costs Moscow very little in monetary terms, for one thing, since
the MPLA pays with American oil revenues for its military hard-
ware and for the upkeep of the Cubans.

The only cost to either side is human, in a war fought with the
senseless terror of land mines. According to one estimate, twelve
hundred Angolan children lose legs every year because no one
can remember which side put which mines where. Munhango

had changed hands so many times in the last three years that our guides neither knew where the other side had planted land mines nor remembered where UNITA had planted its own. And the mines are insidious, hard to see. They look like a pair of wraparound sunglasses folded up and casually discarded. But step on one, and it can blow away a leg. We arrived at Savimbi's train station press conference just after a young UNITA trooper had stepped on one of the mines. Half his right foot was blown off, and as Savimbi spoke the boy lay drugged but conscious on the platform twenty feet away. There was nothing but bloody sinew between the sole of his foot and his shattered tibia. Medics were trying to fold what remained of his foot back onto his leg. I was sure he would die. The nearest doctor was seven hundred kilometers away in Mavinga, over the same rutted roads we had traveled for three days.

Yet the war looks to continue. South Africa is historically so anti-Communist that it will likely continue to train, aid, and occasionally fight beside UNITA.* For the United States it is another matter. It can choose to try to stop the war and negotiate a withdrawal of the Cubans. Or it can continue acting as Pretoria's military ally and the apartheid system's accomplice in the destabilization of an entire region.

If Russia is a mystery wrapped inside an enigma, as Churchill said, then Africa is a mysterious circle made up of intersecting lines. In Africa nothing ever simply exists on its own; something is always part of another story. In Africa I learned how the Angolan civil war is part of another story: sanctions.

---

*Pretoria likes to keep its training and aid of UNITA under close wraps, but on our long trip I saw for myself the close ties between the SADF and the Angolan rebels. At one point I was sitting in the moving truck, stretching my back and neck, unaware that my head was coming dangerously close to getting whacked by a tree. Our armed UNITA escort saved me from a nasty bruise when he shouted *"Passop!"* and I ducked. *Passop* is Afrikaans for "Watch out."

The issue before the U.S. Congress and several European parliaments in 1986 and 1987 was whether to impose blanket economic sanctions on South Africa to register indignation over apartheid and to try to strangle South Africa economically. I learned how difficult it would be to shut down South Africa's economy by sanctions alone. The *pax pretoriana* linked the economies of the interior African states inextricably to the South African economy. If South Africans could, by controlling major rail lines, control what went out of those interior countries, then South Africans could also control what went in — chiefly South African goods. They do: every year South Africa runs a trade surplus of over $400 million with the rest of Africa — good insurance against sanctions, which the white South Africans have feared, and prepared for, for twenty years.

Even though it occupies only four percent of the continent's land area, South Africa accounts for forty percent of Africa's industrial production. It produces more steel and electricity than the rest of the continent, grows thirty-five percent of the continent's corn and nearly twenty percent of its wheat. In 1983 the rest of Africa bought $151 million worth of chemicals from South Africa as well as $124 million worth of metal products and $95 million worth of machinery. Despite an official ban on trade with South Africa, forty-six African countries buy some form of goods or services from South Africa. They can't afford not to. South Africa remains their closest — and cheapest — source of essential materials. And they remain part of South Africa's insurance against sanctions.

Many in the West would like to see South Africa cut off from the rest of the world as punishment for apartheid. Yet while I was there I saw how that would probably never happen. Zimbabwe is perhaps South Africa's bitterest and most vocal enemy on the continent. So it came as a surprise one evening, sitting on the verandah of the Victoria Falls Hotel in western Zimbabwe, when I asked a waiter what kind of beer he served, and he answered, "Lion and Castle," naming South African Breweries' two flagship brands. Another surprise came a few nights later, when I sat down to dinner at the Chobe Game Lodge in far northern Botswana. The wine list was a compilation of some of the best labels from the Stellenbosch and Paarl valleys of South Africa.

Many neighboring countries would not be able to supply basic services if it were not for South Africa. ESCOM, the South African state-owned utility, supplies one hundred percent of Lesotho's electricity, eighty percent of Swaziland's, sixty percent of Mozambique's, and fifty percent of Botswana's. At a profit. The fall in the value of the rand, which came about because of the flight of Chase and other banks, actually made it easier for South African producers to export their goods. Exports will increase.

African trade aside, there are simply too many ways around the 1986 congressional sanctions for them to be totally effective. The U.S. sanctions included a ban on the sale of munitions and petroleum products to South Africa, but Pretoria has been operating under a worldwide arms embargo for more than a decade. It responded to the embargo by forming ARMSCOR, the state-owned munitions company, and now South Africa is an arms and munitions exporter. The South Africans have also been operating under an OPEC oil embargo since 1976. The result: South Africa is today one of the world's leaders in gas-from-coal conversion technology. Pretoria also built up a sizable oil stockpile. Although the stockpiling program cost the country an estimated twenty-two billion rand in premium prices paid on the spot market and in stockpiling costs, the country is in no danger of running out of energy anytime soon.

The U.S. sanctions bill also banned American importation of South African farm products. In December 1985, as the sanctions debate was beginning to heat up, I met a South African fruit farmer at a cocktail party. I asked him if the threat of sanctions worried him. "No," he said, smiling. "I've got this stencil in a shed back on the farm, and it reads 'Produce of Portugal.' "

Many of South Africa's chief exports are vital to the West and are therefore "unsanctionable" — another reason that sanctions cannot bring South Africa to its knees. South Africa produces half the world's gold, for example, and gold is the nation's largest single cash export, accounting for thirty percent of the total value of its exports every year. Gold is something the West cannot do without, and it is unlikely that the United States and European nations would move to restrict their gold imports — because any move to restrict South African gold exports would drive the world price of gold higher and benefit the South African economy.

The same economic rule applies to diamonds and other strategic minerals, because South Africa ranks first in the world in reserves of platinum, chrome, manganese, vanadium, and fluorite and second in the world in reserves of uranium, antimony, asbestos, and phosphate. Most people in the West, except those who attend metallurgy conventions, would never have cause to notice some of South Africa's exported minerals. But vanadium, for example, is crucial for the production of aircraft jet engines, and jets are things the West will not do without.

Proponents of formal sanctions reason that sanctions would make Afrikaners' lives so uncomfortable that they would change their ways. As long as others need South African resources, however, formal sanctions will remain ineffective, and major discomfort will remain a stranger to the Afrikaner. But not to the black.

"Informal" sanctions have already "worked." They began working even before I left South Africa. Foreign companies began leaving, and foreign banks demanded repayment of their loans. Their repayment demands alone will probably do the South African economy more harm than any formal, legislated sanctions would.

South Africa's current accounts surplus in 1986 — its money in the bank — stood at $2.3 billion. Its total foreign debt obligation for 1986, negotiated by Swiss debt mediator Fritz Leutwiler, came to about $2 billion. That means that all but $300 million of South Africa's national earnings had to leave the country to repay foreign debt. That meant a no-growth economy for 1986 and for years to come because South Africa still had $27 billion in long-term debt to repay. With most revenues earmarked to leave the country, companies will not be able to put profits into capital improvements and expansion. There will be few, if any, new jobs created. High-interest domestic loans — the only source of money if foreign markets remain closed off until repayment of existing debt — will likely pull borrowers' profits, and growth, down.

South African economists I talked to estimated that the economy needed to grow at a rate of four to five percent for the country to come out of the recession that had begun in 1981. They also explained that a five percent growth rate was the only way the country could supply jobs for a poor and increasingly unemployed black population of twenty-five million that is growing at the rate of three percent per year. When I left in 1986, the economists were lowering their growth rate estimates for the year to three percent. And prospects for greater black unemployment in the future grew even as the growth rate fell.

As American and European companies disinvested in South Africa, they also lowered South Africa's growth rate. The process of disinvestment involves foreign companies selling their plants and assets to South African companies, and that means that South Africans must spend rands to protect existing jobs instead of to create new jobs. Informal sanctions are in action and are "working." But to whose advantage? That is unclear.

The corporate flight began, in part, because many American and European companies were bothered by the "nuisance factor" of doing business in South Africa — having stockholders' meetings constantly broken up by anti-apartheid protesters. Others were bothered by selective purchase ordinances passed by many American cities in the mid-1980s — laws that banned cities and municipalities from buying products from companies that do business in South Africa.

But most of the sixty-plus companies that left South Africa in

1985 and 1986 — compared with just seven in 1984 — left because they could no longer see any sense in maintaining existing operations in an economy that had been in recession for five years, even if they did give grandiloquent political reasons for leaving. In fact, watching the departure of most Grande Dame American companies was like watching the play within the play of *Hamlet:* the lady protested too much.*

I saw that old gray ladies like GM, IBM, Bell & Howell, and more than sixty other companies could call their story "Not Quite Out of Africa." Leaders of disinvestment drives probably never thought they would be doing GM a favor by asking the troubled automaker to leave South Africa or that for Coca-Cola, disinvestment meant that things go better for Coke.

Most American companies, with the notable exception of Kodak, sold their physical plants to local interests but continued to sell their products in South Africa through licensing, distribution, and technology agreements with the buyers. At the stroke of a pen, they relieved themselves of anti-apartheid pressure at home, got out from under the burden of operating in an unstable economy, and improved their profit margins.

The new owners do not have to operate under the same political constraints that hampered the old owners, and this freedom will increase profit margins for both the new owners and the parent companies. The new owners do not have to conform to the Sullivan Code, the code of practices followed by 160 American companies, which pledged American employers to provide equal pay for equal work for all races and to spend

---

*Pretoria went so far as to restructure the currency to discourage disinvestment. It created the "financial rand" out of thin air, set its worth at about 15 U.S. cents lower than the regular commercial rand, and then decreed that all proceeds from the sale of foreign assets had to leave the country in the form of the financial rand. A U.S. company selling its local plant for 100 million rand would be able to repatriate only $25 million instead of $40 million. Some money-losing companies got around the penalty by structuring their buy-outs around debt repayment — selling for one dollar plus assumption of all debt.

money to train blacks for better jobs. The new employers don't have to abide by those old pledges. They do not have to support education and housing programs, which constituted from five to ten percent of the Sullivan signatories' wage bill. "Funds are going to be damn scarce," said one new owner in the summer of 1986. "And when the pressure is on, it's very obvious what area is going to suffer. I have no choice."

Opponents of disinvestment said that U.S. companies operating under the Sullivan Code were giving their black workers better lives, but the code was undertaken within the framework of apartheid, which by its very nature is unreformable, so the code may never have been able to significantly raise the level of black life. Yet now that those companies have "left," it is undeniable that black workers once employed by those American-controlled companies will see the quality of their lives drop the marginal percentage point or two that the Sullivan Code managed to raise them. It will not be a far drop; just back down to where the rest of black South Africa wallows in the tidal cycle of raised and dashed expectations.*

Throughout the 1970s and 1980s General Motors was among the U.S. companies arguing most stridently in favor of a continued U.S. presence in South Africa. The Rev. Leon Sullivan, the black Philadelphia clergyman who initiated the code that bears his name, was a longtime GM board member, and GM executives in Detroit and Port Elizabeth adamantly insisted that GM's workers' lives would suffer if the company acceded to political pressure and pulled out of South Africa. GM proved the point even before it formally departed.

---

*Before many companies that "left" South Africa joined the run to the exits, they argued that their departures would cause massive unemployment in the black sector. There has been no significant increase in black joblessness because of U.S. companies leaving. The reason? At no time did American companies employ more than one percent of the black labor force.

Two thousand black GM South African (GMSA) workers went on strike the week after the automaker announced it would sell its South African subsidiary to a local management team. Strikers demanded union representation on the new company's board of directors, severance pay when the subsidiary changed hands, and protection of their pension fund. GMSA's American management responded by firing 567 of the strikers and calling in the police when strikers tried to prevent nonunion labor from entering the Port Elizabeth plant. Police used dogs and *sjamboks* to disperse the crowd, something that had never happened before at an American-owned company.

The company's tone became loudly anti-union and, by inference, antiblack. "We will make vehicles, with or without the unions," declared Robert White, GMSA's American managing director. The union, for its part, gave notice that it viewed American management in the same light as it viewed the NP in Pretoria. "If GM management has any sense," said Fred Sauls, secretary of the striking workers' union, "they must climb down from their white pedestals where they sit like members of the privileged white class, and listen to the legitimate demands of the people of South Africa."

I was back in the United States by then, and I saw, sadly, that another line had been crossed. Criticism of Americans was nothing new, but never before had Americans inside South Africa been equated with leaders of the apartheid regime. A tone of voice once reserved for Ronald Reagan and few others was being applied to the largest industrial company in the United States and one of the largest multinational corporations in the world. Labor leaders suggested boycotting all General Motors products in the townships. They even advocated necklacing strikebreakers. A labor-management conflict had escalated into a conflict over apartheid, and on the wrong side of the conflict stood the United States.

The strike showed not only that the anti-apartheid struggle was growing but also that it was becoming increasingly anti-

American, anti-West, and anticapitalist. Disinvestment leaders in the United States had pressed their program with the best of intentions — to help blacks and show them that Americans cared about their plight. They could not have known that the first major U.S. disinvestment would have exactly the opposite impact because of the way the company handled the process.

In the end, apartheid and foreign reaction to it turned the expanding South African economy into a siege economy that could become just another third world economy. Black unemployment will rise as the capital shortage continues. Young blacks reaching employment age will find no jobs available because no money was available to create them. By the year 2000 South Africa's population will have grown to between forty and fifty million, and virtually all of the growth will have happened in the black sector. By the end of the century the number of urban blacks, now roughly equal to the number of urban whites, Coloreds, and Indians put together, will outnumber those other groups by three to one. They will probably be unemployed and, if present trends continue, unemployable, uneducated, and prone to violence.

It was for those reasons and others that a report drawn up by the American consulate in Johannesburg and leaked to the press in late 1986 painted a depressing picture of the country's future. South Africa, the document said, was "closer to becoming just another African state — a chronic debtor, import starved, ridden with ethnic diversities, a repressive regime unable to manage its own domestic constituency in any positive way, whose only leverage is its ability to manipulate foreign governments and attract international attention for better or for worse. This is not an ambiance," the report concluded, "which can attract U.S. trade and investment."

Yet in the end it was clear that the United States did much to bring about the current state of despondency in South Africa, black and white. From Carter and Reagan policies that misjudged and misfired to corporate insensitivity and bankers who pleaded panic or prudence, the trail of the United States runs through South Africa's degeneration like tracks through newly fallen snow. Decency alone should impel the United States to do something about its complicity in the making of a disaster.

Sanctions and disinvestment played an important symbolic and political role in the struggle against apartheid because they showed black South Africans that Americans cared about what happened to *them*. In the context of Reagan policy and corporate behavior, the gesture meant something. Yet it seemed that if Americans and Europeans were serious about ending apartheid and trying to help black South Africans, then opposition to apartheid had to become something more substantial than disinvestment drives and symbolic arrest of American students outside South African consulates. Those gestures cost apartheid's opponents nothing and have been described, not without accuracy, as the moral equivalent of a free lunch.

Rather, it became apparent that fundamental changes had to be made in U.S. foreign policy toward Southern Africa to aid blacks in the region and to make those blacks see the United States as something other than Pretoria's firmest backer. Furthermore, after the U.S. Congress legislated sanctions in the fall of 1986, it became clearer than ever that the Reagan administration had to take the lead in managing U.S. foreign policy toward South Africa or that policy would end up split, contradictory, and confused, with Congress following one policy, the executive another, and business a third. The only people to benefit from that arrangement would be Afrikaners in search of election issues.

It was clear, for example, that support for Jonas Savimbi would have to end. For one thing, helping to end the war in Angola would extricate the United States from a situation in which it helps support the highest infant mortality rate in the world. Child death rates in Angola and Mozambique were the world's highest, UNICEF reported in January 1987, because of the economic destabilization and sheer chaos created by South

African–supported rebel guerrilla movements in those two countries.

Supporting Savimbi casts the United States as the military ally of the apartheid regime in the eyes of black South Africans. The relationship with Savimbi is only one of the factors that make blacks in South Africa mistrust the United States, and that mistrust precludes the United States from playing the role of an honest broker between Pretoria and black South Africans at any time in the future. That role can be played by few *but* the United States: there is no former European colonial power to mediate, as Britain did in Rhodesia. The United States has the stature to mediate, but not the standing. Withdrawing support to Savimbi would help.

Ceasing aid to Savimbi and helping to end the senseless war in Angola would also help break South Africa's *pax pretoriana* grip on the interior of the continent. Ending the war could allow the Benguela railway to start up again, and a functioning Benguela line would free such countries as Zambia, Zimbabwe, and Zaire to trade with the rest of the world without having to traverse South Africa. That alone would extricate those states from the South African sword of Damocles — poised and ready to drop on any interior state that offends Pretoria on matters as diverse as sanctions and the ANC.

For similar reasons — and with the same purposes in mind — it becomes clear that the United States has to resist conservative pressure to aid South African–backed rebels in Mozambique's civil war. U.S. foreign policy should pursue a course that would help Mozambique work toward stability. That, in turn, would help states of the interior escape Pretoria's bully-boy grip on their economies and politics.

Mozambique's Marxist president, Samora Machel, was killed in a plane crash in October 1986, and his death pushed that unstable former colony into deeper uncertainty. Even though South Africa and Mozambique signed a peace treaty in 1984, South Africa continues to fund and back antigovernment guerrillas of the Mozambique National Resistance (RENAMO) in violation of the treaty. RENAMO's guerrilla war against the government in Maputo has caused havoc throughout the nation and, by extension, throughout the subcontinent. Beira, the nation's principal port, is in a state of ruin. The road between Beira and the port capital of Maputo is impassable without military escort because of steady RENAMO attack. The 190 miles of railway line from the Zimbabwe border to Beira works sporadically because of RENAMO sabotage. The economy is in chaos.

American conservatives view RENAMO guerrillas as they view UNITA's — as anti-Marxist freedom fighters. But aiding RENAMO, a hodgepodge of former Portuguese colonials and anti-Marxist blacks, would only further destabilize an already unstable region. Machel's successor as president and leader of the Front for the Liberation of Mozambique (FRELIMO) was Foreign Minister Joaquim Chissano, a moderate Marxist who is generally seen as leaning toward the West. Chissano typifies Marxist African leadership. He once told a group of visiting Western diplomats, "We realize that Marxism doesn't give an explanation of how the world began — but don't expect us to give up this ideology, either."

Chissano looked ready to follow his predecessor's course of keeping close ties to the Soviets while at the same time reaching out to the West for economic assistance. Any U.S. move to support RENAMO would undoubtedly push Chissano further into the Soviet camp. American aid to RENAMO would also wittingly or unwittingly help Pretoria hold the entire region hostage.

Aiding RENAMO would also put U.S. foreign policy at crosspurposes with an existing policy. The U.S. and several European nations already support an ambitious plan called the Beira Corridor Project, and it seemed clear that the United States should continue to support that plan rather than initiate a policy that would ruin it. The Beira Corridor Project was begun in 1985 by several Front Line States, with the ambitious goal of establishing a safe and stable trade route from the interior to the Indian

Ocean. The chief aim of the $280 million project is creating a safe 190-mile rail and road corridor from the Zimbabwe border to Beira. Secondary goals include dredging the port's channel, increasing the dilapidated port's capacity from 1.3 to 5 million tons a year, and raising the railway's capacity from twenty-five hundred tons a day to eight thousand. The project needs help and technical expertise to be completed — everything from locomotives to civil engineers. It seemed clear even when the project began, in 1985, that if the United States wanted to see a stable and prosperous region of Southern Africa, it should do everything in its power to help the Beira Corridor Project succeed.

A healthy Beira Corridor would allow such nations as Botswana, Zimbabwe, Malawi, Zambia, and Zaire, to say nothing of Mozambique itself, to trade with the rest of the world without having to worry about a South African sword poised over their necks. The South Africans showed every intention of using that sword after the United States imposed its limited sanctions in 1986. In late 1986 the puppet homeland of Bophuthatswana, parts of which border on Botswana, announced plans to require all foreign nationals passing through the homeland to acquire Bophuthatswana visas — most significantly, rail engineers from Botswana and Zimbabwe. Since no nations other than South Africa recognize Bophuthatswana as an independent country — or show any sign of doing so — the homeland's actions could have the effect of strangling the economies of the interior nations. No visa, no train; no train, no economy.

Bophuthatswana's gambit showed the importance and immediacy of establishing safe alternative trade routes — and the importance of U.S. support for something like the Beira Corridor Project. It seemed both impolitic and immoral that the United States should do nothing to protect the likely first victims of a sanctions war whose beginning could be traced to Congress's passage of a sanctions bill over presidential veto in the fall of 1986. And helping to establish a safe corridor from Zimbabwe to the Indian Ocean would also allow Zimbabwe to withdraw a quarter of its armed forces from Mozambican soil, where they try to guard the disrupted line. That alone would improve U.S. relations with Zimbabwe.

The Reagan administration all but formally broke its ties with Zimbabwe after a Zimbabwean official rudely and bluntly criticized the United States for its South Africa policy at a U.S. embassy reception in Harare on July Fourth 1986. The Reagan administration subsequently withdrew all aid to Zimbabwe, once the largest recipient of U.S. aid on the continent — again creating the impression among black Africans that the United States was Pretoria's best friend. It seemed clear that substantial aid to Zimbabwe should be resumed if for no other reason than to dispel that impression on the continent and inside South Africa.

But it was also clear that aid should be resumed to show Zimbabwe and the other Front Line States that the United States is willing to stand by them in the event South Africa decides to fight back. American foreign policy of the 1980s seemed insensitive to the needs and aspirations of black Africans, and the United States would rise in the estimation of many blacks if it were seen to be actively involved in the protection and advancement of black-governed nations on the subcontinent. The United States will be able to play no significant role in South Africa or the region until it attains a status of trust with blacks there.

It became apparent as early as 1984, when the most recent South African violence began, that the government of the United States would have to open a dialogue with the African National Congress, if for no other reason than to keep abreast of the politics of an organization that will probably end up ruling South Africa someday. Secretary of State George Shultz met with Oliver Tambo for fifty minutes in Washington in January 1987, and the first-ever talks were cordial. But it became clear in the wake of that meeting that the United States must continue a dialogue with the ANC. The United States may be able to influence ANC policies if it continues contact with the banned organization. But the United States can have no hope of influencing anything if it holds to mainstream Reagan administration policy, which seems to reject dialogue with all but the white minority.

One aspect of the sanctions and disinvestment movement that has always bothered me is that sanctions and disinvestment are easy to walk away from. Many advocates in the summer of 1986 seemed to take the attitude that Congress should pass sanctions and that the sanctions would take care of everything. Yet since there were clear limits to what sanctions could accomplish in the way of punishing white South Africans, it seemed that Americans and Europeans who cared about black South Africans had to take an extra step to help them.

Black South Africans had clear needs even before the beginning of the debate over whether sanctions would hurt blacks more than whites. And those needs remain — tremendous and grim needs in the fields of child health care, preventive medicine, and primary and secondary education. Americans and Europeans who claim to want to help black South Africans have to decide whether to walk away from those needs or whether to address them and deal with them.

A plan of action, originally advanced by the *Economist* of London in July 1986, is to hit South Africa where it is most vulnerable — gold. One reason the price of gold has hovered around $350 per ounce is that 950 million ounces of it sit in the vaults of several central banks around the free world. The artificial shortage is what keeps the price high and also enables South Africa to earn approximately $7 billion for the 21 million ounces of gold it produces each year. The United States holds 263 million ounces of gold; several other Western countries hold 10 million or more each; the Netherlands, strongly anti-apartheid, holds 44 million ounces.

The *Economist*'s bold plan is to arrange for the governors of gold-holding central banks to get together and then notify P. W.

Botha that unless Nelson Mandela and other ANC leaders are released from jail within a specified period of time the banks will begin selling gold from their vaults on the open market. The price of gold would crash "within one hour," the *Economist* estimated, "because private hoarders from Bombay to Brittany would be rushing to sell their gold at crashing prices before the central bank selling began." South African gold earnings would be decimated overnight. Its economy would crash.

The plan is not without its risks and potential setbacks. Allies in the Arab world would howl because many of them converted their oil earnings into gold. So would many other third world governments, which also turned their thin assets into gold as a stable and sure investment. The Soviet Union, a major gold holder and producer, would see its national assets threatened. Playing politics with gold could also undermine the solvency of several leading banks around the world because many followed the safe practice of accepting $350-an-ounce gold as collateral on loans. And selling off more than 500 million ounces of gold could result in a worldwide inflation crisis with currencies losing perhaps half their value because of the psychological shock dealt by the collapse of the gold market. Perhaps the central bank governors could formulate a buy-back plan to ease the adjustment back to a stable gold price.

Yet the beauty of the *Economist*'s plan is that it could work. The NP cabinet contains many jingoes, but few understand economics and many actually fear the subject for its complexity. A massive gold dump may be enough to scare them into releasing Mandela and beginning negotiations.

It has been clear since the recent cycle of violence began in 1984 that the release of Nelson Mandela and other ANC leaders was probably the only way to ease South Africa into a peaceful future. Any plan to secure his release is worth consideration for that reason alone. A peaceful future negotiated with Mandela — possibly with the United States acting as broker — is also probably the only way to ensure that the West will continue to have a steady supply of strategic minerals and diamonds well into the next century.

Securing Mandela's release is probably also the only way to alleviate a bloodbath. Ending apartheid will cost. The West can have a say in determining that cost. It can act — and act significantly — or it can continue with the *grand geste*, which costs nothing and will only make the final cost higher than ever imagined.

Seven

THE WILL TO RULE

I was out of africa, and I didn't want to be, watching a country I had grown to love unravel at a distance.

The government did its best to stop the flow of news out of the country, but I learned from friends in Johannesburg how far things continued to fall under the permanent state of emergency. Soweto and other townships remained bloody battlegrounds. The UDF-AZAPO war continued, and the streets of Soweto remained impassable after dark because of the war. Black police showed no sign of ending their campaign to kill as many comrades as they could find. The government began conscripting unemployed blacks and loosing them on the townships as special constables, giving them less than a month's formal training. The black-on-black violence grew worse than ever.

Lucky Mbatha, my chief Soweto stringer, gave up his *Newsweek* string and found a job at the Chamber of Mines. He called me on his son's first birthday — the bureau had gone in on a christening gift nine months before — and I could hear the baby chortling happily on Lucky's knee over four thousand miles of empty space. But things were going badly, Lucky said. Soweto was such a mess that he'd moved his family out of the township and into a small flat in the Hillbrow section of Johannesburg, a whites-only area that in recent years has become an illegal melting pot. He'd had to make a choice, he explained, and he chose the risk of pass arrest in Jo'burg over the risk of his family's getting killed in Soweto. "I don't go out much," he said with a laugh. "But hey, man, it's bad there. The outlook in the townships is real bad."

The arrests continued, and opposition politicians released figures showing that some of the blacks held in custody were aged ten, eleven, and twelve. The war between Chief Buthelezi's Inkatha organization and the UDF showed no sign of ending. In late January 1987 gunmen carrying automatic rifles stormed a township outside Durban, killing thirteen, including seven children. Residents of the township accused the gunmen of being Inkatha followers bent on killing a noted UDF leader at his home.

The "KwaNatal option" died. A power-sharing plan worked out by moderate blacks and whites in historically liberal Natal province, the option was one of the few live signs of genuine hope during my time in South Africa. The option called for the political unification of Natal with the homeland of KwaZulu, which rests entirely within its borders, and a two-chamber legislature elected by voters of all races. It was thought that if the option were allowed to go ahead on an experimental basis — and actually worked — then it could be applied to other parts of the country as well. But in late 1986 the government in Pretoria rejected the option, saying it "will lead to domination" of the whites of Natal by blacks.

Little seemed to have improved since I had left the country, and the collision courses set by South Africans, black and white, saddened me. I could see even before I got to the country in the first place that South Africa was headed for terrible violence unless something was done to avert it, and I spent a lot of my time in South Africa — and after — trying to figure out what that "something" was. Anyone who has lived in that country with the Vusis and the Killers and the Dave Kuims wants to find that "something," perhaps because we human beings cannot accept the notion of an entire country committing suicide. I came to learn that to hope for peaceful change in South Africa is to hope for change in the soul of the people, mostly the soul of the Afrikaner. What I saw while I lived in South Africa did not leave me with great cause for hope.

One sultry, humid day in January 1986, Peter Younghusband, Mark Peters, and I flew to Durban to talk with Alan Paton. We wanted him to compose an essay for *Newsweek*'s international edition about the Afrikaners he had written so much about, and we sat in Paton's red screened porch, over tea, trying to iron out what he would write. The lush green hills of Natal spread before us, and the white-maned and grizzled Paton, still lively at eighty-three, grumbled over his assignment. At one point he tucked his chin into his neck, like a turtle, and peered at us over his glasses. "Can the Afrikaner divorce himself from his history?" he growled. "That's what you're asking. Can he overcome the corruption of his own history?"

I saw in many places, and on many occasions, how close history still is to the Afrikaner.

One place was Peter Younghusband's farmhouse outside Paarl. The house was built in 1792, and it is unique in South Africa because the Afrikaans language was invented in it. Peter's long dining room table held the books, papers, and inkstands of the Burgers who codified and compiled the language in the 1870s. The barn beside the house was the first schoolhouse where Afrikaans was used as the regular medium of instruction. A visitor sitting by the pool or lounging outdoors might see a head pop up over the whitewashed wall and ask, in hushed, museum tones, if it would be possible to look at the barn and see the table. These weren't neighbors, but people who had driven from Johannesburg or Cape Town. The Afrikaner and history are as warp and weft; there is no question of divorce.

I also saw the Afrikaner's marriage to history at the Voortrekker Monument, Afrikanerdom's holiest of holies. The monument, which sits on a hill outside Pretoria, is a memorial to Bloukrans, Blood River, and all of the Great Trek. Every year on

December 16, the Day of the Covenant, thousands of Afrikaners gather at the monument to honor their history and keep it alive. Entering the place is like entering a church. A sign outside warns — and one can almost hear the nasal Afrikaner voice intoning: "Visitors must be suitably dressed, e.g.: adults with bare feet, ladies wearing shorts and gentlemen in sleeveless vest-type shirts will not be admitted." Nor is the sign an idle warning. One afternoon in February 1986 my wife took a visiting American friend to see the monument. My wife was wearing a pair of stylish knee-length culottes, and no sooner was she up the long flight of steps to the monument than a woman attendant swooped down on her and wrapped a long skirt around her waist.

The eeriest part of the monument is standing at the top of that long flight of steps before entering the monument itself. I walked those steps one hot January day, went through a wall into a garden, and turned around to see the view — the natural thing to do after climbing a long flight of steps.

Ox wagons. Scores of them, carved in bas-relief on the inside of the wall. There was no doubt I was inside a *laager*. Monuments are sacraments, outward signs of inner beliefs, and there was no mistaking this monument's assertion that life was safest inside a *laager*. Nor is there any misunderstanding the deeper meaning of those bas-relief oxen and their wagons. The Afrikaners will continue to honor the *laager* for as long as they honor the Day of the Covenant. Forever.

Stone carvings inside the monument depict the progress of the Great Trek, and they make up a "G.I. Joe" cyclorama of mausolean proportions: stabbing spears and booming muskets; blood; treacherous blacks; conquered blacks; victorious whites. The massacre at Bloukrans. The retaliatory massacre at Blood River. The message to Afrikaners is clear: past is present and present is past. South African whites will continue to survive if they keep the wagons circled.

It is hard to imagine the Akrikaner changing after seeing his icons — his wagons, muskets, even the portrait of a dour woman in the museum next to the monument, Johanna van der Merwe, remembered for the twenty-two spear wounds counted in her body after Bloukrans. It is hard to think of the Afrikaner prying loose the wait-a-bit thorns of his own history because the thorns have become a part of his very makeup. All modern cultures are shaped by history in varying degrees: the Kleenex society of 1980s America obviously to a lesser degree than the Chinese or the German cultures of the same era. The modern Afrikaner is defined by his relationship with his past, a living, breathing past that is brought before him every day of his life.

Part of every white South African's school curriculum, for example, is something called *veldskool,* or bush school. It would be the equivalent of requiring all children in the United States to attend a week-long political Outward Bound course at least once during high school. Groups of kids go on long marches and learn map reading, tracking, and assault tactics. They stand guard around a fire at night, and they must keep it going. Sometimes the nights are interrupted by mock attacks. The afternoons and evenings are taken up with political films and lectures, most of which concern the dangers of communism and terrorism and emphasize history, hardiness, and the moral purity of frontier Voortrekker life.

White South African children are fed a steady diet of heroic Afrikaner history in school as well — studying the tales of the Great Trek for three consecutive years. The white school system also nurtures the myths that spring from any people's history. A 1981 study by the University of South Africa (UNISA) analyzed fifty-three standard secondary school texts used in both black and white schools and found that they promoted several myths that the study called "harmful to the process of encouraging harmony between the different racial groups." Some of the myths identified by the study: whites are superior to blacks; the Afrikaner has a special relationship with God; South Africa rightfully belongs to God; the Afrikaner is militarily ingenious and strong; the Afrikaner has a God-given task in Africa. With myths like those forming the intellectual diet of South Africa's future white leaders, there can be little legitimate hope for South Africa's whites changing the way they view the world around them.

Another myth identified by the UNISA study was that "legitimate authorities should not be questioned," and to my mind white observance of that myth looms very large in preventing harmony between black and white. White South Africans bow to authority in a way that far exceeds British habits like "queuing up" and respecting bobbies. On the first day of the permanent emergency in June 1986, with virtual martial law in effect, I noticed a heavily armed soldier reach into his right trouser pocket, pull out a coin, and feed a parking meter. A week later, after a bomb exploded in Johannesburg and police cordoned off several blocks of the city for several hours, meter maids came along and ticketed all the cars at expired meters inside the roped-off area. Questioning authority or straying from accepted norms is not in the makeup of the white South African.

And that is important. The notion of questioning authority has historically been a liberalizing influence in Western society and a force for peaceful change. The very assumption that authority can be questioned is what brings about debate and new solutions to new problems in Western cultures. Some of the debates can be pretty lively: U.S. congressmen in the 1840s, after all, took to caning each other in the well of the House, and sessions I've attended in Ottawa and Quebec City sounded more like bilingual barnyards than parliamentary debates. But those forums and the debates that took place in them have over the years produced laws and compromises that allowed countries to avoid wars, depressions, divisions, and hatreds. In South Africa, where authority is not to be questioned, there is no debate. With no debate there can be no negotiation, and with no negotiation there can only be a hardening of the lines.

Instead, white South Africans view the settlement of disputes and problem solving in terms of legitimate authorities who hand down rulings in the manner of a feudal overlord or guardian — Hannes Luus's *voogskap*. The way Afrikaners talk about power sharing with blacks underscores that view: they speak of "giving blacks power sharing." The government's term for the accommodation of black political aspirations is "a political dispensation for blacks" — something that is dispensed from above, handed down from the pulpit. Since black South Africans show few signs of accepting anything that is dispensed from above because the process smacks of condescension and paternalism, hope for a peaceful resolution of South Africa's future must be sadly diminished.

The settlements of civil wars elsewhere in Africa could serve as models for bringing peace to South Africa, except that South Africa lacks a thread common to those other wars and their endings.

The white minorities in Rhodesia, Algeria, Angola, and Mozambique all lost the will to rule. The Afrikaners have not yet arrived at that state of mind. Nor are there many signs that they are anywhere near approaching it.

Gaullist France and newly socialist Portugal decided to end the civil wars in their African colonies because the wars had become expensive domestic issues. France and Portugal simply withdrew from Africa and declared the former colonies independent.

Finding peace was a different matter in Rhodesia, probably the closest to the South African situation, at least in terms of politics and chronology. After declaring a Unilateral Declaration of Independence (UDI) from Britain in 1965, the Ian Smith minority government became an international pariah. International sanctions were imposed, and the white minority began fighting a fifteen-year bush war against several black nationalist groups. The independence of Mozambique in 1975 cost the UDI government in Rhodesia a vital oil pipeline, and the Rhodesian economy began to crumble. By 1978 whites were pressed into spending half their time in the armed forces, and by the end of 1979 whites in Rhodesia conceded the inevitability of black rule. Britain came in and began a process of negotiation that covered two years. Britain's involvement proved vital because when a black majority government emerged at the end of the Lancaster House talks, as they were known, most white Rhodesians were guaranteed British citizenship if they wanted it. But paramount in the transition from UDI Rhodesia to black majority–ruled Zimbabwe was that Ian Smith and the other entrenched whites lost the will to go on fighting.

Yet most white South Africans (unlike white Rhodesians) do not have a mother country to return to. Some South Africans of British descent would be granted admission to Great Britain as their counterparts were in Rhodesia. But to many Anglos and certainly to all Afrikaners, South Africa *is* the fatherland. Afrikaners have as little affinity for the Netherlands or France, where many could trace their roots, as they do for Greenland or Antarctica. Events of the last several years seemed to show that the Afrikaners' response to the continuing civil war was the opposite of the Rhodesians'. The Afrikaners' will to rule was growing stronger.

A limited state of emergency in 1985 was followed by a permanent state of emergency in 1986. The South African government all but banned black organizations such as the UDF, COSATU, and the SACC. It responded to unrest in schools in Soweto and the eastern Cape by closing more than seventy of them. The government responded to protests in one township near Pretoria by simply closing the township down and moving residents to another township. Press restrictions in effect when I left the country were broadened in December 1986 so that witnessing, much less reporting, virtually any antigovernment activity was made an offense punishable by heavy fines and imprisonment. Even printing blank spaces in newspapers, to show they were being censored, was made against the law. Hardly signs of giving up.

Another sign of the continuing will to rule was P. W. Botha's call in 1987 for a special whites-only election. Many of us in the foreign press had long speculated that Botha would call a special election, even though he did not have to call one until 1989. Botha turned seventy in 1986 and visibly wearied of the job of governing his country. But he could not step aside and turn over the reins of government with the country in turmoil and Afrikanerdom split. He would have to unite the White Tribe first — and proclaiming a permanent emergency, virtually banning all opposition, and cracking down on the press were all part of the same strategy. The Afrikaners had to be brought together so that their long and hard rule would not fall into immediate jeopardy. If simply frightening all whites into the *laager* was the only way to achieve unity, then so be it. The NP won the May 1987 election handily. But the two right-wing parties increased their share of the vote by thirty percent. As Dave Kuim had predicted fifteen months earlier, the Conservatives became the official opposition in Parliament.

There was once speculation that when P. W. Botha stepped aside he would hand over power to one of his *verligte*, enlightened, Cabinet ministers, such as Pik Botha or Gerrit Viljoen. Pik Botha's chances were badly damaged when he told the foreign press that he could foresee a day when there might be a black state president in South Africa. P. W. Botha came down on his foreign minister with both feet before a full session of Parliament. Pik Botha had been out of line, the president said, and had apologized. Viljoen, a former chairman of the Broederbond, seemed to lack the political base to run successfully for leader of the NP caucus, which is tantamount to election as president.

Instead, events seemed to favor two conservative ministers, F. W. de Klerk, the national education minister and powerful leader of the NP in the party's Transvaal stronghold, and Chris Heunis, the minister for constitutional planning and development and P. W. Botha's hand-picked successor as leader of the NP in the Cape Province.

They are both *verkrampte* — hard line. De Klerk was the one who shouted me down at a press briefing when I challenged his assertion that busing had been made illegal in the United States. One other time, during a long flight from Johannesburg to Cape Town, I got into a conversation with him about Nelson Mandela. He declined comment on whether Mandela was going to be released, but then, as we were leaving the plane, he started shouting at me across the cabin. "If you were a South African, which party would you support?" he bellowed. "Eh? Eh? Probably the PFP. You worthless liberals are all alike." De Klerk told a group of us in the foreign press that schools would remain segregated "for as long as my party is in power."

Heunis, tall, husky, and more urbane than de Klerk, is no less conservative. He forced P.W. to backpedal on several reform initiatives, including the ill-fated "Rubicon" speech of August 1985, which was supposed to promise reform and ended up promising nothing.

There was also speculation that Botha's successor would be able to continue Botha's original reform program. The rank and file would have been polled, would not have to be polled again for another two years, and reforms could go on. But that speculation seemed without foundation. There was no evidence that any successor, no matter how *verligte,* would try — or would be able — to mandate reforms culminating in the genuine sharing of power between black and white. As long as the rank and file resist change, there is no chance of leadership advancing radical reforms that would put Afrikaner unity at risk. A loss of unity would put rule at risk.

Until the mass of Afrikanerdom shows a willingness to advance toward a more democratic and less authoritarian state in South Africa, there can be no reform of a significant nature. Reform, by its very nature, is a forward-looking process; chances for increased reform become difficult, at the very least, when leadership spends most of its time constantly looking to its rear for support. It seemed more likely, sadly, that the rank and file — in their *veldskools,* their mines, and their farms — would demand a tightening of repression along with a tightening of the *laager.* Not only have the mass of Afrikaners not given up the will to rule; they have not begun to give up the idea of ruling.

South Africa's blacks, in the meantime, showed no sign of abandoning *their* will to rule. The government's *kragdadige* — forceful — measures only made the blacks' hunger for liberation greater — and increased the danger that the masses would continue to control the direction of politics in the black sector as well as the white.

In South Africa, the masses in black politics are black youth: that huge, roiling, and critical mass of population that thinks nothing of throwing a brick at a Casspir or of necklacing a *shebeen* owner. The massive crackdown on anti-apartheid protest that began in June 1986 may have been intended to control black youth. It will only make them less controllable.

Older blacks knew the challenge they faced in satisfying and controlling their youth, and for a time they were able to contain them. The National Education Crisis Committee (NECC), which grew out of a Soweto parent-teacher organization, recognized as early as 1984 that township schools had ceased to function normally. Their children, they also saw, not only were getting no education but also were setting off from home in the mornings to find school doors closed — either by police or by boycotts — and were turning to other alternatives: stoning Casspirs, necklacing informers, and routing black police from the townships. The NECC decided that for black children to be controlled, black parents and teachers would have to take over the schools.

At first the greatest stumbling block to taking over the schools was not the white government but the black children. Many wanted to boycott their inferior schools. Others took the attitude "liberation now, education later." But over the Easter weekend of 1986, parents, teachers, and students of the NECC locked themselves into a church in an Indian township outside Durban — Inkatha tried to stop the meeting — and debated the boycott question. The parents and teachers won. They persuaded the kids to go back to school with a pledge that the

NECC would take over control of the schools from the Department of Education and Training, the white body that oversees black education.

It was called "people's education," like its 1976 Soweto counterpart, and it flourished, although briefly. Black parents felt that if they could keep their children in school, then the children could be helped. Teachers told the children to draw pictures — simple crayon sketches — so they could express their anger and frustration in some way other than throwing rocks at Casspirs or necklacing policemen. Just drawing the pictures was an act of release. Also, parents could see in the pictures what troubled a child and then try to channel the anger and trouble in some constructive way.

I saw some of those student drawings once, and they showed how depressed and angry the children were. One drawing depicted South Africa as a volcano, with the people inside it about to erupt. One boy's drawing showed life as a traffic light, with green representing permission from the government, yellow as "danger from both sides," and red as a signal to stop his education. Another drawing was simply a flower and under it the words "Education Is Happiness."

The trouble with people's education was that it encouraged compromise by both sides, blacks and Afrikaners. Any move toward better education — and controlling black youth — required compromise just because of the flammable nature of young black hatred. The Afrikaners tend to see any compromise on any issue as a defeat. The Department of Education and Training disapproved of people's education because people's education meant the DET was no longer in control of the schools. So the government sent the army into the townships and closed the schools. The children went back to throwing rocks at Casspirs. People's education died, a good idea whose time had come and for that reason was quashed.

Dismantling people's education was just one of Pretoria's ways of seeming to make black youth less controllable. Possibly of greater consequence was what the government did to other blacks who were trying to control the young comrades: it threw them in jail.

Black activists in their late twenties and early thirties — the Soweto generation — had been trying for nearly two years to harness the comrades' bleak and bitter anger. The South African Council of Churches (SACC) and the United Democratic Front (UDF) worked closely with black youth and tried to make them focus their hatred. They aimed to add some discipline to anti-apartheid activities of young comrades like Killer and Bongani and Vusi Mabaso and Scarface Toni Fuck You Montana. But what the Soweto generation saw as discipline and compromise the Afrikaners saw as dangerous opposition. Most of the twenty thousand arrested on and after June 12, 1986, were the controllers, the handlers, the compromisers. Countless others are on the run from the police.

My mind ached, seeing how those arrests would make the anti-apartheid struggle less disciplined, less focused. The struggle will now become more *tsotsi* — wild-eyed hooliganism, simple thuggery. Several studies carried out by social scientists around the country in 1985 and 1986 found a direct link between *tsotsi* violence and the level and authority of community-based organization. The former diminishes as the latter rises. Now that community-based organization has been all but shattered, the level of *tsotsi* violence seems sure to rise.

I listened to many scenarios for South Africa's future while I lived there, and the only two elements they had in common were that they were all equally depressing and that they all discounted the participation of the Anglo community. The Anglo liberals Alex Boraine and Frederick van Zyl Slabbert will continue trying to build bridges between black and white, and they may attract some converts. The body of Anglo South Africa, though, seemed inclined to do little more than sit by the pool and watch. As it always had.

All of the scenarios I heard involved violence, in varying degrees. Many seemed to accept an escalation in the ANC campaign of violence. Some saw the ANC moving into concerted guerrilla warfare not only against government installations but also against Western industrial interests, as a way to force those industries either to close down or leave. Almost all scenarios involved an increasing number of civilian casualties as a result of the ANC's widening warfare. Many spoke of "degenerative collapse" — South Africa descending into Lebanon-style civil war, with the ANC guerrilla war compounded by continuing and widening township unrest.

One scenario, appropriately apocalyptic, came from the Rev. Nico Smith, the former Broederbond member who became the minister in Mamelodi, outside Pretoria. Smith sat in his study telling me this scenario of his, and he looked tired. His eyes, behind the smoked glasses, were drooping. He ran his big Orange Free State hands through his thinning hair and sighed. I was always touched by the contrast between how Smith sounded and how Smith looked — he looked so Afrikaner, so big and coplike, but he sounded so gentle.

He slumped back in his couch and looked distractedly at the beamed ceiling of his study. "It could happen the day the black leaders are released from jail," he said quietly. His voice was soft and fluttering. "The black youth will run rampant through the streets of Pretoria and every other major city. Every white will have a gun. There will be a major slaughter on both sides. It could cause a slaughter of human beings that would be unimaginable."

Smith sat up straight, suddenly, and leaned forward, as if pleading with me. "My only hope is that in the aftermath, black youth will have felt their obsession for liberation to be quenched, satisfied," and Smith gritted his hands into tight fists. "It is also my hope that whites will have realized that they have to talk — that five million whites cannot keep twenty-five million blacks down, that they will realize that they cannot keep saying 'Ons is baas' — we are masters." Smith was talking so fast he was almost praying. Then he slowed, and he looked solemnly at the floor. "It is my hope that the revolution will be cathartic in this way, to bring about understanding and peace in the end."

Smith looked up from the floor and paused. He took a deep breath, then, and shook his head. Sadly. "The revolution is inevitable," he said softly, holding his hands before him, as if presenting a tangible proof. "It is around the corner, and it is impossible to ignore it. My only hope is that it will offer some kind of catharsis to purify us all." He paused again, and again clenched his hands into fists. "Something to make us think of people as people and not as black and white."

"You know," he said, breaking off his scenario. "I got a phone call the other morning. It was before dawn and I wondered what it could be. I picked up the receiver, and it was a former student of mine calling from the United States." Smith paused, looking down from the ceiling, bemused. He started talking again, his soft voice humming over the words gently. "He wanted to know if he should come home. If he stays in America he will have a good life. If he comes home, his life could be a mess. He wanted to know what he should do."

"So what did you tell him?" I asked.

"I told him he must come back," Smith said, his big Afrikaner shoulders hunched over, his hands on his knees. He shook his head slowly. "I told him this is not a time to run away. We all helped create this situation. We never considered the consequences. We didn't shout loud enough when we should have. We all must try to undo what we have done, as difficult as it may be."

"What did he say to that?" I asked.

Smith gave a small, grim laugh. "He said, 'How do you unscramble scrambled eggs?'" And Smith grunted again, a small laugh. "I told him I didn't know, but that we had to try to find a way. The revolution's coming."

* * *

It is up to the Afrikaner to find a way principally because the Afrikaner is the one in the position to give. All the blacks can give further are their lives, and I saw, just before I left the country, that blacks will never relent in their struggle.

Literally just before I left the country, I was walking into the international terminal at Jan Smuts Airport with my wife and son and my friends. The terminal was in its usual state of evening chaos because all flights to Europe and the United States leave around the same time. We were headed through the forest of suitcases and milling bodies for the departures area, and off to my right, whom should I see but Winnie Mandela.

She was seeing some friends off on a flight, and she stood out in the bustling horde, nearly glowing in a white kaftan, white headscarf, and sparkling beaded jewelry. I noticed how she threw back her head and laughed with her friends, and the sound came out happy and clear.

I looked at her and she looked at me, and we both smiled in greeting.

"Come here, Matthew," I said to my son, gently. "I'd like you to meet someone."

We walked over to Winnie Mandela, my son's small hand in mine. I had once told Winnie that Matthew was under the impression that Nelson Mandela was a personal friend of mine because I was always jetting off to Cape Town to "see" him. She had laughed heartily when I told her, and I could see the look of recognition in her eyes as Matthew and I crossed the twenty yards of airport linoleum toward her.

She smiled broadly as I extended my hand. "I'm sorry to hear about your troubles," she said quietly, her teeth and jewelry sparkling in the light. "And this must be your little boy, who thinks you are Mandela's friend?" she said, her voice rising.

She laughed lightly and squatted down to my son's eye level. "Matthew," I said, also bending over. "This is Mrs. Mandela. Would you like to say hello?" He frowned a five-year-old frown and kept his hands behind his back.

Winnie smiled and held her hands out together, as in a cup. "You know, Matthew," she said in her sing-song Xhosa voice, softly, "you and your Mummy and Daddy would not have to leave South Africa if my husband were not in jail," and Matthew moved over to hug my leg.

"Would you like to come back?" she whispered. Her voice carried even over the echoing din of the busy terminal. "We will gladly have you back, my husband and I."

"No."

"Well," she laughed, "we will see that you three can all come back. Soon. We'll have you back after the revolution."

"So much for children," I said with a shrug as the two of us straightened up. I lifted Matthew and held him on my hip, and Winnie smiled at us. She reached out her hand and patted Matthew gently on the knee.

I offered her my hand, and we shook goodbye again. "I just wanted to say goodbye," I said, "and to thank you and to say good luck."

Winnie smiled again and fluttered her eyelids as we shook hands. Her white headscarf set off her black skin and the whites of her eyes. We began to walk together, and she turned her head slightly in my direction. "We'll have you back soon," she said, slowly, amused. "These are the last kicks of a dying horse. The Boers are now running scared. There is no way they can stop us. We will win in the end. I know that. We will win in the end."

Then Winnie Mandela walked through the doors and out into the parking lot, her white robes fluttering in the winter wind behind her. She held her head high and her chin erect, as if certain that she, and her brothers and sisters, would win.

Afterword

GONE

I was lucky that the plane, for once, did not stop to refuel in the Cape Verde Islands and instead flew nonstop from Johannesburg to London. I had a Scotch somewhere over Botswana and then a glass of wine with the appetizer. I fell asleep at ten and did not wake until we were somewhere over Portugal at six the next morning. It was, I realized, the only decent night of sleep I'd had in five days.

We landed at Heathrow, and my old friend from Chicago, Donna Foote of *Newsweek*'s London bureau, met me at arrivals. She had found me a lovely room at the Dorchester, and I spent much of the next week on the phone, trying to help my wife coordinate the packing and moving from Jo'burg. Diane put everything together with amazing speed, and we made plans to link up in New York on what turned out to be New York's orgiastic Statue of Liberty celebration on July Fourth. I was not in the mood.

I was lucky to spend time in London when I did, because it turned out that Mark Peters and his girlfriend, Sheila Watt, were also there. Sheila had won two tickets for the Wimbledon men's finals, and the two of them had decided to make a week's vacation out of it. They arrived two days after I did, and we spent much of the next week together. It was good — no, lekker — for me just to have someone to talk South African with. Weebits and peaches, whingers and pozzies, cozzies and baby veal. The three of us crawled the pubs and dinner spots, talking Jo'burg talk.

One day I had the Dorchester put together a picnic for us to take out to Henley for the boat races. Sheila blanched at the Dorchester silver and tablecloths as well as the fine fare laid out on them. The cost, she said. Peters looked up with a smile. "Fuck 'em if they can't take a joke, eh Rick?" and we giggled under the warm June summer sun.

Donna Foote gave a small dinner on my last night in London, and Mark and I were joined by another South Africa hand, Associated Press photographer Greg English, who had shared an office next to ours. It was so terribly odd. At one end of the outdoor table sat Donna and her British friends, talking refined British politics. And at the other end of the table, like three conspirators, huddled English and Peters and me, drinking all of Donna's wine and howling over South Africa. The evening ended, and I think Donna was glad to see us go.

I boarded my BA flight to New York the next afternoon, and was nicely settled in with a book and a glass of wine when the in-flight movie came on. I usually don't watch in-flight movies, but when the opening scenery came on the screen I grabbed for my headphones and plugged them in as fast as I could. The movie, which I had never seen but whose soundtrack I knew almost by heart, was *Out of Africa.*

I sat in the darkened cabin, my chin resting on my left knee. "I had a farm in Africa, at the foot of the Ngong Hills . . ." I began to cry. It all came back, the music making me think of it all: the aloes in the garden, the *monstro delicioso,* the bougainvillea, the birds of paradise.

Karen Blixen's Kenyan sky was my sky in the Transvaal, and it made me remember baking under the blinding sun at mass funerals, prisons, and riots. The sight of the brown Kenyan savannah made me want *my* savannah, the veld. It even made me want to be back crashing through fifteen hundred kilometers of Angolan *bundu,* and I laughed at that and cried at the same time, the sort of thing that gives you hiccups.

I suppose I was due for a good weep, and weep I did, thinking of all the people I was leaving behind. I thought of our house-keeper and her husband, Ann and Saul Molefe, and how Saul had taken time off from work on my last day to come home and wish me well and say goodbye. Ann had come up to my wife a few days later — I was gone by then — carrying a small paper package. "Saul says we must give you this, Ma'am," she said. It was a beautiful batik of an African woman carrying a clay pot on her head, her *bubba* wrapped in a blanket on her back.

I thought of Joel, our gardener. We had given him magazines and newspapers and shoes, paid him well and given him loans when he needed them. I think he liked us because we worked alongside him — cleaning the pool, cutting brush, rewiring out-door lightbulbs — and didn't give orders in the Afrikaner fash-ion. He was a man of very few words, and my wife was shocked, after the deportation order came, when Joel approached her and made what, for him, amounted to a speech.

"Ma'am," he said, "I want you to go back to America and tell people what is happening here. Tell them what the Boers are doing to our country." And he walked away with tears in his eyes.

I remembered how on my last day I had gone to say goodbye to Joel. He was in a small fenced garden we had cleared out together. It had once been used for growing aloe seedlings, and all of us were going to share it for growing vegetables. He was leaning on a hoe, and his eyes were wet and milky.

"I think I'm going to have to leave this afternoon, Joel," I said, shaking my head. "I wanted to say goodbye."

Joel rolled his eyes. "I will never forget you as long as I ever live," he said, crying. I was taken aback and embarrassed. But then, I realized, the Mannings were probably the first whites who ever treated Joel as a human being.

"Never forget that this is your country, your land."

"I won't," Joel said, shaking his head.

"*Hlala kahle.*" Stay well.

"Hamba kahle." Go well.

I thought, too, of Lucky as I sat there crying in the BA 747 over the Atlantic. He had spent my last days in the country looking like a beaten dog. We had worked wonderfully together, and I missed him. On my last day he had slipped into my office while I was away at our last lunch and had left a card, one of those all-occasion cards that the card companies produce by the gross. But coming from Lucky it meant something. I wiped away my tears as Robert Redford and Meryl Streep flew over Kenya, and I reached into my carry bag for the card.

"Hope," it read in flowery script, "is not pretending that troubles don't exist. It is the trust that they will not last forever, that hurts will be healed and difficulties overcome. It is faith that a source of strength and renewal lies within to lead us through the dark and into the sunshine." Coming from a black South African, it meant a lot. It even made me stop crying. I took a series of deep breaths and ordered a double Scotch from the steward.

I closed my eyes and thought of them all, of Vusi and Killer and Bongani, of Seth and Murphy and Thabo; and of Dave Kuim, Hannes Luus, and Jan Leroux. I smiled, then, taking a sip of Scotch, glad I had made that last insert into that last story out of Johannesburg. It happened the way it often does with reporters on deadline, a small voice calling for tone, for shape, the one last sentence that will add by rounding and, I mused, by complicating.

I was walking through the kitchen, and Diane was upstairs packing a bag for me for the first time in seven years of marriage as I was about to start the process of transmitting the last story on that last day. I ran, then, into my office across the *stoep* and called up my story on the computer. Into the top of the last paragraph I inserted the sentence I'd been looking for: "One cannot share tea and rusks with Willem Kleynhans and leave South Africa condemning all whites." I took another sip of Scotch, then, glad that I had made that last change.

The BA flight bounced into New York, under a pall of humidity and enforced and largely plastic patriotism that July Fourth weekend. I didn't want to be there. I wanted to be back in Jo'burg, with the people, all the crazy, fractured, and splintered people. And I have never ceased wanting to be there, ever since.

Readjusting to life in America came easier after we were able to reclaim some of our things once they arrived by boat from Durban. We got out the basket Mark and I bought in Alldays, and we use it for a laundry hamper. Matthew's Christmas decorations, made the year before in South Africa, hung on our tree in the country. One thing that never left us, though, was Ann's batik of the woman, her clay pot, and her *bubba*. We had it stretched and framed as soon as we could. It hangs over our bed and, probably, we agreed, always will. A simple reminder of giving; of the goodness of the human spirit; and of the indomitable will of the burdened and oppressed to be free.